Martin Jörg Schäfer, Alexander Weinstock
Theatre in Handwriting

**Theatre Studies** | Volume 157

**Martin Jörg Schäfer** teaches Modern German Literature and Theatre at Universität Hamburg. His research examines literature, theatre and theory from the eighteenth century to the present with a focus on the (historical, theoretical and praxeological) relationships between theatre and text.

**Alexander Weinstock** works as a dramaturg at Theater an der Ruhr in Mühlheim an der Ruhr. His research focusses on literature and culture of the eighteenth century, models of aesthetic education, and the history and theory of theatre.

Martin Jörg Schäfer, Alexander Weinstock
# Theatre in Handwriting
Hamburg Prompt Book Practices, 1770s-1820s

[transcript]

The publication of this volume was funded by the Deutsche Forschungsgemeinschaft (DFG, German Research Foundation) under Germany's Excellence Strategy - EXC 2176 'Understanding Written Artefacts: Material, Interaction and Transmission in Manuscript Cultures' - project no. 390893796.

**Bibliographic information published by the Deutsche Nationalbibliothek**
The Deutsche Nationalbibliothek lists this publication in the Deutsche Nationalbibliografie; detailed bibliographic data are available in the Internet at https://dnb.dnb.de

This work is licensed under the Creative Commons Attribution 4.0 (BY) license, which means that the text may be remixed, transformed and built upon and be copied and redistributed in any medium or format even commercially, provided credit is given to the author. For details go to https://creativecommons.org/licenses/by/4.0/
Creative Commons license terms for re-use do not apply to any content (such as graphs, figures, photos, excerpts, etc.) not original to the Open Access publication and further permission may be required from the rights holder. The obligation to research and clear permission lies solely with the party re-using the material.

**First published in 2024 by transcript Verlag, Bielefeld**
**© Martin Jörg Schäfer, Alexander Weinstock**

Cover layout: Maria Arndt, Bielefeld
Cover illustration: Staats- und Universitätsbibliothek Hamburg Carl von Ossietzky, Theater-Bibliothek: 728, Die Sonnen Jungfrau. Schauspiel in fünf Aufzü-gen, folios 29v and 30r.
Print-ISBN 978-3-8376-6965-7
PDF-ISBN 978-3-8394-6965-1
ISSN of series: 2700-3922
eISSN of series: 2747-3198

# Table of Contents

**Acknowledgements** .................................................................................. 9
Abbreviations ............................................................................................. 10
Digital Dataset .......................................................................................... 10
Note on Translations ................................................................................ 10

**Chapter 1. Introduction** ........................................................................ 11
I.   Setting the Scene: A Manuscript Culture in an "Age of Print" ............ 12
II.  The Hamburg Theater-Bibliothek Collection and Its Context ........... 18
III. Framework and Outline ..................................................................... 29

**Chapter 2. Prompting and Its Written Artefacts: Anecdotal Evidence** ..... 35
I.   Prompting as a "Necessary Evil" in Eighteenth-
     and Nineteenth-Century German Theatre ........................................ 36
II.  A Question of Honour: Taking Care of the Written Artefacts
     of Prompting and More ...................................................................... 42
III. Prompt Books in Reading: At the Prompter's Whim ......................... 50

**Chapter 3. Writing and Paper Practices in the Prompt Books
of the Hamburg Theater-Bibliothek** ....................................................... 57
I.   The Format and Use of Prompt Books ............................................... 58
II.  Adding and Retracting Dialogue and Stage Directions .................... 62
III. Types and Functions of Other Additions and Retractions ............... 72
IV.  The Material Performance of Prompt Books .................................... 78

**Chapter 4. Creating a Prompt Book, Two at a Time: Scribes and Multi-
Layered Revisions for the Hamburg Production of Kotzebue's
*Die Sonnen-Jungfrau* (1790-1826)** ........................................................ 81
I.   Doubling Down: Two Prompt Books for *Die Sonnen-Jungfrau*
     at the Theater-Bibliothek .................................................................. 81
II.  *Theater-Bibliothek: 728* as a Not-So-Fair Fair Copy ...................... 87

III. The Error-Prone Dynamics of Copying: Unintentional Gender Trouble .............. 94
IV. Reshaping *Theater-Bibliothek: 728* – Tweaking a Play for the Stage ................. 99
V. Going It Alone: Fair Copy *Theater-Bibliothek: 1460*,
   Assisted Reading, Technical Instructions ................................................. 113
VI. Reworking the Play, Reshaping *Theater-Bibliothek: 1460* I:
    Political Pressure in 1813 ..................................................................... 123
VII. Reworking the Play, Reshaping *Theater-Bibliothek: 1460* II:
     Discovering the Heroic Dreamer in 1823 ............................................... 133

**Chapter 5. Prompt Book Practices in Context:
The "Hamburg Shakespeare" between Handwriting and Print,
the Audience and Censorship Demands (1770s–1810s and beyond)** ......... 141
I. The German Shakespeare in Print and Its Relationship to Theatre ................ 142
II. The 1776 *Hamlet* and Its Relationship to Print ............................................... 146
III. The 1776 *Othello*: Adapting *Theater-Bibliothek: 571*
     from Various Printed Sources ................................................................ 153
IV. In Search of an Audience: Hasty Prompt Book Revisions
    in *Theater-Bibliothek: 571* ..................................................................... 159
V. Prompt Books on the Censor's Desk: Handwriting, Print,
   and Shakespeare .................................................................................. 167
VI. A 1778 *König Lear* Print Copy and Its 1812 Context ......................................... 171
VII. Appeasing the Censor: The Handwritten Revision
     of *Theater-Bibliothek: 2029* in 1812 ...................................................... 176

**Chapter 6. Doing Literature in Theatre: Schiller's Adaptation
of Lessing's *Nathan der Weise* between Prompting
and Stage Managing (1800s–1840s)** ................................................................ 187
I. A Closet Drama, an Adapter's Work in Progress,
   and Two Related Written Artefacts ........................................................ 189
II. The Author as Adapter: Schiller's Template in *Theater-Bibliothek:
    1988a* and *Theater-Bibliothek: 1988b* ..................................................... 194
III. The Work of the Inspector in *Theater-Bibliothek: 1988a* ................................. 201
IV. Transforming a Print Copy into a Prompt Book: Technical Requirements
    for Creation and Use in *Theater-Bibliothek: 1988b* ................................. 209
V. The Evolution of an Adaptation I: Simultaneous or Non-Simultaneous Use ...... 222
VI. The Evolution of an Adaptation II: Negotiating Christianity in Public ............. 235
VII. Entangled Purposes, Complementary Materialities ....................................... 242

**Chapter 7. Outlook** ........................................................................... 245

**List of Figures** ................................................................................. 253

**Bibliography** ..................................................................................... 255
I. List of Written Artefacts from the Theater-Bibliothek ................... 255
II. List of Databases and Datasets ............................................. 258
III. List of Other Sources .......................................................... 258

# Acknowledgements

The research for this book was funded by the Deutsche Forschungsgemeinschaft (DFG, German Research Foundation) under Germany's Excellence Strategy – EXC 2176 "Understanding Written Artefacts: Material, Interaction and Transmission in Manuscript Cultures", project no. 390893796. The research was conducted within the scope of work at the Centre for the Study of Manuscript Cultures (CSMC) at Hamburg University.

More specifically, the idea for this book emerged within the scope of the "Multilayered Written Artefacts" group. We are profoundly indebted to all of our colleagues who introduced us to the depths, shallows, and intricacies of manuscript studies. It was only by comparing "our" prompt books with written artefacts from other regions, periods, and fields that we were able to map out their special features. Our thanks go to Sebastian Bosch, Christian Brockmann, José Maksimczuk, Ivana Rentsch, Thies Staack, Eva Wilden, and Hannah Wimmer. For their general support at the CSMC, we would also like to thank Michael Friedrich, Kaja Harter-Uibopuu, Konrad Hirschler, Karsten Helmholz, Eva Jungbluth, and Christina Kaminski. We were lucky to be able to build on recent research on the holdings of the Hamburg Theater-Bibliothek and are deeply grateful to Bernhard Jahn, Jacqueline Malchow, and Martin Schneider for sharing their work with us. We are also thankful to the staff of Staatsbibliothek Hamburg and its "Handschriftenlesesaal" for always providing smooth access to "our" prompt books. Deciphering the prompt books from the Hamburg Theater-Bibliothek collection was just as much a collaborative effort as creating and using these prompt books seem to have been. Vast areas of our analyses were the result of staring at Zoom screens together during the Corona pandemic. Without the input, effort, perceptiveness, and sharp wit of Anna Sophie Felser, Tobias Funke, Hannah Göing, and Sophia Hussain, this book would not have been possible. These four were also largely responsible for the digital dataset we have made available to anyone who would like to further comprehend or continue our work. Many heartfelt thanks! We would also like to express our gratitude to Lydia J. White for correcting, amending, and always improving our English. Last but not least, we would like to show our appreciation to Laura Bach, Luisa Dietsch, Anna Sophie Felser (again), Mirjam Groll, and Niklas Heupel for adding the finishing touches while getting the book ready for publication.

## Abbreviations

L: *Theater-Bibliothek: 2029* (prompt book for the 1812 production of W. Shakespeare's *König Lear* [*King Lear*], based on a copy of the 1778 print edition of F.L. Schröder's 1778 adaptation). Digital access: https://resolver.sub.uni-hamburg.de/kitodo/HANSd27842.

Nm: *Theater-Bibliothek: 1988a* (inspection book for the 1803 production of F. Schiller's adaptation of G. E. Lessing's *Nathan der Weise* [*Nathan the Wise*], manuscript). Digital access: https://resolver.sub.uni-hamburg.de/kitodo/HANSh3323.

Np: *Theater-Bibliothek: 1988b* (prompt book for the 1803 production of F. Schiller's adaptation of G. E. Lessing's *Nathan der Weise*, based on a copy of the 1781 print edition of Lessing's play). Digital access: https://resolver.sub.uni-hamburg.de/kitodo/PPN1727958179.

O: *Theater-Bibliothek: 571* (prompt book for the 1776 production of F. L. Schröder's adaptation of W. Shakespeare's *Othello*, manuscript). Digital access: https://resolver.sub.uni-hamburg.de/kitodo/HANSh1815.

S1: *Theater-Bibliothek: 728* (correction copy for the 1790 production of A. v. Kotzebue's *Die Sonnen-Jungfrau* [*The Virgin of the Sun*], manuscript). Digital access: https://resolver.sub.uni-hamburg.de/kitodo/HANSh1978.

S2: *Theater-Bibliothek: 1460* (prompt book for the 1790 production of A. v. Kotzebue's *Die Sonnen-Jungfrau*, manuscript). Digital access: https://resolver.sub.uni-hamburg.de/kitodo/HANSh2452.

## Digital Dataset

Under http://doi.org/10.25592/uhhfdm.13916, we have made "manuals" available containing metadata and explanations of technical instructions, diacritical signs, and abridgements. We have also included additional data (such as enrichment transcriptions) depending on the focus of the respective analysis.

## Note on Translations

Unless stated otherwise, translations are our own.

Some of the translations of F. L. Schröder's *Gesetze des Hamburgischen Theaters* are based on George W. Brandt (ed.): *German and Dutch Theatre: 1600–1848*. Cambridge/New York 1993.

Some of the translations of G. E. Lessing's *Nathan der Weise* are based on the 1805 translation by William Taylor: *Nathan the Wise*. London/Paris/Melbourne 1893.

# Chapter 1. Introduction

This study proposes that we conceive of the theatrical prompt books created and used in Hamburg in the late eighteenth and early nineteenth centuries as written artefacts[1] that connect literary texts with theatrical processes, discourses, and practices on a material level and in a performative fashion.[2] Many of the observations that we will make in this book can be adapted to different, more general contexts;[3] however, they do have specific objects, namely those in the particularly rich Theater-Bibliothek [Theatre-Library] collection, located in Hamburg, and its more than 3,000 prompt books, created between around 1750 and 1880. While the rise of modern European theatre since the sixteenth century had depended on the proverbial emergence and dominance of letterpress printing, a distinct and internally diverse manuscript culture persisted within European theatre. In many historical contexts, the most prominent surviving written artefacts are prompt books that were created to ensure the technical and textual repeatability of the production in question (sometimes over decades). The term *prompt book* derives from the fact that prompters were the prime users of these volumes. During performances, prompters would whisper cues from the prompt book to help actors out with forgotten or mangled lines. The Hamburg Theater-Bibliothek collection mainly consists of written artefacts created for this purpose, but the prompt book was also the theatre troupe's master copy for the production of a play. The need to maintain prompt books and to regularly revise them according to both intra- and extra-theatrical requirements meant that the primary *fair copies* were constant-

---

1 Throughout this study we will employ the term "written artefacts" as meaning either manuscripts in the literal sense, i.e., written by hand, or printed books that are enriched by handwriting.
2 This study builds on various shorter texts in which we have outlined our thinking and taken firsts steps in analysing our material. Cf. Schäfer 2021; cf. Weinstock 2022; cf. Schäfer/Weinstock 2023; cf. Weinstock 2024; cf. Weinstock/Schäfer 2024.
3 To some extent, our analytical framework is valid for the overall manuscript practices of modern European theatre. However, historical and local particularities apply for each and every prompt book. Nevertheless, prompt books from eighteenth and nineteenth century German spoken theatre as stored in extensive collections in Berlin, Cologne, Munich, Vienna, and Weimar largely work in a similar fashion.

ly being enriched with interacting layers produced by different writing tools, in multiple hands, and with the additional involvement of other paper practices such as gluing, cutting, and folding. These processes have resulted in a unique material biography for each prompt book – a *material performance* for all intents and purposes, deserving of attention in its own right. In this volume, we will employ thick description and close analysis coupled with broader contextualisation to examine the multi-handed creation and handwritten transformation of selected prompt books from the Hamburg Theater-Bibliothek, their complicated relationship to print, their responsiveness to the (real or perceived) demands being made by audiences and the authorities, and the complex (both aesthetic and technical) processes involved in adapting a play to the stage. (Cf. figure 1.)

*Figure 1: textual and material enrichments in a prompt book for Lessing's* Nathan der Weise *(Nm, 44v and 45r).*

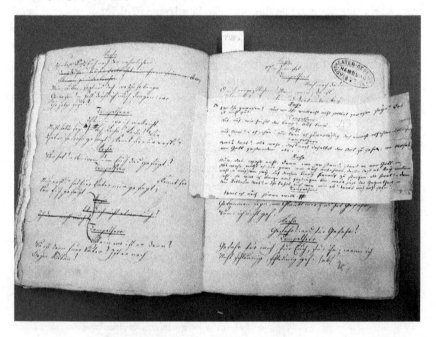

## I.   Setting the Scene: A Manuscript Culture in an "Age of Print"

Discussions of European spoken-word theatre have traditionally relied on a fundamental distinction being made between drama and performance, i.e., between reading and watching, the text and its performance, where the spoken word is just one of many theatrical elements. The scholarly discussion of European theatre has largely adhered to this distinction since the dividing-up of text and performance in Aristotle's *Poetics*.[4] It has viewed the written artefacts involved, such as the prompt books in our Hamburg context, as resources that we can use to gain knowledge about either the play as a text or the play in performance. From this perspective, prompt books and other written theatre artefacts have long been viewed as objects that provide helpful information about the textual basis or historical particularities of a theatre production. On the one hand, there is a literary text, spelt out to varying degrees depending on the theatre tradition, the time, and the circumstances, but it always contains the words to be spoken, the characters to be played, and the actions to be performed on stage. On the other hand, there are the events that take place on that very stage. What transpires on stage does not necessarily take into account the action that has been written down and prescribed. Instead, performers might be allowed to do virtually anything they want: to improvise scenes and dialogue depending on the mood of the audience, to make up parts that are sometimes only outlined in writing (or that the actors have simply not memorised that well), or to forget about language altogether and indulge in purely physical action.

Scholars of literature, theatre, and both forms of cultural expression have either privileged the text, emphasised the fleeting experience of the unique performance, or argued for some complex form of entanglement between the two.[5] However, surprisingly little attention has been paid to the various written artefacts that have been produced and used in theatres.[6] Aside from all the written documents necessary to sustain theatre operations (bank statements, contracts, playbills, tickets, etc.), the performance itself primarily relies on *scripts*[7] that set out in writing what is to be repeated the following day (or the following year, or a decade later) and what is (sometimes implicitly) left over to convention or chance: which words are to be uttered by the actors and when, where they are supposed to enter and exit the stage, when the lights are supposed to be dimmed, when the curtain is supposed to fall, etc. If circumstances change, so too must the script (which nonetheless can never completely capture what "really" transpires during

---

4 Cf. the notorious section 26 of Aristotle 2013.

5 Cf. Phelan 1993; cf. Halliwell 1986; cf. Malone 2021. In a vein similar to ours, Kaethler, Malone, and Roberts-Smith argue that "the term promptbook holds a complicated place in theatre history and textual studies, both of which recognise promptbooks as texts interested in stage action, but also make assumptions that lead to ongoing misunderstandings of their history and nature" (Kaethler/Malone/Roberts-Smith 2023, 4).

6 Any reference to the manuscript practices of theatre is conspicuously absent in the authoritative *Cultural History of Theatre*. Cf. Leon 2017; cf. Marx 2017. For an overview of previous research cf. Kaethler/Malone/Roberts-Smith 2023, 4–10. They primarily build their argument on the discussion of prompt books for Shakespeare-performances in the English speaking world. Cf. Shattuck 1965; cf. Werstine 2012.

7 Cf. Schechner 2003, 68; cf. Müller-Schöll 2020.

a performance). Situated between text and performance, theatre relies on written artefacts that are constantly being reshaped and that do not necessarily remain in the hands of the same people in that process.[8] Martin Schneider has recently proposed viewing prompt books as "media" that store performance history.[9] Mark Kaethler, Toby Malone, and Jennifer Roberts-Smith have recently called attention to prompt books as "polychronic actants" within the practices that make a performance possible.[10] While Schneider, Kaethler, Malone, and Roberts-Smith focus on prompt books as a means to reconstruct productions and performances, our endeavour has taken a complementary perspective on the material dimension of the written artefacts we are examining, i.e., on the ways in which their context and use have transformed them into something that not only "remains"[11] of the performance but also facilitates future ones.

In twenty-first-century, globalised, experimental performance art, scripts can consist of intricate digital spreadsheet files or, conversely, just of a bundle of scribbled notes for the stage set-up.[12] If no words are spoken, there is no need to write down any words. If they are improvised, only an outline needs to be jotted down or memorised. What needs to be written down digitally or by hand depends on the customs of the artists, the demands of the performance space, and overall conventions. This is a truism that can be applied to European theatre culture. A tradition stemming from the sixteenth century that would retroactively be seen as the "rebirth" of ancient Greek theatre shifted the dramatic text into the centre of attention.[13] It stood side by side with other traditions that relied on extemporisation, often that of the spoken word as well. There is no reliable information about whether the text excerpts we have from the Italian *commedia dell'arte* or Ger-

---

8   From the point of view of our study, the relationship between text and theatrical performance (or overall theatrical production) would need to be reconsidered. A performance would neither consist of the "execution" of the dramatic text in the Aristotelian or Hegelian sense nor would the text solely provide "material" to be used at will. Other metaphors such as the "transformation" of a dramatic text into a performance, the text as an "instrument" to be tailored and interpreted, or the dramatic text as interface between literature and theatre would also need to be tweaked to take the open-ended processes that take place in a prompt book into account. For these processes, cf. the following chapter. For the respective concepts, cf., for example, Weimann 2000 ("instrument"); cf. H. T. Lehmann 2006 ("material"); cf. Worthen 2010 ("interface").

9   Cf. M. Schneider 2021: Schneider uses a slightly different conceptual framework to study prompt books and related written artefacts in their historical contexts from the Middle Ages to contemporary theatre. While Schneider focuses on prompt books as a means to reconstruct the productions and performances in question, our endeavour focuses on the material dimension of the respective written artefacts.

10  Cf. Kaethler/Malone/Roberts-Smith 2023.

11  For a discussion of the non-transitory aspects of theatre performances, cf. R. Schneider 2012.

12  Cf. Müller-Schöll 2020, 77–83.

13  Cf. Brauneck 2012, 127–190; cf. Dupont 2007.

man travelling theatre (*Wanderbühne*) derive from written artefacts that were used in the theatre or taken down by audience members.[14]

It is this text-based aspect of the European theatre tradition that our study is interested in. The dramatic scripts that have survived from different contexts often include paper files with performers' parts written out in ink (often stitched together as a booklet[15] while the etymology of, for example, the German "Rolle" [part, role] is literally roll, i.e., a scroll), as well as set-up lists for the technical teams (decoration, scenery), and, most prominently, handwritten master copies of the play and any additional information. These were usually paper quires which were stitched together and bound into what were referred to as "prompt books". (For the context we are interested in, there is next to no record of any draft and trial versions of their respective content.) Once assembled into a fair copy, prompt books were then updated with whatever writing tool was available when the need for an update arose (and, in our context, sometimes decades later). Once other technologies became widely available, such as print copies of plays (when they were used as performance versions), mechanical typewriters, and different photocopying methods, the use of handwriting began intermingling with those new technologies and tended to be used for updates such as corrections and notes. The more effective the other technologies became, especially with the rise of digital tools, the more handwriting shifted to the margins. But, at least in the German context, prompt books were still being created in handwriting well into the early twentieth century.[16] Moreover, anybody who has worked backstage in any role at one of the "grand houses" in recent years can testify to the pervasive use of handwritten lists and notes in the second decade of the twenty-first century, despite the widespread availability of PCs, printers, and tablets.[17]

Depending on the historical period and context, a written artefact of this kind in Germany might have remained in the care of one of the following figures: the *principal* [*Prinzipal*], i.e., the owner, chief executive, or artistic director of one of the travelling German troupes that, during the eighteenth century, began settling down in fixed places; the *artistic director*, a figure who only emerged in European theatre in mid-nineteenth century; the *inspector*, who, in Germany, has been similar in many respects to contemporary stage managers since the late eighteenth

---

14 Cf. Münz 1979, 53–60; cf. Kotte 2013, 160–164.
15 Cf. Maurer-Schmoock 1982, 98.
16 Take, for example, the early twentieth century written artefacts from the two "grand houses" in Hamburg. The theatre collection at Staatsbibliothek has mostly handwritten prompt books from Schauspielhaus while from the neighbouring Thalia Theater there are interleaved print copies with handwritten notes.
17 From conversations with Anna Sophie Felser, we know that handwritten notes are at least prevalent at the contemporary Hamburg Opera.

century but who also has overall management responsibilities for the company's day-to-day operations[18]; or someone who had responsibility for the prompt books as a librarian or at least custodian. As we will elucidate below, the person in charge of the master copy in the German context at the turn of the nineteenth century was often actually the prompter themselves.[19] When the respective caretaker changed, so too did the person who would potentially update the prompt book. But, as we will see in the Hamburg context, any person who was responsible for artistic or technical aspects of the performance could, of course, pick up the quill or pencil. Well-guarded from possible rivals, prompt book creation and upkeep were usually a multi-handed endeavour spanning a long period of time. The objects held in the Hamburg Theater-Bibliothek, generally books for the prompter and sometimes the inspector, bear witness to such multi-layered effects.

While taking the Hamburg Theater-Bibliothek with its late eighteenth- and early nineteenth-century materials as its point of reference, this volume will also propose that we reconsider the significance of written artefacts in the modern European theatre tradition more generally. Our study suggests that we view prompt books as the centrepiece of a specific manuscript culture which developed in European theatre from the sixteenth century onwards. A "particular manuscript culture to which a given manuscript belongs" can be understood, as Jörg Quenzer puts it, as "the milieu in which it was and is produced, used and transmitted".[20] By revealing the multi-layered traces of their regular use over weeks, years, and decades, we will show that prompt books are written artefacts of interest in their own right. We will put their material biography – i.e., the material traces of use accumulated by a prompt book over time and the modifications it has undergone in the course of its existence – on display in what we refer to as the inherent *material performance*[21] of their intersecting layers. Each prompt book performatively connects the multiple agents and technologies that make up the theatre as an overall set of cultural practices.[22] In doing so, a particular practice of handwriting comes into view which outlasted the arrival and dominance of movable type printing in Europe by several centuries.

---

18  There was also a *Theatermeister*, which might be more idiomatically translated as "stage manager". Cf. Schröder 1798, 36f.

19  Cf. Maurer-Schmoock 1982, 88–101.

20  Quenzer 2014, 2.

21  We re-apply and redefine scholarly approaches to the material experiments with books and print conducted by the artistic European avant-gardes of the early twentieth century. We borrow the term "Materialperformanz" from Julia Nantke (Nantke 2017, 77).

22  Our study complements the renewed interest in the materiality of printed books in the European "age of the books". Cf. Spoerhase 2018; cf. Fuchs 2020; cf. Bartelmus/Mohagheghi/Rickenbacher 2023.

# Chapter 1. Introduction

The intricate relationship between the growth of the vibrant trans-European theatre culture of the early modern world and the rise of letterpress printing and the ensuing, sprawling book market has been well documented.[23] What is commonly referred to as the European "age of print"[24] or the "age of the book"[25] (which is, to some extent, ongoing) had a significant influence on the reemergence of theatre on a grand scale, whether in the growing metropolises of England, France, or Spain, or beyond, e.g., in the German-speaking countries. Convincingly, Julie Stone Peters has argued in a major study that, from the sixteenth century onwards, print was one of the most important factors in shaping "early modern" and "modern" understandings of the theatre as an institution along with the dramatic genres represented in it. Printed playbills advertised performances to great effect. Newspapers and their critics amplified feedback and attention. Dedicated journals fostered fan cultures and critical discussions alike. Not least, the new accessibility of plays in print copies created links between the reading public and the theatre-going public.[26] No matter how widespread manuscripts remained within theatre contexts until the nineteenth century, it was print that effected the "rebirth" of European theatre on a grand scale.

Adding to the scope of Stone Peters's study, our undertaking has a complementary focus: it aims to grasp the multiple ways in which handwritten prompt books were crucial in everyday theatre practice, i.e., in specific artistic and practical processes, and how they interacted with their social context. The rise of European theatre may have been externally fuelled by the printing press, but internally, everything that was not printed would, of course, be written down by hand. Long before and long after the advent of the printing press in Europe, handwriting was not an indicator of uniqueness in the theatre or anywhere else (which is how handwritten letters and manuscripts by literary authors were perceived from the eighteenth century[27]); handwriting was therefore (and often still is) pragmatic in nature.[28] On the level of day-to-day theatre operations, putting something in print may just not have been worth the effort or might even have been counterproductive. Thus, the theatre cultures of early modern and modern Europe developed specific practices for writing by hand and creating manuscripts. For many practical reasons, the format of these manuscripts often emulated the most successful format of the European "age of print", the bound book, as they were stable, move-

---

23 Cf., above all, Stone Peters 2000.
24 Cf. Clair 1976, for example.
25 Cf. Giesecke 1998, for example.
26 Cf. Stone Peters 2000, 93–112.
27 Cf. Benne 2015.
28 Cf. Quenzer/Bondarev/Sobisch 2014.

able, storable, and constantly updatable all at once.[29] But it is the distinct writing and paper practices of prompt books' initial handwritten creation and subsequent use that sets them apart from, firstly, the uniformity and quick reproducibility aimed at by the printing press and, secondly, other instances of pragmatic writing.

## II. The Hamburg Theater-Bibliothek Collection and Its Context

Our approach is local but also serves as an example of the persistence of manuscript practices in European theatre. The Hamburg Theater-Bibliothek sports a particularly rich collection that bears witness to the activities that were taking place in one of Germany's leading theatre centres at the time. The roughly 3,050 prompt books in its collection pertain to 2,100 plays from all spoken word and musical theatre genres that were being performed at the Hamburgisches Stadt-Theater [Hamburg City Theatre] at Gänsemarkt (formerly the Comödienhaus [Playhouse] and the Deutsches Nationaltheater [German National Theatre], then the Théâtre du Gänsemarkt during the French occupation) under various principals from around 1750 until 1880. Most of these artefacts are bound paper manuscripts with cardboard covers of various sizes made from inexpensive material. About 500 of them are print copies of plays that were commercially available with new covers, extra glued-in sheets, and handwritten supplements, while the rest are entirely handwritten – whether the plays were available in print or not.[30] Prompt books for productions staged from the 1770s to the 1810s and in the early 1820s form the overwhelming majority (approximately three quarters) of the collection. Although a number of them remained in use after 1827, when the building was given up for a new one at Dammtorstraße that is now home to the city opera, our study focuses on the prompt books created during the Gänsemarkt era. (Cf. figures 2, 3, 4.)

---

29  Cf. Latour 1986, 19f., 25–39.

30  The manuscripts and prints have been indexed for the digital Kalliope library catalogue (https://kalliope-verbund.info/). Each index includes a short description of the material status of the artefact that contains information about its length and the types of amendments that have been made to it. A short overview of the *Theater-Bibliothek* collection and its digital representation is given in Neubacher 2016. Since a recent DFG project in Hamburg has catalogued the playbills at the Comödienhaus, which later became the Stadt-Theater, the dates of the performances and their changing participants can now be identified in many cases; cf. Jahn/Muhle/Eisenhardt/Malchow/M. Schneider (https://www.stadttheater.uni-hamburg.de).

*Figure 2: a handwritten and a printed prompt book for Shakespeare's* Maaß für Maaß [Measure for Measure] *(Theater-Bibliothek 514, 122 and 123, and Theater-Bibliothek 948b, 32 and 33).*

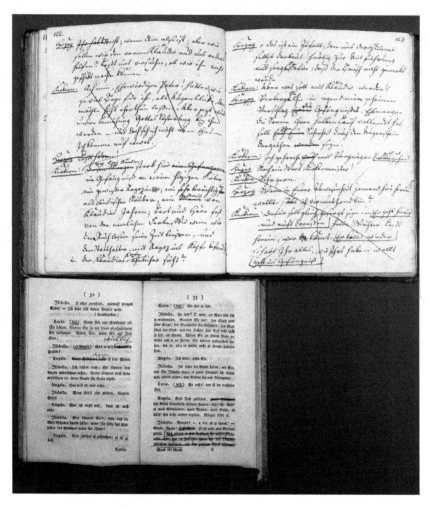

*Figure 3: the front cover of an 1815 prompt book for Shakespeare's* Othello *(Theater-Bibliothek: 586a).*

*Figure 4: the complete cover of* Theater-Bibliothek: 586a.

The Theater-Bibliothek is also a treasure trove for musical materials used by the orchestra, a fixture at the Stadt-Theater (and at most German theatres at the time).[31] Melodramas[32] and operas were a staple in the repertory; musical numbers and ballets were often used as preludes or epilogues.[33] At the turn of the century, more and more plays were being performed without musical elements supplementing the spoken text and without any musical preludes or epilogues either. However, the orchestra sprang into action during the interludes between acts, when stage scenery needed to be changed. The privately run theatre was bound by contract to employ the official city orchestra, at least for these interludes.[34] It may be partly for this reason that hardly any connections between the prompt books and the sheet music can be found; the latter will therefore not feature prominently in our study.

In the Anglophone world, *prompt book* has come to mean any text in book format in which a stage version and additional stage instructions are recorded. While a prompt book in the strict sense means the written artefact used by the prompter, prompt books in a more general sense can refer to the written artefacts either used by the respective equivalent of stage manager or created by an artistic director (to put forward their aesthetic vision in formats that ranged from notebook

---

31 Cf. Mühle 2023; cf. Neubacher 2016, 29–34.
32 Cf. Rentsch 2016.
33 Cf. Jahn 2016.
34 Cf. Malchow 2022, 162.

scribbles to fully fleshed out descriptions, especially from the twentieth century onwards) and their assistants (to obtain a record of all the technical information). In English, *prompt book* can have many meanings such as part book, memorial book, stage manager's book, or preparation copy. Prompt book might also refer to a commercially traded printed book containing the text of a stage adaptation of a certain production.[35] However, in the German context, these different written artefacts are referred to as director's books (*Regiebücher*, previously *Dirigierbücher*), inspector's books (*Inspektionsbücher*, sometimes synonymous with, sometimes distinct to *Inspizierbücher*), or published stage adaptations (sometimes referred to as *publizierte Bühnenfassungen*).[36] For the sake of convenience, this study will use *prompt book* as an overall term of reference but will draw occasional distinctions when necessary. In most cases, categorisation as a prompt book is in fact correct in the strict sense: we are examining the written artefacts used by prompters. For a short period towards the end of the eighteenth century, the texts of stage adaptations in Hamburg were sometimes printed for commercial publication, but they did not explicitly advertise their connection to the stage. The concept of the artistic director (and his "own" book) only emerged in the mid-nineteenth century.[37]

In addition to prompt books in the strict sense, the Hamburg Theater-Bibliothek collection also contains a number of *inspection books* to be used backstage. *Prompt books* and *inspection books* often come in pairs for the same production. It is relatively certain that these books were used in tandem. However, there is often no definite way of determining whether this characterisation was made upon the creation of the written artefact or at a later point in time. Some of the written artefacts referred to as prompt books include content that was presumably required by the inspector (casting, set, and prop lists, entrances and curtain calls) and vice versa. Sometimes, it seems to have depended on the circumstances whether one written artefact served both purposes or two written artefacts were created separately. In the following, we will make this distinction where required, but we will examine both types as part of the Hamburg manuscript practices that this study is interested in.

The period spanning the 1770s to 1820s on the Hamburg Stadt-Theater stage was a significant period of theatre history in the German-speaking world. It was the first time that a theatre at a fixed location that was not a court with a patron proved that it could be economically successful and was praised by critics as artistically sophisticated. The beginning of this period was shaped by Friedrich Ludwig Schröder who, as principal and lead actor but also as adapter of plays and

---

35 Cf. Brockett 1999, 346; cf. Beal 2008, 318–320; cf. Pavis 1998, xvi, 362. (Pavis solves the problem of wording by subsuming the different written artefacts under the term "staging book".)

36 Cf. Düringer/Barthels 1841, 177.

37 Cf. Roselt 2015, 9–15.

playwright, achieved renown for his innovative, proto-realist aesthetics and his new style of "natural" acting, with the theatre revelling in Schröder's afterglow after his retirement.[38] In the second half of the eighteenth century, Hamburg had become one of Germany's theatre hubs, despite the ongoing reservations of the local clergy.[39] The short-lived attempt in the late 1760s to establish a *Nationaltheater* [national theatre] at the recently built Comödienhaus [playhouse] at Gänsemarkt is well known. Due to Lessing's involvement and the direction he outlined in his *Hamburgische Dramaturgie* [*Hamburg Dramaturgy*], the period 1767–69 has been canonised in literary and theatre history as the origin of a specific kind of "German" theatre that aimed to educate civil society.[40] Things were more complicated in practice. The repertory of the Nationaltheater still included the usual entertainment provided by the theatres of the time, such as ballet, pantomime, and light opera.[41] The high regard in which the Nationaltheater was held was in large part due to the acting prowess of the theatre company originally established by Konrad Ernst Ackermann, who had commissioned the construction of the Comödienhaus in 1763 and then leased it to the Nationaltheater. He went on to become one of its lead actors and returned as a principal after the endeavour's economic failure. As an actor, he was one of the pioneers of the new realist acting style, and as principal he introduced ensemble-based working methods that were unusual for the time (brought about by holding group rehearsals instead of relying on individual extemporisation).[42] After his death in 1769, his wife Sophie Charlotte and stepson Friedrich Ludwig Schröder (then just twenty-five) took over as co-principals and built on Ackermann's legacy. Schröder's fame as principal and actor soon stretched far beyond Hamburg's borders. Such was his popularity that, when his coffin was ceremoniously transported to the graveyard in 1816, mourning crowds are said to have lined the streets.[43] Sophie Ackermann retired in 1780. Except for a three-year stint in Vienna, Friedrich Ludwig Schröder headed up the theatre and its company until 1798 and returned for another one-year stint as co-principal during the French occupation from 1811 to 1812.[44] In the meantime, Schröder, and after his death his heirs, leased the theatre building and its repertory of plays, which was stored in the prompt books, to the principals. It was only when the theatre moved to its new building on Dammtorstraße in 1827 that a handover of the rights

---

38 Cf. Hoffmann 1939; cf. Litzmann 1890–1894; cf. Jahn 2016.
39 Cf. Geffcken 1851.
40 Cf. Haider-Pregler 1980.
41 Cf. Jahn 2016.
42 Cf. Malchow 2022, 226–238; cf. Kotte 2013, 266f., 293–295.
43 Cf. Meyer 1819b, 415.
44 Cf. Meyer 1819b, 317–322.

to the archive, i.e., the prompt books, was negotiated.⁴⁵ It is these objects that form the backbone of the Theater-Bibliothek collection. Many of them have speckled brown cardboard covers, indicating that they had been part of Schröder's own collection at some point.⁴⁶ While Schröder's handwriting is all over these specific prompt books, and often accompanied by an authoritative final stroke of his pen, his is but one of many hands. (It is well known that Schröder often worked with collaborators for his stage adaptations.⁴⁷) Over time, the handwriting of the respective decision-makers dissolved into the web of different layers that enrich a given prompt book.

The prompt books that are now assembled in the Theater-Bibliothek collection were of vital importance to the new aesthetics developed by Ackermann and then Schröder in line with the views of eighteenth-century German-speaking intellectuals and critics who, influenced by the French theatre tradition of the seventeenth century (*le théâtre classique*), were demanding a major overhaul of the theatre. As part of the wider cultural transformation of the theatre's social reputation, adherence to the literary text was posited as a central element of this new aesthetics. Proponents called for new modes of interacting, moving, and speaking on stage to represent complex new dramatic characters and conflicts. Instead of relying on extemporisation, these characters and their conflicts were written down beforehand as literary texts. Thus, acting was to be based on the dramatic script being staged. In other words, the performance became increasingly subject to the text – at least as a theoretical goal that, in the late eighteenth century, frequently did not correspond to practice.⁴⁸ However, Ackermann's and then Schröder's troupe were renowned for spearheading developments. In order to become such a stable point of reference, the text had to be written down. The new theatre aesthetics was accompanied by its own manuscript practices, relying on the prompt books that also served as master copies and templates for the actors' roles.

Many of the practices pioneered or consolidated by Schröder are documented in his *Gesetze des Hamburgischen Theaters* [*Laws of the Hamburg Theatre*], a list of regulations. Schröder published an early version in 1792, and an extended version circulated within his theatre until his first retirement in 1798.⁴⁹ Schröder insisted on

---

45  Cf. Uhde 1879, 6f.
46  Cf. Uhde 1879, 14.
47  Cf. Hoffmann 1939, 18–21; cf. Malchow 2022, 99; cf. Chapter 5.
48  Cf. Münz 1979; cf. Krebs 1985; cf. Graf 1992; cf. Fischer-Lichte/Schönert 1999; cf. Meyer 2012.
49  We are referring to the internal 1798 version as stored in Hamburg Staatsbibliothek. An initial, slimmer version of the Gesetze des *Hamburgischen Theaters* [*Laws of the Hamburg Theatre*] was published in 1792 in a periodical named *Annalen des Theaters* [*Annals of the Theatre*]; cf. Schröder 1792, 3–22. An English translation, titled *Hamburg Theatre Regulations*, is included in Brandt 1992, 108–114. Schröder's first draft of *Laws* which was published in 1781 was similar to rules and regulations of other theatres of the time. Cf. M. Schneider 2018, 104.

collective rehearsals to enhance the understanding of a text and its corresponding enactment on stage.[50] Schröder insisted (or at least tried to insist) that actors and actresses would know and understand their parts precisely rather than improvising them. Schröder also worked on abandoning the habit prevalent among actors of simply standing still whenever they did not have anything to say.[51] Now, everybody had to continue playing their parts, albeit silently, with the purpose of keeping up the illusion of the fictitious world.[52]

The actors' lines and cues were delivered to them on loosely bound handwritten sheets, most of which have been lost in the Hamburg context and are not contained in the Theater-Bibliothek.[53] However, the stage adaptation of the play itself was key: a handwritten copy containing the complete text and frequently additional relevant information about, e.g., actors, props, technical effects, and entrance cues (stage left, stage right), as well as lighting, music, sound effects, etc. Anyone with good enough handwriting, whether aspiring actor or professional scribe, could be employed (and compensated) to copy actors' parts or the fair copy of a whole prompt book.[54] Only a few prompt books from the Theater-Bibliothek can be attributed to a distinct hand with certainty. All copyists were overseen by the prompter, who sometimes went to work copying themselves.[55] There was generally one prompter per German theatre company at the turn of the century – usually a man, in Hamburg a woman until 1776.[56] As stated above, and as we will elaborate upon in the next chapter, the Hamburg prompter was also the librarian and archivist responsible for a company's prompt book collection as a whole and all

---

50 Cf. Malchow 2022, 250–261.

51 Cf. Malchow 2022, 261–264.

52 For an overview of the new modes of rehearsing and staging that emerged in the late eighteenth century as well as Schröder's contributions to the transformation of the respective practices, cf. Maurer-Schmoock 1982, 168–202; cf. Hoffmeier 1964, 97–104.

53 The notable exception are all five part books for August Klingemann's one-act play *Die Matrone von Ephesus*, which he published as *Die Witwe von Ephesus* [*The Widow of Ephesus*] in 1818. The catalogue of Theater-Bibliothek lists a prompt book, an inspection book, as well as booklets for all five parts: Theater-Bibliothek: 492a, Theater-Bibliothek: 492b and Theater-Bibliothek: 492c1–5. The written artefacts are dated ca. 1811. Since they include a censor's note they are firmly to be placed within the French period. However, apart from the censor's approval, there are no traces of use whatsoever. There is also no testimony of the play ever having been performed (for example, in Jahn/Mühle/Eisenhardt/Malchow/M. Schneider (https://www.stadttheater.uni-hamburg.de)). Perhaps the reason that these written artefacts have been preserved is precisely that they were not given out to actors.

54 Cf. Maurer-Schmoock 1982, 98.

55 Cf. Chapter 2.

56 Cf. Malchow 2022, 253.

the other written artefacts created at Schröder's company.[57] They were expected to make sure that as few members of the company as possible had access to the full texts.[58] Schröder's *Gesetze* clearly state in the second law "den Souffleur betreffend" [concerning the prompter]: "Er soll daher die Rollen eines Manuscripts von zwey und mehreren Personen schreiben lassen" [Therefore, he should have the roles in a manuscript copied by two or more people].[59] If several scribes were copying separate sections of the play, e.g., specific actors' lines and their cues, it reduced the risk that any one of them would take off with a copy of the whole play.

Such secrecy was long deemed necessary because the repertoire, i.e., the manuscripts of the plays in the company director's possession, contributed to the company's economic success and standing. It allowed theatres to stage plays that had not been published in print and that other companies did not own. Standing out like this could be crucial in the competitive field of professional theatre, where directors ran their companies as independent entrepreneurs, touring from town to town and fair to fair. In the limited time they spent in one fixed place, they tried to attract as many paying spectators as possible.[60]

However, towards the end of the eighteenth century, an increasing number of companies stopped touring constantly as it was now possible to work at a permanent location, like Schröder's company did in Hamburg. Due to restrictions on the number of days they were allowed to perform there, Schröder's company continued to do a lot of travelling, but they earned more and obtained more local Hamburg permits over time.[61] An increase in professional stability was accompanied by the growing need to vary their programme in order to keep the local audience interested.[62] The periods between productions grew longer, and their reliance on the written records of stage adaptations and technical arrangements increased. In order to diversify their repertoires, company directors also asked authors or the directors of other companies for copies of certain plays, which, if they received a favourable assessment, were copied by the prompter and then included in the company's own repertory. Another option was to put on contests between playwrights – in the anticipation that they would enter usable material. Sometimes,

---

57 Cf. Schröder 1798, 28.
58 An overview of the tasks and the requirements can also be found in Schröder 1798, 28–30.
59 Schröder 1798, 28; Brandt 1992, 112.
60 For the performance conditions and structure of a theatre company in Germany in the eighteenth century, cf. Maurer-Schmoock 1982. For the specific Hamburg circumstances, cf. Malchow 2022.
61 Cf. Malchow 2022, 238–246.
62 From 1750 to 1800, the population of Hamburg increased from 75,000 to 130,000. The opera that was located on the site of the Stadt-Theater held 2,000 spectators. It can be assumed that the Stadt-Theater had a similar capacity. Cf. Malchow 2022, 138–152.

authors also sent in plays on their own initiative in the hope that they would be staged.[63] Either way, manuscripts remained guarded secrets but were circulated more and more frequently among theatres thanks to the relaxing of policy regarding the exclusiveness of company repertories. However, this only increased the number of possible hands and layers revising, updating, and thus enriching prompt books. (Cf. figure 5.)

*Figure 5:* Theater-Bibliothek: 641, 13v and 14r. *Joseph Marius von Babo's heroic tragedy* Die Römer in Teutschland *(created presumably shortly before 1780) was a contribution to a writing contest.*

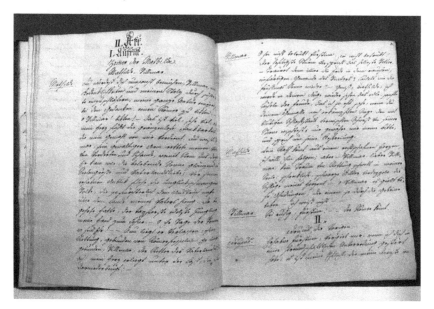

As previously mentioned, from the second half of the eighteenth century onwards, playwrights were having their plays published in print more often and were thus positioning themselves within a growing literary market. While many plays had become easily available as print copies, the specific adaptations used for the stage were still valuable.[64] A print copy could only be aligned by hand with the stage adaptation if the changes were not too drastic and the text remained legible. In most cases, a handwritten version, the fair copy, would be created from the template at hand: The principal might have made some adjustments to a printed book

---

63  Cf. Neubacher 2016, 24–27.

64  Up until the nineteenth century, company directors in European theatre capitals kept up the habit of sending scribes to copy another company's adaptation of a play live over the course of a few nights of its performance. Cf. Stone Peters 2000, 219–225.

or a manuscript sent in by an author – or, as sometimes in Schröder's case in the 1770s, he might have developed his own adaptation of one of Shakespeare's plays. The fair copy was then enriched with any updates that were made after the quires had been stitched and bound together as a book, whether in short-term fixes such as corrections of obvious errors or in long-term transformations, e.g., when a play had been on hiatus for few years and technical conditions had changed, or lines needed to be adapted to reflect the assumed new popular taste. Principals, actors, inspectors, and prompters would come and go; prompt books often remained in use for decades. They developed their own material biographies, which were written by multiple hands (often the principal, the prompter, and any other person in charge) and enriched over long periods of time.

It is these internal dynamics of creating and updating prompt books that our study is interested in and aims to situate within their respective contexts. German (and other European) prompt books at the turn of the nineteenth century and beyond are generic in nature; they follow predictable and repeatable patterns. A prompt book used in Weimar or Vienna during the same period does not look much different from one in the Hamburg collection. Even though "[t]here is no standard operating process for marking prompt-books: Annotations are determined by the individual prompter, stage-manager, or recorder"[65], the conventions of prompt book notation and the symbols used in them are often vaguely similar on both national and international levels; some of them have remained stable over time.[66] However, due to their long-term use, each prompt book has also become a unique written artefact – each a beast of its own. While general patterns are quite easy to observe, each and every prompt book is also an individual rabbit warren of multiple layers of writing and diverse paper practices. The following chapters aim to work through the *they're all the same but they're all unique* conundrum by continuously negotiating the relationship between the overall context and the individual prompt books.

---

65 Malone 2021, 20.

66 It is instructive to compare the abbreviations Düringer and Barthels named in the respective article of their 1841 insiders' German theatre lexicon to the notation practices Arne Langer has compiled for the prompt books of 19th century European opera. The similarities point to widespread overarching practices, the differences probably to a large scope of variation (rather than a difference in genre). Cf. Düringer/Barthels 1841, 9–12; cf. Langer 1997, 155–170.

## III. Framework and Outline

Our study originated at the inter- and transdisciplinary Centre for the Study of Manuscript Cultures (CSMC) at Universität Hamburg, more specifically within the research cluster "Understanding Written Artefacts". We have made full use of this stimulating and collegial environment and have tried out points of view that were new to us. Not least, the CSMC lab performed a scientific ink analysis on a prompt book to allow us to better distinguish between certain layers of writing, which is part of Chapter 5. Wherever productive, we have introduced, adapted, and applied manuscript studies methods and terminology, which have generally been developed for objects produced before the European "age of print" and "age of the book". Their foundations lie in the *material philology* approach put forward by Stephen Nichols, who perceives a text as something "fundamentally unfixed, always open to new inflection" and therefore as something without a "definitive expression".[67] We have found this to be a very apt description of the business of a dramatic text, which was always unfinished, as it was written down and then revised in a prompt book, which itself was regularly changed on a material basis.[68]

Moreover, our open concept of the written text allows us to draw on the 1970s *critique génétique* approach regarding the development of literary manuscripts. Having said that, we do not follow the in part inherent glorification of the individual artistic process and do not attribute any teleology to it. *Critique génétique* conceives of the dynamics of writing processes as, in the words of Almuth Grésillon, a "performative act of becoming text"[69] which takes place in the written artefacts that form the "avant-texte"[70] of an oeuvre. If we take a *critique génétique* perspective on an "open set of writing processes",[71] then theatre texts are a particularly interesting case. Since they are connected to the "stage world", texts written for the theatre are subject to its dynamics and are constantly being adapted to meet the requirements of the stage: "In principle, there is no such thing as a *ne varietur* 'version' of a theatrical work, since each new production can lead not only to new

---

67 Nichols 1997, 17.
68 As Mark Kaethler, Toby Malone, and Jennifer Roberts-Smith put it, a prompt book is a "process" (Kaethler/Malone/Roberts-Smith 2023, 10) rather than a stable entity. In Shakespeare scholarship, this is already state of the art: "What the promptbook remembers is not an event but the movement towards and across events, always marking process." (Holland 2010, 13) The dramatic text "is not an object at all, but rather a dynamic process that evolves over time in response to the needs and sensibilities of its users" (Kidnie 2009, 2).
69 "text before the text", Grésillon 2010, 304.
70 "Performance-Akt der Textwerdung", Grésillon 2010, 304, 291.
71 "ensemble ouvert des processus d'écriture", Grésillon 2016, 12.

versions, but also to new textual twists."[72] Grésillon also points out that theatre texts "are often 'two-handed' writing, i.e., the product of several writers", which is due to the "encounter between a written text and data belonging to the world of the stage (actors, voices, gestures, set, space, lighting)".[73] This applies to prompt books in particular because in most cases they are created, used, and updated by people who belong to the "stage world".

Nevertheless, our aim is to describe and analyse the performative dimensions Grésillon identifies not only with respect to the content of prompt books but also to the extent that they are constitutive for the materiality of a single, multi-layered written artefact. We are interested in the *material performance* and processual dynamics of the prompt books used in the theatre. Although prompt books are sometimes fascinating to behold as objects, ours is not an aesthetic interest but a practical one. Our endeavour clearly reflects a renewed interest in praxeological aspects of literature and theatre.[74] Our interest is related to the interest in writing as a cultural technique,[75] especially in the vein of what has been called research into the "writing scene",[76] i.e., the ways in which writing, its instruments, and its bodily and cultural conditions interact.[77] We examine the writing and paper practices that went into creating and using prompt books, as well as the feedback loops that prompt books formed with their contexts: their material biographies created by various hands over long periods of time; their relationship to a culture increasingly dominated by print, a commercial book market, and notions of individual authorship[78]; the connections between prompt books and the external demands being made by audiences and the authorities; and the internal aesthetic, technical,

---

72 "univers scénique", "L'œuvre théâtrale ne connaît en principe pas de version *ne varietur*; puisque chaque nouvelle mise en scène peut entraîner non seulement de nouvelles visions, mais aussi des rebondissements textuels", Grésillon 2008, 266.
73 "sont souvent de l'écriture 'à deux mains', c'est-à-dire le produit de plusieurs scripteurs", "rencontre entre un texte écrit et des données appurtenant en propre à l'univers scénique (acteurs, voix, gestes, décor, espace, lumière)", Grésillon 2008, 249.
74 Cf. Martus/Spoerhase 2022 for the practices of the humanities themselves; cf. Kershaw 2011 for the 'practice turn' of theatre and performance studies.
75 Cf. Zanetti 2012.
76 Cf. Campe 2021; cf. Stingelin/Giuriato/Zanetti 2004.
77 However, while writing scene research tends to focus on resistances thematized or staged in literature in the structure of writing processes, we are interested in their execution, their causes and effects, and their dynamics in the prompt book itself.
78 Tobias Fuchs argues that the status of authorship in the mid- and late eighteenth century is linked to a publication in print, cf. Fuchs 2021. In emerging copyright laws, authors became the individual creators of individual works – their own works. The authors' name vouched for the quality of the works, through which authors position themselves within a growing literary market. Authors' authority over their works thus combined an aesthetic dimension with economic and ultimately also legal aspects, cf. Plumpe 1979; cf. Bosse 2014.

and practical considerations of adapting plays to the stage. All the prompt books we will examine in the following chapters were subject to the pushing and pulling that took place within this multipolar forcefield. However, each chapter will place special emphasis on only one or two aspects of the prompt book in question. We have also supplemented our discussions digitally with links to scans of the prompt books that we will examine and manuals laying out how we think it best to decipher them, as well as several overviews of layers that we have identified and transcriptions that we have made during the course of our work.[79]

After two more general chapters, three case studies will examine individual prompt books or pairs of prompt books within the milieu that constituted their specific manuscript culture. After this introduction, Chapter 2 will outline the practice of prompting in Germany in the late eighteenth and early nineteenth centuries. The fact that prompting depended on someone reading in a hushed voice from a prompt book is often taken for granted. In contrast, our account draws out the intricate relationship between prompter, prompting, and prompt book, while paying particular attention to Schröder's Hamburg troupe. Chapter 3 will then take a manuscript studies approach to present the most common writing and paper practices employed in the prompt books of the Hamburg Theater-Bibliothek. In Chapter 4, close analyses of two prompt books for August von Kotzebue's *Die Sonnen-Jungfrau* [*The Virgin of the Sun*] will take a look behind the scenes of creating and updating multi-handed and multi-layered prompt books. This is the only example of a preserved trial copy in which the Kotzebue's play was first written down and then revised for what became the actual prompt book for the 1790 production. Both fair copies were distributed between several scribes to prevent bootlegging. The chapter will go on to analyse two revision periods in 1813 and 1823, during which the prompt book, which was used until 1826, was revised by several hands and writing tools. Chapter 5 will then assume a broader perspective by situating Schröder's 1770s Hamburg adaptations of Shakespeare at the intersection between plays published in print and their stage adaptations. In a second step, the chapter will retrace these interconnections with regard to the hasty revisions Schröder made to the prompt book for *Othello* (to better tailor the failing 1776 production to public tastes) and the longevity of his 1778 production of *König Lear* [*King Lear*] in Hamburg (a print copy of which was revised to meet censorship requirements in 1812). After that, Chapter 6 will zoom in on the practical and technical implications of revising a play for the stage. An adaptation by Friedrich Schiller of G. E. Lessing's 1779 dramatic parable *Nathan der Weise* [*Nathan the Wise*] was copied by hand into an inspector's book, while a print copy of Lessing's original version was reworked by hand into a prompt book by employing various paper

---

79 Cf. http://doi.org/10.25592/uhhfdm.13916 (Felser/Funke/Göing/Hussain/Schäfer/Weinstock/Bosch 2024).

practices. Both written artefacts then took on lives of their own as the play was intermittently staged over a period of forty years between the 1800s and 1840s. Finally, Chapter 7 will run through the ways in which we hope our study can be productive for the disciplines we have drawn on, i.e., theatre, literary, and manuscript studies.

We do not intend to give a (quantitative) overview of scribes, users, revisers, or, for that matter, of genres, periods, or any other patterns that can be observed in the prompt books of the Hamburg Theater-Bibliothek collection. Here, a lot of valuable research has been and remains to be done. Our research is deeply indebted to the work carried out by Bernhard Jahn, Jacqueline Malchow, and Martin Schneider[80], especially to their effort to reconstruct the Stadt-Theater programme for the period 1770–1850 from playbill leaflets and other sources.[81]

We will not be able to do justice to every aspect of the Hamburg repertory with its focus on comedies[82], and operas[83] as well as its inclusion of prologues[84], one-act plays, and interspersed musical numbers. Although there are three prompt books for the same production in a few cases (a separate prompt book for arias alongside a libretto prompt book, and one for the inspector[85]), there is next to no interaction between the prompt and inspection books on the one hand and the musical material on the other. Similarly, prologues and one-act plays seem to have been reused only when they still suited requirements; the respective written artefacts were rarely enriched or reshaped, and also warrant a quantitative approach.

The prompt books examined in this study were chosen on the basis of how representative they are of prompt book practices from that time. We will describe their content and material form in relation to those practices. The plays that make up their content might not proportionally represent the entire repertory, but they do reveal perspectives that we find paradigmatic in one way or another. Kotzebue's *Die Sonnen-Jungfrau* stands for the crowd-pleasing, entertaining plays that dominated the repertory. Moreover, the Stadt-Theater not only emphasised its productions of Shakespeare, Lessing, and Schiller in order to underline its own artistic quality – those authors and their plays were also very popular. However, by no means had they already achieved the canonical status that they would come to enjoy over the next two centuries. Instead of demonstrating the diversity of what then comprised the "canon" (which, again, would require a more quantitative approach), we aim to

---

80 Cf. Jahn 2016; cf. Malchow 2022; cf. M. Schneider 2023; cf. M. Schneider 2024.
81 Cf. Jahn/Mühle/Eisenhardt/Malchow/M. Schneider (https://www.stadttheater.uni-hamburg.de).
82 Cf. Dennerlein 2021.
83 Cf. Neubacher 2016, 29–34.
84 Cf. Özelt/Schneider 2024.
85 Cf. the written artefacts for Salieri's opera *Axur*: *Theater-Bibliothek: 1403a* (for the inspector), *Theater-Bibliothek: 1403b* (for the libretto without the arias), *Theater-Bibliothek: 1403c* (for the arias).

demonstrate how entirely uncanonical later canonised plays were when analysed as part of prompt book practices at the turn of the century – as texts that were in flux, inconsistent, and always up for a potential revision.[86]

A well-established (and largely justified) historical narrative generally associates the period spanning the mid-eighteenth to mid-nineteenth centuries with the emergence of new cultural norms and concepts, including notions of individual authorship (which expressed themselves in copyright laws) and works of art (such as dramatic texts) that were no longer beholden to outside authorities. The theatre of that period both relied and did not rely on those notions, and the material biography of a prompt book exposes their multi-layered underbelly. On some heavily revised or glued-over prompt book manuscript pages, the truism that every text consists of a web of intertextual quotations has become a material reality. The same applies for the truism that every theatre production is a collective endeavour.[87] While none of the multiple hands and tools that co-created and continuously updated a prompt book could have laid claim to authorship as it appeared on the playbill leaflet, these prompt book practices nevertheless provided the critical infrastructure[88] that made the staging of "plays" by "authors" possible in the first place.

---

[86] If there is a common thread running through the plays in these prompt books, it is how, in the distinctly local world of prompt book creation and use, the content of the plays depicted the greater world outside of Hamburg. In line with the changing fashions of the time, *otherness* stepped onto the Hamburg stage as the "Moor" Othello whose agency runs counter to the staple exotic moor characters in other 1770s dramatic texts. In the 1790s, the fashionable Incas in Kotzebue's *Sonnen-Jungfrau* [*Virgin of the Sun*] served as exotic elements while at the same time delivering a thinly veiled mockery of the German present. In the 1800s, it was the backdrop of Orientalism that led to the discovery of Lessing's much earlier play, set in Jerusalem during the Crusades, for the stage. The practices that reworked the plays and thus reshaped the prompt books often made reference to this *otherness*: Othello's unsettling agency, the Incas' too-close-to-home monotheism, the changing negotiation of religion in *Nathan der Weise*. Such changes cannot be separated from their manifestations in the material biography of the respective prompt book.

[87] Cf. Weigel 1952.

[88] Cf. Etzold 2023.

# Chapter 2. Prompting and Its Written Artefacts: Anecdotal Evidence

Much of our knowledge about the work done by eighteenth- and nineteenth-century German prompters, and, by extension, the written artefacts they used, is anecdotal in nature.[1] Prompters were only talked about when they had to intervene, i.e., when the performance did not run as smoothly as it should have. In doing their job, prompters – and their written artefacts – appeared disruptive and exposed small mistakes.[2] Aside from being perceived as a general nuisance, disruptions that were deemed especially funny, telling, or revealing were passed on, retold (perhaps in a more pointed fashion), or became folklore. When examining the work of prompters, *fact and fiction*, i.e., claims to truth and the emphatic pleasure taken in fabulation, become indiscernible and reinforce one another. To complicate matters even further, a great number of the anecdotes in question can be found in theatre chronicles and almanacs compiled by the prompters of the time for extra income.[3] What would later be perceived as "knowledge" of the work of prompting in the emerging theatre lexicons and histories of the nineteenth century seems to be greatly indebted to this amalgamation of lore and storytelling. This makes it all the more important to use the frequently anecdotal evidence as a steppingstone to learn more about the work of prompters on the basis of their written artefacts – considering how these stories were told and what they left out.

---

1 For the theoretical power of the anecdotal, cf. Gallop 2002.
2 For the insight gained through interruptions, cf. Latour 2005, 81–83.
3 Cf. Ulrich 2022; cf. Žigon 2012.

## I. Prompting as a "Necessary Evil" in Eighteenth- and Nineteenth-Century German Theatre

When, at the onset of the nineteenth century, prominent members of the local Hamburg audience lodged a complaint with the management of their once renowned Stadt-Theater about the overall quality of performances,[4] one of their main points of contention was the unwelcome, continuous interference of the prompter during the performances. Actors played up to fifty different parts a year, often a different one every night.[5] Although most of them played parts according to their *Rollenfach* [role type] (the young lover, the dame, the old bully, the young hero, etc.), there were too many lines and cues to memorise,[6] and it was impossible to be on point all the time or, sometimes, to even become familiar with one's part at all. Enter the voice of the prompter, which was not always able to meet its main requirement, namely to be heard by the actors but not by the audience.[7] The latter thus regularly witnessed the prompter at work: prompters feeding actors forgotten lines and helping out with missed cues became a constant feature of performances in Hamburg. But witnessing the prompter at work did not mean seeing them. The prompter's voice was strangely placeless; it was on the stage and yet it was not. The prompt box, from where the voice emerged, was a "Verschlag unter dem Podium des Proszeniums gerade in der Mitte zwischen den beiden Beleuchtungslampen"[8] [hutch under the proscenium podium, right in the middle, between the two lighting lamps], as it was described in a mid-nineteenth-century dictionary. This box was open towards the stage but protruded only slightly into it so as to make space for the prompter's head – and their arms in the event the prompter was also tasked with lighting and putting out tallow candles on the ramp. Thus, the prompter was both on and off stage. They were simultaneously in the light and in the dark, in the heat and in the cold. A humorous piece in one of the growing number of theatre almanacs described them as suffering from the "Last von Kälte oder Hitze; denn er verschmachtet ja im Sommer, in mitten der ihn von beiden Seiten einkeilenden hundert Lampen"[9] [burden of cold or heat; for he languishes in summer, in the midst of the hundred lamps wedging him in from both sides]. Shielded in a way

---

4 Cf. M. Schneider 2017, 281–287.
5 Cf. M. Schneider 2017, 10; cf. Malchow 2022, 274–282; cf. Ulrich 2008, 218–222.
6 Cf. Tkaczyk 2012.
7 "Die Hauptaufgabe des Souffleurs ist, von dem Schauspieler verstanden und von dem Publikum nicht gehört zu werden." (Düringer/Barthels 1841, 1003) [The main task of the prompter is to be understood by the actor and not heard by the audience.]
8 Blum/Herloßsohn/Marggraff 1846b, 13.
9 Holzapfel 1823, 114. (Holzapfel's compilation Neuer Almanach quotes a speech by then Stadt-Theater director Friedrich Ludwig Schmidt in honour of the recently deceased prompter Heinrich Barlow.)

that emanated as little light as possible, the audience could not see that someone was both up and down there with a copy of the lines to be uttered on stage by the actors, simultaneously reading along, observing, attentively listening, and anticipating any potential pitfalls. While the audience was bothered by the sometimes unintelligible whispers or, occasionally, by the all too comprehensible interjections, prompters did not conjure their words out of thin air. Rather, they relied on the written artefacts they had with them in the dim light of their hutch. It was these stable, storable, portable, and updatable written artefacts[10] which the whole performance was based on. They went unneeded and unnoticed during the performance if lines had been sufficiently memorised, but were always at hand in the event they had not – and also somewhere close by during the everyday work of the theatre company, just in case it seemed like a good idea to brush up a tried and tested play that might fit well with the audience's current tastes.

Much of this situation was historically specific to German spoken-word theatre. During the eighteenth century, prompters had become an integral part of theatre companies.[11] Slowly, touring companies started to settle down in permanent locations as they had in Hamburg – but without enough of a population base to repeatedly perform a given play in house, sometimes not even more than once a year. During the eighteenth century, German critics notoriously called for a "purification of the stage",[12] i.e., for educational plays and stagings based on literary texts to be performed instead of the playful extemporisation of loose narrative patterns. While adherence to such theoretical demands was mixed in practice and varied from company to company, as well as from region to region, a long-lasting trend had nevertheless been set. The amount of text that actors were expected to commit to memory grew exponentially[13] and, with it, the need to provide a remedy whenever the flow of a performance stalled. This was when prompters helped out on a more than regular basis.[14] Since the prompters themselves could not possibly learn all the lines by heart, they needed written artefacts containing lines from the play to help them along. What the Hamburg audience heard was the prompter reading from a prompt book as softly as possible.

---

10 Cf. Latour 1986, 19f., 25–39.

11 Cf. Maurer-Schmoock 1982, 97f.

12 "Gereinigtes Theater", cf. Heßelmann 2002.

13 In addition, the authorities in some cities such as Vienna seized the opportunity to tightly control every word that was uttered on stage. Texts had to be submitted and authorised prior to performances. Moreover, there was always the chance that a policeman would be present to control the faithful recitation of the lines. Cf. Ulrich 2008, 221.

14 It was only when the state began owning or at least supporting German theatres that their reliance on the prompter decreased. For this transition period in Hamburg, cf. Brauneck/Müller/Müller-Wesemann 1989, 98–155.

The audience's complaints about the profuse reliance on prompters, and therefore their written artefacts, was a staple of intra-theatrical discussion about aesthetic standards and technical requirements during the first half of the nineteenth century. The high demands placed on the actors by the ever-changing repertory of plays ran counter to prevailing notions of what an ideal performance should look like. The late eighteenth century prided itself on its new acting style developed and refined in Schröder's company, the "natürliche"[15] [natural] Hamburg style of acting, intended to convey the impression that the audience was witnessing an only ever so slightly enhanced truth on stage. This style fit in well with the predominance of prose plays that were being put forward by the playwrights of the time.[16] A shift in the early nineteenth century saw renewed emphasis being placed on the artifice of acting as developed in Iffland's declamatory Berlin style and in the strictly metrical style of the new dramas being influenced by Goethe's and Schiller's Weimar aesthetics.[17] As constant background noise, the prompter's murmuring undermined both aesthetic concepts – the illusion of nature and the artifice of art. Both were exposed as something that had been created by the cranking nuts and bolts of the theatre apparatus. Instead of embodying characters and creating an artistic illusion onstage, even the most personal of means that such characters brought to the table – their words – were being injected from an obscure place inside the theatrical infrastructure – and read in a hushed voice from an unseen written artefact.

A practitioner like Friedrich Ludwig Schmidt, who had first been an actor before becoming a co-principal at the Hamburg Stadt-Theater from 1815 to 1841, mused in the 1820s on the ugly sight of the "Kapsel des unterirdischen Orakels" [capsule of the subterranean oracle] that was the prompt box containing its inhabitant. While the figure of Hanswurst had (supposedly) been chased from the eighteenth-century boards, the ideal nineteenth-century stage would now have to be purged of the prompt box, which was a stand-in for the prompter – and, by extension, for the written artefacts they used:

> Gelänge es den "Einhelfer", wie man früher in ehrlichem Deutsch sagte, ganz zu verbannen, so wäre damit eine wahre Herkulesarbeit geglückt. O welch ein unschätzbarer Reiz wäre der Schauspielkunst gewonnen, wenn die Kapsel des unterirdischen Orakels nicht mehr mitten im Vordergrunde der Bühne figurirte, – sie, die in jeder Hinsicht ein schreiender Übelstand ist und an die nur hundertjähriger Schlendrian uns gewöhnen konnte![18] [If the "helper", as they used to say in straight-

---

15  Malchow 2022, 187.
16  Cf. Kob 2000, 137f.
17  Cf. Heeg 1999.
18  Schmidt 1875, 139.

forward German, could be banished completely, it would be the achievement of a true Herculean task. O what inestimable charm would be gained for the art of acting if the capsule of the subterranean oracle no longer figured in the foreground of the stage – in every respect it is a glaring nuisance to which only a century of carelessness could have accustomed us!]

By the mid-nineteenth century, the irritating, excessive reliance on prompters and their written artefacts had made it into the new German theatre lexicons and encyclopaedias (being published by insiders above all for other insiders). In their 1841 *Theater-Lexikon*, Philipp Jakob Düringer and Heinrich Ludwig Barthels grumbled:

> Die englischen Theater haben ihren Souffleur in den Kulissen stehen, und brauchen ihn nur, im Falle Einer stecken bleibt; die Franzosen haben den Souffleurkasten wie wir, und ihr Souffleur schlägt nur die Perioden an; bei uns hat der Arme am meisten zu tun, denn leider nur zu oft ist er dazu da, um das ganze Stück vorzulesen, mindestens in jedem Stücke einige Rollen.[19] [The English theatres have their prompter standing in the wings, and only need him in the event that an actor gets stuck; the French have the prompter's box like us, and their prompter only cues a new period; in our theatres, the poor man has the most to do, for unfortunately, he is all too often there to read out the whole play, at least some roles in each.]

The reliance on a written artefact is implied but not explicitly stated. As the mediator between written artefact and actors, the prompter was proclaimed to be the metonymical root of the problem. In their competing 1846 lexicon, Blum, Herloßsohn, and Marggraff gave the continuous grind of the everchanging repertory as the reason, if not an excuse, for German actors' dependence on the inhabitant of the prompt box:

> Man hat häufig das franz. Theater als mußtergültig ausgestellt [...] und auf die leider nicht zu verkennenden Folgen hingedeutet, welche die fortdauernde Thätigkeit des deutschen S.s auf die Darstellung hat. [...] [M]an vergißt indessen, daß in Frankreich 20 bis 30 Proben stattfinden, wo in Deutschland höchstens 3 [...]; daß ein Stück täglich so lange hintereinander fort gegeben wird, bis das Publikum sich gleichgültig gegen dasselbe zeigt, während in Deutschland täglich Anderes und unersättlich Neues verlangt wird. [...] Die fortdauernde Thätigkeit des S.s ist also in Deutschland ein nothwendiges Uebel [...].[20] [The French theatre has often been

---

19  Düringer/Barthels 1841, 1004.
20  Blum/Herloßsohn/Marggraff 1846b, 11f. The thoroughly practical problem of the prompter on the German stage is discussed in terms that are highly theoretical and even metaphysical. This discourse is a prime example of what Jacques Derrida has analysed as the logic of the "danger-

described as exemplary [...] and hints have been made at the unmistakeable consequences of the continuous activity of the German p[rompter] for the theatrical presentation. [...] However, one forgets that in France, 20 to 30 rehearsals take place, while in Germany 3 at most [...]; that a play is performed every day, day after day, until the audience has become indifferent to it, while in Germany something different and insatiably new is demanded on a daily basis. [...] Therefore, the continuous activity of the p[rompter] in Germany is a necessary evil.]

In spite of all attempts at explanation, the unpopular but intimate relationship between German actors and prompters – and implicitly with their written artefacts as well – was constantly being panned and slammed by critics and academics. In his influential 1843 *Wissenschaftlich-literarische Encyklopädie der Aesthetik* [*Encyclopaedia of Aesthetics*], Hebenstreit demonstrated his abhorrence for the customary "Kunst auf den Souffleur zu spielen"[21] [art of playing to the prompter], an idiom that even received its own entry in Düringer and Barthels's lexicon.[22] According to Hebenstreit, instead of presenting a fleshed-out character, the actor became a lifeless puppet, a "Maschine, die durch den Souffleur aufgezogen wird"[23] [machine wound up by the prompter]. Biting remarks about actors' ineptitude were legion in the proliferation of chronicles and almanacs compiled by working or former nineteenth-century prompters as well as in the first overviews of modern theatre history. Actors came to stand in front of the prompt box "wie angepicht"[24] [as if pinned down]; they repeated empty interjections while waiting for "das fehlende Wort" [the missing word] and seemed more "zu Hause"[25] [at home] in the prompt box than in their roles. The most damning judgment that could be made about a performance was "daß der Souffleur an dieser Bühne die Hauptperson sei"[26] [that the prompter is the main character at this theatre]. The audience is said to have taken it with composure, even amusement, when a popular but forgetful actor found the prompt box empty one evening and, as a matter of course, declared: "Verzeihen Sie, ich kann nicht weiter spielen, der Souffleur ist

---

ous supplement" (Derrida 1984, 141): something that is, on the one hand, necessary to produce a stable, coherent identity of some sort but that, on the other hand, undermines that very stability and coherence in that it is external to such an identity. Even more to the point, the voice of the prompter spells out what Derrida has called "[l]a parole soufflée" (Derrida 1978, 169) at the heart of Antonin Artaud's twentieth-century theatre aesthetics: the horror of an external force which has infected the performers' (and humanity's) core by whispering in its own words and thoughts.

21  Hebenstreit 1843, 726.
22  Cf. Düringer/Barthels 1841, 85.
23  Hebenstreit 1843, 726.
24  *Allgemeine Theater-Chronik* 1845c, 459.
25  *Allgemeine Theater-Chronik* 1846, Nr. 116, 462.
26  Devrient 1848, 108.

nicht auf seinem Posten"[27] [Excuse me, I cannot play any further, the prompter is not at his post].

It was only on rare occasions that prompters themselves were noticed as participants in the performance rather than as disembodied voices – when the usual procedures were interrupted by their mistakes or defiance. On such occasions, commentators struck a good-natured or amused tone, e.g., when a prompter was even more moved by the play than the audience and burst into tears: "[e]in seltenes Kompliment für Dichter und Darsteller"[28] [a rare compliment for poet and performer]. But normally, the pervasiveness of the "necessary evil" that everything depended on, although it needed to be obscured at every turn, found an outlet in epithets that were simultaneously flowery and biting:

> "Theatralischer Schachtmeister und Hütten-Inspector", "Unentbehrlicher Versteckspieler", "Declamatorischer Rede-Fluß-Schleusenmeister", "König der Echo's", "Urquell der ästhetischen Ergötzlichkeiten", "Ohrenbläser und Wort-Eingeber", "Hebebaum des versunkenen Thespis-Karren", "unterirdischer Magnet der Oberwelt", "Magister legens", "Theoretischer Universal-Schauspieler und dramatischer Revisor", "Grundstein vom Tempel Thalia's"[29] [Theatrical shaft master and hut inspector, indispensable hide-and-seek player, declamatory speech-flow lockmaster, king of echoes, fountainhead of aesthetic delights, ear blower and word feeder, lever of the sunken Thespis cart, subterranean magnet of the upper world, magister legens, theoretical universal actor and dramatic revisor, foundation stone of Thalia's temple]

The joke in most of these metaphors and descriptions is that the hidden emergency responder is another actor in the play – or even its "main character" – drawing on the discrepancy between the significance of the prompter for the performance and their insignificant and thoroughly humble position at their workplace. However, all of these descriptions either take for granted or ignore the fact that prompters themselves were not the originators of the lines they fed the hapless actors. Prompters were not "universal actors" but, first and foremost, readers. And with them down in the "shaft", they had written artefacts from which they read in a hushed voice. Indeed, the joke would lose its punchline if it referred to this self-evident technical requirement. The work of the prompter depended on an auxiliary item, a written artefact that contained a version of the dramatic text that was to be performed. Prompters were therefore special kinds of readers who had to be alert to any discrepancies between what was recorded in the written artefact and

---

27  Devrient 1848, 278.
28  *Allgemeine Theater-Chronik* 1845b, 304.
29  As compiled by Paul S. Ulrich 2008, 223.

what was actually transpiring on stage. In fact, the written artefacts, the prompt books, were the truly "indispensable" "foundation stones" of performances. The actors fully relied on the prompter's ability to make good use of the prompt book – to reliably read along, to know when to intervene, to restore order when someone bungled up a passage or jumped to an entirely different part of the play, and to anticipate any potential problems.

It is only when we examine the entanglement between the written artefact, the prompter, the actors, and the overall infrastructure of the work at a theatre company that the role that prompting played in eighteenth- and nineteenth-century German theatre comes into view. Importantly, prompt books provide more than enough evidence of the theatrical practices implemented on stage at a given point in time and attest to how a given literary text was adapted. It was the practices implemented with and upon these written artefacts that tied many of the knots that these entanglements consist of. Therefore, the focus of this study is on the prompt books themselves and the ways in which they lent "affordance"[30] to such entanglements. The following chapters will try to explain in depth why and how this was the case. But for now, let us retrace the relationship between prompters and their written artefacts in more (anecdotal) detail.

## II. A Question of Honour: Taking Care of the Written Artefacts of Prompting and More

As we will explain over the course of this study, the written artefacts used in the prompt box contained the lines of a company's specific version of a given play as well as any additional information the prompter might require. The prompters usually took care of the "Zeichen zum Anfangen und Endigen des Acts, die Verwandlungen, Tag und Nachtmachen u.s.w."[31] [signs at the beginning and end of an act, the transformations of the scene, light cues for day and night etc.]. The orchestra conductor was usually located at the back of the box, towards the audience, and could be notified of any action that needed to be taken by a knock. The equipment in the box varied depending on the technical equipment on stage, as did the cues that needed to be recorded in the prompt book. In an opera house, the prompter might have been able to operate the bellows with their feet or might have had bell pulls to notify stage workers of impending tasks.[32] On a stage without a prompt box, they might have whispered the words from the side of the stage as was custom in English theatres. The Hamburg Stadt-Theater stage at Gänsemarkt

---

30 Gibson 1986, 130–134; cf. Levine 2015, 6–11.
31 Blum/Herloßsohn/Marggraff 1846b, 11.
32 Cf. the article "Zeichen" [signs] in Düringer/Barthels 1841, 1136–1139.

was not particularly technically sophisticated,[33] but anecdotes relay that it had a conventional prompt box from which lines could be fed and signs could be given.

The prompter also acted as the librarian at Hamburg's Stadt-Theater in the late eighteenth and early nineteenth centuries. At least, this is how Friedrich Ludwig Schröder, the long-standing Hamburg principal, described the prompter when he put forward his *Gesetze des Hamburgischen Theaters* [*Laws of the Hamburg Theatre*], the internal code of conduct for his company that Schröder formulated as a set of rules and regulations and then printed and circulated in the 1790s. The first of the "Gesetze den Souffleur betreffend" [Regulations concerning the prompter] immediately states that "er zugleich Bibliothekar ist" [he is also the librarian]. However, this definition characterised the prompter as being somewhere between a bookkeeper in the literal sense, i.e., as caretaker of all written artefacts, and a scribe. The prompter "muss die Bücher in gehöriger Ordnung erhalten, und bey dem Verluste seiner Ehre kein Manuscript ohne Anfrage weggeben, und jede Entwendung zu verhüten suchen, damit Autor und Director nicht Schaden leiden" [has to keep the texts in good order and must not give away any scripts without authorisation at the risk of forfeiting his honour, and he must try to prevent any theft so that neither the author nor the director suffers any damage]. The books in question included a "Hauptbuch der Rollenvertheilung" [main book of casting] with notes about sets, props, and running time; a "Hauptbuch der Garderobe" [main book of wardrobe]; a "Requisitenbuch" [prop book]; and a "Decorationsbuch" [scenery book][34]. In Schröder's theatre, the prompter also produced most of the other written artefacts, no matter their function. These ranged from "circulars" which needed to be sent around and signed by everyone concerned to all written artefacts used on stage: "Er schreibt die Briefe, welche nebst den Schriften und Büchern auf dem Theater zu seinen Requisiten gehören"[35] [He writes the letters, which, alongside the writings and books, belong to his props at the theatre]. In short, prompters operated something akin to an "office" in the modern administrative sense in that they presided over the interface between all stored written artefacts and their utilisation. At the same time, they were the main users of this living archive.[36]

Rather incidentally, Schröder's regulations also tell us that the prompter was involved in copying out the various roles of the actors, who as a matter of convention only received their lines and cues in a small booklet: "Wenn er Zeit und Lust hat, selbst Rollen zu schreiben, so werden sie ihm bezahlt"[37] [If he has the time and inclination to write out parts himself he will receive [extra] payment]. In practice,

---

33 Cf. Malchow 2022, 138ff.
34 Schröder 1798, 28; Brandt 1992, 112.
35 Schröder 1798, 29; Brandt 1992, 113.
36 Cf. Meynen 2004, 11.
37 Schröder 1798, 29; Brandt 1992, 113.

this also referred to the writing of the content of the prompt books. Jacob Herzfeld, one of the co-principals in Hamburg from 1798 to 1826, stated in the 1800s that he preferred the handwriting of Heinrich Barlow, the Stadt-Theater prompter from 1796 until his death in 1820, to that of every other scribe.[38] One of his later co-principals, Friedrich Ludwig Schmidt, stated in Barlow's obituary that the prompter spent a lot of his spare time "mit Abschreiben von Stücken und Rollen [...]. Er war ein solcher Geschwindschreiber, daß er nach einer mäßigen Schätzung in den lezten vierzehn Jahren [...] mindestens 28,000 Bögen à 3 Schilling geschrieben haben muß"[39] [with copying plays and rolls [...]. He was such a fast writer that, by a conservative estimate, he must have written at least 28,000 sheets for 3 shillings each in the last fourteen years].

As we explained in the introduction, the role of the librarian came with huge responsibility. Before the advent of copyright laws, a successful play was a valuable commodity. Companies did not want to share their plays, and playwrights could only expect to be paid by the principal if their new work was not commercially (or otherwise) available in print yet. Therefore, Schröder's regulations tasked the prompter with "preventing theft". The previously quoted second rule codified a common eighteenth-century practice by decreeing it mandatory to "have the actors' parts [in a play] copied by two or more persons". Thus, none of the scribes and none of the actors would have a copy of the complete play in hand that they could sneak out.

At this point in theatre history, actors were usually familiar with the play as a whole. Building on Ekhof and his own stepfather Ackermann, Schröder had employed reading rehearsals and later introduced the practice of rehearsing the whole play. Actors now worked as an ensemble, but those who spontaneously jumped in as substitutes were not usually given access to the complete play. This made their work difficult since the play to be performed in the evening was often only announced the evening before or on the day of the performance itself. Karoline Schulze Kummerfeld, who would later star as Iphigenie, wrote of Clara Hoffmann, prompter in the Ackermann company: "Die war auf die Bücher wie der Teufel auf eine Seele. Kurz, ich bekam's nicht. [...] Daß ich nicht [...] ganz so gespielt, wie ich hätte sollen, war kein Wunder"[40] [She was after the books like the devil after a soul. In short, I didn't get it. [...] It was no surprise [...] that I didn't perform as I should have].

---

38 Barlow was "der einzige, dem wir das copiren der mcpte anvertrauen" (quoted in Neubacher 2016, 25) [the only one we entrust with copying the manuscripts]. In Chapter 6, section 5, we discuss supplements to *Nathan der Weise* written by Barlow.

39 Schmidt 1875, 141f.

40 Schulze-Kummerfeld 1915, 105f.; cf. Maurer-Schmoock 1982, 98f.; cf. Malchow 2022, 219.

The caution taken by Schröder and his predecessor was well-founded: prompters were popular first points of contact (often behind the principal's back) for those in search of a specific play or stage adaptation. In his essay on the prompter in German theatre, nineteenth-century actor Hermann Schöne recalled some of the widely circulating anecdotes:

> An Johann Fr. Schütze in Hamburg schrieb ein kursächsischer Buchhändler ganz ehrlich (!) und rund heraus: "Sie kennen ohne Zweifel den Souffleur der Schröderschen Bühne. Senden Sie mir doch gelegentlich durch ihn (oder mit seiner Hilfe) Manuskripte Schillerscher Stücke. Ich will sie gut bezahlen." – Holtei erzählt vom Souffleur W. beim Königlichen Theater in Berlin, daß er einen verbotenen Kleinhandel mit abgeschriebenen Manuskripten betrieb. In späteren Jahren verfielen neue Couplets und Einlagen aller Arten, trotz Vorsichtsmaßregeln der Urheber und Eigentümer, den Geiersgriffen der Souffleure, welche Abschriften machten und verkauften, bis endlich die Gesetze zum Schutze des geistigen Eigentums diesem Standrechte ein Ende machten.[41] [To Johann Fr. Schütze in Hamburg, a bookseller from the Electorate of Saxony wrote in a quite frank (!) and uninhibited manner: "You undoubtedly know the prompter at Schröder's stage. Please occasionally send me manuscripts of Schiller's plays through him (or with his help). I will pay you well for them." – Holtei tells the story of the prompter W. at the Royal Theatre in Berlin, who ran a small, forbidden trade in copied manuscripts. In later years, despite the precautions taken by authors and owners, new couplets and inserts of all kinds fell into the vulture's grip of prompters who made and sold copies, until the laws for the protection of intellectual property finally put an end to that privilege.]

Thus, in Schröder's day, the prompter-librarian was the weak link in protecting the written artefacts from wider circulation. Only the prompter's "honour", as Schröder's *Gesetze* referred to it, stood between their safe-keeping and the abuse detailed by Schöne.

Being promoted to librarian, a position of considerable responsibility, was at odds with the historical reality of the profession. In the mid-eighteenth century, prompters were often actors who had just started out or who had too little talent for the stage.[42] One Johann Christian Brandes had to start with "zugleich Rollen schreiben, [...] die Stelle eines Souffleurs vertreten, und auch in den Baletten mitfiguriren"[43] [copying parts, [...] taking the place of the prompter, and also performing in the ballets all at once]. The responsibility for the written artefacts may have organically developed out of the subordinate activity as a copyist but altogether

---

41  Schöne 1904, 135; cf. Ulrich 2008, 224ff.
42  Cf. Maurer-Schmoock 1982, 98.
43  Brandes 1799, 173.

represented a qualitative leap: a promotion from the lowest rank in the company to the position of librarian responsible for everything.

Goethe's famous bildungsroman *Wilhem Meisters Lehrjahre* [*Wilhelm Meister's Apprenticeship*] (published in the mid-1790s), which is also an ironic itinerary through recent theatre history, demonstrates a playful take that nonetheless gets to the point in question. When the prompter of a company (that is more or less based on Schröder's in Hamburg) moves up to the position of actor (in a twofold sense, as he takes on the role of lead actor in the traveling theatre company in *Hamlet*), a drifting youth named Friedrich (who had been following around the company staging *Hamlet* out of love for another actor) is swiftly employed as prompter. Once their theatrical careers come to an end, he and his mistress hide away in a library and read books out loud to each other without understanding them.[44] In the 1820s sequel *Wilhelm Meisters Wanderjahre* [*Wilhelm Meister's Journeyman Years*], Friedrich is then promoted to the role of professional archivist.[45] While the two latter parts of the storyline no longer take place within the realm of theatre, they clearly spell out the development from prompter to archivist-librarian that underlies Schröder's conflation of the two positions: the prompter becomes an archivist by mechanically reading out lines which would not normally concern them at all.

A good century after Brandes started out as a prompter and copyist, the new theatre lexicons and encyclopaedias listed the librarian as a separate profession but still proposed that their work could be done in tandem with another administrative role such as that of secretary, inspector, or, thirdly, prompter.[46] The question is, however, to which extent Schröder's 1790s or Düringer and Barthels's 1840s ideal was put into practice on a larger scale. When the Hamburg Stadt-Theater moved to its new building at Dammtorstraße (now home to the opera house), a new owner had to negotiate with Schröder's heirs to gain the rights to use the company's collection of prompt books. When Schröder died in 1816, he was still the main owner of all the written artefacts, which he, and after him his heirs, leased to the company. A late-nineteenth-century history of the Stadt-Theater claimed that, ten years later, the collection, precursor to today's Theater-Bibliothek, did not have a proper caretaker and was in a sorrowful state. The supposed librarian is not named but seems to have been someone not wholly devoted to the task at hand:

> [ein] beliebiger Mann, der auf die Soufflirbücher und Rollen Acht zu geben hatte, denn von einer wirklichen Fürsorge, welche die Direction der Bibliothek gewidmet hätte, war gar keine Rede. Es sind durch Unkenntniß und beispiellose Schleuderei Schätze und bibliographische Seltenheiten ersten Ranges rettungslos zu Grunde

---

44 Cf. Goethe 1988a, 554–559.

45 Cf. Goethe 1988b, 334f.

46 Cf. Düringer/Barthels 1841, 162.

gegangen. Die werthvolle Büchersammlung, welche Schröder mit Liebe und Sorgfalt angelegt hatte [...] – Alles ist zersprengt, zertrümmert, zerstört, theilweise nach Gewicht an Käsehöker verhauft worden, weil die Directoren einer Bühne wie das Stadttheater in Hamburg diesen Dingen das gebührende Interesse selten oder nie gewidmet haben.[47] [The library was left in the hands of a random man who had to take care of the prompt books and actors' parts, for there was no question of any real care given by management to the library. Treasures and bibliographical rarities of the most important kind have been lost due to ignorance and unprecedented recklessness. The valuable collection of books which Schröder had built up with love and care [...] – Everything was shattered, smashed, destroyed, and some of it sold by the pound to cheesemongers, because the principals of a theatre such as the Stadttheater in Hamburg have seldom or never devoted the proper interest to these things.]

The sale of written artefacts like prompt books to the local cheesemonger is an extreme example of what Schröder's "first law of theatre concerning the prompter" was supposed to prevent – "at the forfeiture of his honour". However, such "honour" turned out to be a rather fragile concept in the context of Schröder's theatre regulations and warrants closer inspection.

In effect, the appeal to the prompter-librarian's "honour" did not fit in neatly with the rest of the regulations, especially the ones concerning the actors, which take up most of the space. Internal regulations had existed in European travelling theatres since the sixteenth century but proliferated in the German-speaking world since the 1780s.[48] Schröder had been using his own "Theatergesetze" (literally "theatre laws") adopted from other troops since the 1780s, and, in 1792, he presented his own regulations, which were considered particularly progressive because they proclaimed bilateralism: "Gesetze müssen Dämme sein gegen Despotie [...] und Heftigkeit der Direction; Dämme gegen Nachlässigkeit, Unsittlichkeit und Heftigkeit der Schauspieler. Die Direction muß weder willkürlich strafen noch entschuldigen können"[49] [Laws must be dams against despotism [...] and the wrath of the principal; dams against negligence, immorality, and the vehemence of actors. The principal should not be able to either punish in an arbitrary fashion or to make excuses]. This was to guarantee the welfare of everyone: through professional performances as recorded in the prompt book – and therefore through a flourishing treasury. As travellers, the members of a theatre company had no civil rights well into the nineteenth century. If principals could present their regula-

---

47 Uhde 1879, 14.
48 Cf. Bishop/Henke 2017, 29–31. For the German context since the 18th century, cf. Dewenter/Jakob 2018.
49 Schröder 1798, 4.

tions when applying for a performance permit, the company would seem at least concerned about order, and it was more likely they would obtain the permit.[50]

Accordingly, the regulations often address members' public conduct. Even the slightest impression of the petty crime and prostitution associated with travelling folk was to be avoided. However, instead of, for example, self-organised "arrest" Schröder's *Laws* stipulated fines for misdemeanours: betraying trade secrets or spreading false rumours, being late for rehearsals, and missing performances were all punishable by fines of up to a month's salary.[51] In most theatre regulations of the time, the director stood apart from those affected by the "laws", much like the sovereign in Hobbes's *Leviathan*.[52] As in most other theatre regulations, in Schröder's *Laws* there were no regulations pertaining specifically to the principal either. However, the other "laws" not only applied to him as well, but the principal, i.e., Schröder, also paid double the fine in each case.[53] The former absolute ruler of the theatre world did not lose any of their power but was now inside and outside the rule of (theatre) law at the same time.

Many penalties imposed on actors concerned their knowledge of their parts and forbade them from deviating from the given text. What was seemingly self-evident – the text needed to be memorised, rehearsed, and reproduced in the performance – was thus guaranteed by a plethora of minor threats of punishment. Earlier in the eighteenth century, an army of soloists generally stood around, uninvolved, until it was their turn to speak. Now, the small penalties imposed by Schröder's *Laws* were intended to create a coherent ensemble performance in which every actor came across as if they were uttering their lines naturally.

Reading Schröder's Hamburg theatre regulations alongside Michel Foucault's *Discipline and Punish* is illuminating – in particular Foucault's famous chapters about the transformation of state law in the eighteenth-century France from sovereign power (tied to the person of the sovereign) to disciplinary power.[54] Like in Foucault's text, in Schröder's *Gesetze*, it was no longer about a theatre sovereign acting despotically against a band of tramps who could scatter to the four winds overnight and thus escape the principal's tyranny. In 112 paragraphs of minute detail, Schröder's *Laws* name as many offences as imaginable and decree what Foucault calls "the gentle way in punishments"[55] for all of them: just severe enough to deter and thus to maintain order within the company and on stage.

---

50 Cf. Dewenter/Jakob 2018, 9.
51 Cf. Schröder 1798, 10–18.
52 Cf. M. Schneider 2018, 107–111.
53 Cf. Schröder 1798, 21.
54 Cf. Foucault 1995, 73–103.
55 Foucault 1995, 104.

The attention to detail in this, in Foucault's words, "microphysics of power"[56] within the theatre company finds its equivalent in the aforementioned aesthetics of the "natural" acting style that dominated in Hamburg. In the prompt books, psychological scores are recorded in detail, including Schröder's famous pauses, for example, before and during King Lear's outbursts of madness.[57] In many performances, however, the psychologically accurate portrayal did not stem from the much-vaunted "reality" that was to be presented on stage but, to a considerable extent, from the prompt book read out from the prompt box. Moreover, the whispered speech was always the precursor to the fine, which was to be avoided by memorising the part.

However, as previously stated, the prompter was not threatened with fines like everybody else when it came to the upkeep of the prompt books. This is where the "forfeiture of honour" in the event of loss or unfair surrender of the book made its entrance, which was the prompter's penalty. Losing one's honour was both a minimum and maximum punishment – but it did not quite fit in with the disciplinary regime of small penalties put forward in the other regulations. On the contrary, honour and loss of honour were the principles of the form of power that preceded disciplinary power in Foucault's paradigm shift. According to the famous description by Montesquieu, honour and loss of honour were part of a monarchical, absolutist form of government.[58] Disgraced noble people who had forfeited their honour were exposed to contempt and would probably be expelled from court. One can extend this argument to less noble realms: being ostracised from her family might have proven dangerous and even fatal for a woman who had "lost her honour", but such danger fell outside the purview of the law, and that was precisely the point. Similarly, the prompter's honour could not be regulated by the principles of the "rule of law" promised by Schröder's regulations. Honour thus had no place in the "disciplinary society" analysed by Foucault but was firmly established in the previous power relationship outlined in *Discipline and Punish*, i.e., that of the sovereign power which lets live and makes die but does not care much about how life is organised. Was a person exposed to contempt perhaps expelled from theatre society and thus left to their own devices, but robbed of the protection of the sovereign? Who would take responsibility for the vast number of written artefacts without an extensive handover? Did the threat ultimately remain empty because the prompter-librarian was too knowledgeable and thus, in their own "subterranean" way, too powerful? Ultimately, it was not only the principal who was both inside and outside the law in Schröder's regulations but also the prompter, who was responsible for preserving and using (and often enough

---

56 Foucault 1995, 26.
57 Cf. Chapter 3, section 3.
58 Cf. Montesquieu 2004, 154f.

creating) the written artefacts used in prompting. Just like the prompter in their box was both on and off stage, their position as caretakers of the written artefacts also gave them an at once powerful and precarious position within and outside of the theatre company's day-to-day operations. The prompter was the least and most important member at the same time; the prompt books they took care of and read out in a semi-loud fashion formed the basis of the whole theatrical endeavour – and yet this endeavour only worked in the proper sense when the prompter's existence was forgotten as much as possible during the performance.

As a matter of fact, the question of honour seems to be historically tied to the Schröder era and perhaps to the Hamburg company. When Düringer and Barthels came up with their own proposition for theatre regulations half a century later, prompters were subjected to "gentle punishments" specific to their occupation but based on the same overall principles that were in place for everyone else.[59] But what might have come down to loose wording in Schröder's *Gesetze* still shines a spotlight on the both central and marginal place occupied by the task of taking care of the prompt books.

## III. Prompt Books in Reading: At the Prompter's Whim

In mid-nineteenth-century theatre lexicons and encyclopaedias, the prompter comes across as something of a quick-witted polymath, with the knowledge required to maintain a constant overview of the play's action, all its minutiae, and all the interdependencies between the various details. Prompters were perceptive enough to decide then and there how to fix what had gone off the rails, i.e., to lead actors back to passages they had skipped, to introduce rough summaries when needed, or to leave out skipped passages if they were no longer necessary. The prompter had to be "ein Mann von Bildung"[60] [an educated man]. Their capabilities consisted "in einem großen Interesse an der Sache, [...] in Kenntnis lebender und todter Sprachen und in der Beurteilungskraft, ob eine vom Schausp. übersprungene Stelle unbeschadet wegbleiben, oder zum Verständnis des Ganzen derselbe wieder darauf zurückgebracht warden muß"[61] [in a great interest in the overall matter, [...] in knowledge of living and dead languages, and in the power of judging whether a passage skipped by the actor can be left out without harm, or if, for the understanding of the whole, the actor must be brought back to it]. This meant, first of all, having "Geistesgegenwart in verwickelten Fällen" [presence of mind in complicated cases] and might even have included "kleine verbindende Extempo-

---

59  Cf. Düringer/Barthels 1841, 1175.

60  Düringer/Barthels 1841, 1004.

61  Blum/Herloßsohn/Marggraff 1846b, 12.

re's" [small connecting extemporisations] that were improvised on the spot by the prompter and then given to the actors as if they were their regular lines.[62]

In addition to the play, the ideal prompter was also highly familiar with the actors performing it: "Er muß den einzelnen Schauspielern ihre Eigenheiten ablauschen und ihre Schwächen genau studiren"[63] [He must come to learn the idiosyncrasies of the individual actors and study their weaknesses carefully]. In theory, the prompter thus needed to be able to predict potential deviations from the text by becoming familiar with the actors' quirks and foibles. In practice however, prompters often found themselves confronted with the highly diverse demands made by actors. A humorous poem that can be found in one of the prompters' almanacs goes to the heart of the matter:

> Oft ruft einer: "Lassen Sie sich sagen,
> Mir souffliren Sie heut' Wort für Wort!"
> Jene bittet: "Mir nur angeschlagen,
> So komm' ich gewiß gut auf Sie fort."
> "Mir das erste Wort von jeder Zeile!"
> (Ruft der Dritte hastig hinterdrein;)
> "Und bei mir, mein Bester, keine Eile,
> (Spricht der Vierte) und nicht zu sehr schrein'!"
> Will dem Fünften nun die Red' nicht munden,
> Spricht er nach der Vorstellung Verlauf:

---

[62] "Die Hauptaufgabe des Souffleurs ist, von dem Schauspieler verstanden und von dem Publikum nicht gehört zu werden. [...] Geistesgegenwart in verwickelten Fällen, dazu nöthige Kenntniß fremder Sprachen, müssen ihn in den Stand setzen, das Stück im geregelten Gange zu erhalten, indem er mit gehöriger Ruhe immer über der Darstellung wacht, bei eingetretenen Stockungen oder Verwirrungen, selbst durch kleine verbindende Extempore's, welche er dem außer Fassung gekommenen betreff. Schauspieler soufflirt. Ebenso muß ein tüchtiger Souffleur im Augenblick übersehen und zu beurtheilen im Stande sein, ob das Springen (Ueberschlagen) eines Schauspielers dem deutlichen Verständnisse des Ganzen keinen Eintrag thut; in diesem Falle kann und muß er mit- u. nachspringen, im andern aber muß er den Schauspieler wieder zurückführen und die nöthigen Reden mit etwa nöthigen Einleitungen souffliren." (Düringer/Barthels 1841, 1003f.) [The main task of the prompter is to be understood by the actor and not heard by the audience. [...] Presence of mind in complicated cases, the necessary knowledge of foreign languages, must enable him to keep the play in order, by always watching over the performance with a proper calmness, in the event of stagnation or confusion, even by small connecting extemporisations, which he then whispers to the actor who has lost his composure. In the same way, a competent prompter must be able to see and judge at a moment's notice whether an actor's skipping of a passage is not detrimental to the clear understanding of the whole; in this case he can and must go along and follow, but in the other case he must lead the actor back again and prompt the necessary speeches with all necessary introductions.]

[63] Düringer/Barthels 1841, 1004.

"Sagen Sie, was machten Sie denn unten?
Heute paßten Sie gar nicht auf!"[64]

[Often, someone calls: "Let me tell you,
You are prompting word for word for me today!"
Asks another: "For me only the first words [of the section]
then I'm sure I'll get along well with you."
"For me the first word of each line!"
(Calls the third hastily after her)
"And with me, dear friend, no hurry,
(Speaks the fourth) and don't shout too much!"
If the prompting is not to the liking of the fifth,
He speaks about it after the performance:
"Tell me, what were you doing down there?
Today you weren't paying attention at all!"]

This rendition of the text in all the various modes required by the actors is linked to the ever-attentive gaze shifting back and forth between what is happening on stage and the prompt book positioned at reading distance from the body. Prompt books thus made for peculiar reading: they were not read line by line, but always between the scene taking place on stage and the scene of writing; prompters were always shifting between reactive and proactive reading, constantly switching between silent or murmuring reading or reading aloud while stuck in a cramped, uncomfortable, and only half-lit space. Depending on what the emergency was, the switch from silent reading to reading in a hushed voice (or the switch from reading to improvising) had to be properly timed.

The actors did not just depend on each other's timing but, above all, on that of the prompt book reader. In the half-light of the prompt box, however, the prompter's reading had to react to the whims of the actors and the uncertainties of their interactions, had to negotiate between them or get ahead of them to put the action on stage back into the order prescribed by the written artefact at hand.[65] The prompter's reading of the prompt book regulated how the action penned down in the written words was converted into action on stage, but in the most complex of manners.

---

64 Quoted after Ulrich 2008, 222.
65 As John Durham Peters has it, writing is the medium capable of reversing the flow of time. In writing, spoken language is not lost to time but stored and can be revived again (cf. Peters 2015, 261–266). However, a written-down play is a particular beast in this respect. When performed, it does not only reverse time but reconverts that which has been taken out of the flow of time into the duration of the performance.

The lexicons and almanacs of the nineteenth century take it for granted that, as written artefacts, prompt books had to be conducive to such complex reading operations. They therefore largely state truisms but keep silent about the specific affordances of the prompt book. According to the *Allgemeines Theater-Lexikon*, it is "am besten geschrieben und auf jeder Seite mit einem weißen Rande versehen"[66] [best written by hand and has a white margin on each page]. "Wir bemerken hier nur [...], daß es jedenfalls auf hartes Papier, deutlich und groß geschrieben, [...] sein muß"[67] [We only note here [...] that it must in any case be written on hard paper, clearly, and in large letters]. However, such truisms either were not historically true at all or did not smoothly translate into practice. The handwriting in a great number of prompt books at the Theater-Bibliothek is not particularly tidy. Frequently, it appears that readily available print versions were favoured over existing manuscripts as the basis for prompt books.[68]

The entries in the *Allgemeines Theater-Lexikon* have the character of prescriptions or at least wishful thinking. They thus demand meticulous organisation when updating prompt books: "Gewissenhaft muß er im Streichen und Einschieben der Zeichen in das Soufflierbuch sein, um seinem Nachfolger das Geschäft zu erleichtern"[69] [He must be conscientious in crossing out and inserting the symbols in the prompt book to make the business easier for his successor]. In contrast, the entry in Düringer and Barthels seems more grounded in reality. They demand "Schonung der Bücher" [care for the books] as they were "oft zum Erschrecken zerfezt u. so verstrichen [...], daß kein Mensch mehr Sinn u. Verstand herausfinden kann" [so ragged and so crisscrossed [...] that no-one can make sense of them anymore].[70]

However, the demand for clarity underscores one of the main requirements of prompting: that the prompter did not hesitate, instead making quick decisions about what needed to be read in a perhaps "ragged and crisscrossed" prompt book that they potentially had taken over from someone else. The lexicons record this as the speed and attentiveness of the prompter who had to react to the actors' whims by speedily deciphering the proper text. But vice versa, the actors were also at the mercy of the prompter. It was the latter who made the decisions in the heat of the moment on a given day: "Auf der andern Seite muß der S. wieder so gewissenhaft sein, nicht willkührlich zu springen, entweder aus Bosheit, um einzelne Schausp. in Verlegenheit zu bringen, oder in der Ab-

---

66  Blum/Herloßsohn/Marggraff 1846a, 36.
67  Blum/Herloßsohn/Marggraff 1846b, 15.
68  Cf. Düringer/Barthels 1841, 1006; cf. our Chapters 5 and 6.
69  Blum/Herloßsohn/Marggraff 1846b, 12.
70  Düringer/Barthels 1841, 1005.

sicht, das Stück umso schneller zu Ende zu bringen, was auch schon da gewesen"[71] [On the other hand, the p.[rompter] must be so conscientious as to not jump arbitrarily, neither out of malice, nor to embarrass individual actors, or with the intention of bringing the play to an end all the more quickly, which is not unheard of]. Instead of ensuring the play could be repeated in exactly the same way every time it was performed, reading from the prompt book became a source of arbitrariness, capriciousness, and even a variation of the despotism Schröder wanted to guard against with his regulations.[72] This might have happened voluntarily or involuntarily as the person in the prompt box might have missed the signs of the actors' failure or might have been anything but quick-witted. In this vein, the *Allgemeine Theater-Chronik* of 1845 takes up an anecdote from the Hamburg Stadt-Theater from the late 1810s, which can be found in various publications from the 1820s onwards and seems to have become popular lore:

> Der alte Souffleur Barlow in Hamburg [...] war manchmal fast wie geistesabwesend. Eines Tages machte er plötzlich mitten im Stück sein Buch zu und verschwand; zwar entstand eine Stockung, einer der Schauspieler aber fand sich glücklicher Weise, der imstande war, die erledigte Stelle, für den Augenblick wenigstens, zu besetzen. Aber auch dieser verschwand, als er kaum sein Werk aufgenommen hatte, bei den Füßen nämlich von Barlow zu sich herabgezogen, der jetzt ärgerlich vor ihm stand und sagte: "Herr, wenn ich gewollt hätte, dass jemand souffliren sollte, so wäre ich selbst im Kasten geblieben."[73] [The old prompter Barlow in Hamburg [...] was sometimes almost absent-minded. One day he suddenly closed his book in the middle of the play and disappeared; there was a hold-up, but, fortunately, an actor was found who was able to fill the vacancy, at least for a moment. But he, too, disappeared before he had scarcely taken up his work, being pulled down by the feet by Barlow, who now stood angrily before him and said: "Sir, if I had wanted someone to do the prompting, I would have stayed in the box myself."]

This example illustrates, in exaggerated fashion, how the supposedly merely auxiliary position of the prompter implied a peculiar position of power: prompters decided whether to help ensure the smooth running of a performance or not, whether to support the actors or not, whether to do their job inconspicuously or to interpret it according to their own whims. The "hold-up" in the example cited

---

71 Düringer/Barthels 1841, 1005.

72 In the vein of Walter Benjamin and Paul de Man, Bettine Menke argues that reading in general operates by creating (rather than deciphering) ever-shifting constellations of meaning, cf. Menke 1993. From this point of view, the reading of prompt books "in the heat of the moment", as it were, extrapolates a broader structure of reading.

73 *Allgemeine Theater-Chronik* 1845a, 248; cf. Schmidt 1875, 139–148; cf. Holzapfel 1823, 113–116.

here was not caused by forgotten or messed-up lines, but by the absence of a certain person, without whom nothing seemed to work. The peculiar place occupied by this person comes into view as the dim, much-ridiculed in-between place of the prompter's box. (Barlow's obituary joked that he would now be in the coffin exactly where he had been most alive all his life.[74]) But in his subordination, the prompter Barlow is also a distinctive kind of ruler here. Whoever ventures in (as a substitute prompter) can be pulled down out of the above-ground order altogether. But such power retains a strange status of potentiality; it takes place in the subjunctive and only decrees one thing: that no one else should occupy this space of power: "If I had wanted to, I would have stayed." But only in its absence does the "will" of the prompter manifest itself at all. Barlow's power is capricious in that it only becomes visible when it fails – it only can subvert and disturb the order of the performance it is there to guarantee. As long as prompters did their job, they did not seem very important or powerful at all.

Once more, the part that written artefacts played in prompting is ignored in this anecdote. However, the anecdote still accounts for the precarity, power, and capriciousness of the prompter, as they left material traces in the actual written artefacts. The frequently crossed-out lines had to be deciphered on the spot by this one person who made instant decisions about what was actually written there. Weeks, months, or years after the creation or last use of the prompt book, the prompter had to decipher corrections made some time ago by their own or an alien hand. Whenever a performance was put in jeopardy by a crisis of forgotten or mangled lines, the prompter became the prompt book's autocratic reader – and was simultaneously at its mercy.

For outsiders or twenty-first-century readers like the authors of this study, prompt books can develop their very own pull due to their striking visual features. Artefacts that, in the context of their time, were designed to ensure the repeatability of the text in question sometimes take an idiosyncratic turn or simply remain illegible – and not (only) because the material has been worn down by time, a pencil has faded, or one's knowledge of *Kurrent*, i.e., German cursive is not good enough. The text and the corrections made to it were sometimes jotted down fleetingly. The writing seems almost private and is certainly hard to decipher if not done regularly. In the heat of the moment, the prompt book reader has to make a tough call – make a call on a whim – as to what a certain line or word is supposed to mean and whether it means anything at all (cf. figure 6).

---

74 Cf. Schmidt 1875, 142.

*Figure 6:* Theater-Bibliothek 1989b, 54.

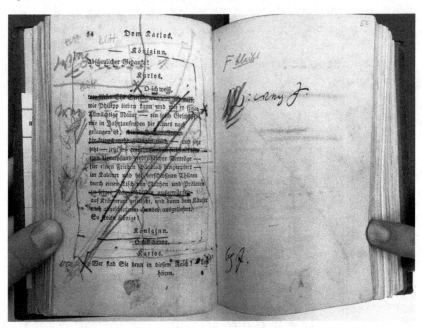

The next chapters will delve into some of the written artefacts from the Hamburg Stadt-Theater collection, the Theater-Bibliothek, in order to demonstrate how these written artefacts were created in order to ensure the repeatability of a given text during a performance. However, these chapters will also frequently point to the unpredictable aspects that emerged in the everyday use of prompt books by prompters.

# Chapter 3. Writing and Paper Practices in the Prompt Books of the Hamburg Theater-Bibliothek

Prompt books were not fixed entities; rather, they were revised and updated depending on the circumstances. The content of a play might have had to be changed overnight due to a negative audience reaction; two scenes might have had to be condensed into one in order to reduce the number of lighting changes when a play was taken up again after a decade; a character might have had to be played by an actor of a different build and age, making it ridiculous to address the character as "young man" on stage. These are all examples of updates that we will be discussing in the course of this study. The prompt book had to be reshaped to adapt to all of them: by adding or retracting words (character lines or technical instructions for the lighting, music, and sound effects), sometimes by intervening on a material level (by folding, cutting, or gluing sheets of paper together). The material biography of a prompt book thus consists of what we refer to as the "layers"[1] it accumulated over time. This term must be employed loosely as it is often difficult to tell where one layer of a prompt book ends and another begins. As we will see, the "original" fair copy made for a play's premiere was sometimes heterogeneous from the outset, written in different hands or stitched together from various sorts of paper. Sometimes, a number of writing tools would work in concert during a certain stage of revision, but not necessarily simultaneously. Indistinguishable hands and writing tools were sometimes clearly working against each other. While the prompt books at the Hamburg Theater-Bibliothek are nearly always multi-layered, this study will refrain from providing overviews of the boundaries between the various layers. Instead, it will provide thick descriptions of the writing and paper practices that, in their entanglement, make up the material biography of a prompt book.

---

1 Cf. Maksimczuk/Möller/Staack/Weinstock/Wolf 2024. For the concept of multilayered written artefacts, cf. Beit-Arié 1993.

With Dickmann, Elias, and Focken, we define *writing practices* as any act of dealing with written artefacts that is "routinely performed by a large number of people".[2] We will mainly be focussing on operations of what Gumbert calls "enrichment": performing writing operations to add and retract text in a play or to update technical information that concerned the prompter. With Pethes, we understand "paper practices"[3] to be more technical operations by which a written artefact was changed materially, namely by folding, cutting, or gluing paper together within the object. In the following, we will introduce the main operations that can be observed at the Theater-Bibliothek, which we will then elaborate upon in the subsequent chapters.

## I. The Format and Use of Prompt Books

Prompt books can and, indeed, should be viewed as auxiliary means of gaining a deeper understanding of the history of a given production or the stage adaptation of a literary text.[4] Nevertheless, this study proposes taking an additional point of view: when examining prompt books in themselves as part of a manuscript culture, the unique quality and development of each prompt book as a material object comes into view. As we will argue below, the shape that a prompt book took on in the course of its practical use can thus be described as a performance in itself, i.e., performative in the broad sense of being processual rather than static – and also of manifesting on a material level rather than on the level of signification.[5] The material performance of a prompt book can, then, contribute to our understanding of the history of a specific production. The Hamburg Theater-Bibliothek serves as one example of this, although, as stated in the introduction, the practices employed in other German-speaking theatres of that period did not considerably differ. The differences between them had more to do with particular creators and users.

The content of the prompt books at the Hamburg Theater-Bibliothek was usually written down in German cursive handwriting (called *Kurrent*) on folded paper quires and penned in whatever commonplace ink was available at the time. The quires were then bound together between plain cardboard covers. As the books were mere objects of utility in the theatre and of no particular value as artefacts in

---

2 "Schriftpraktiken", "die mehrere Personen routiniert vollziehen" (Dickmann/Elias/Focken 2015, 139). Dickmann, Elias, and Focken contrast writing practices with a more general concept of "Schrifthandlungen" [writing actions].

3 Cf. Pethes 2019, especially 99–104. While paper tools, according to Pethes, are "sheets, files, or staplers", paper practices are procedures "such as turning, stacking, filing, ripping – as well as including folding and gluing household papers and paper toys" (Pethes 2019, 100f.). These concepts are derived from a general notion of paper technology as developed by Hess and Mendelsohn 2013.

4 Cf. M. Schneider 2021.

5 Cf. Nantke 2017, 77.

themselves, the materials used to make them were generally fairly cheap. In rare cases, different types of paper were used for one and the same book, apparently for the sake of convenience.[6] When the text of a play performed by the company closely resembled the version of the play that was commercially available in print, a print copy was sometimes chosen as the first layer and then enriched by hand. Approximately one-sixth of the objects stored at Hamburg's Theater-Bibliothek were made on the basis of printed books, i.e., normal print copies targeting the reading audience of the day were used as the fair copy for the respective prompt books. However, there are rare cases of interleafed print copies with extra pages for writing on that seem to have been created as prompt books. These were handy as far as enrichments were concerned but bulky to carry around and use in the prompt box. Either way, everything else was then added by hand, just like in the handwritten exemplars, thus creating hybrid forms between handwriting and print.

Size and colour vary slightly from prompt book to prompt book: some of the dimensions of the written artefacts that will be discussed later include 16.5 × 20.5 cm for *Theater-Bibliothek: 571*, a prompt book for William Shakespeare's *Othello*; 17.5 × 22 cm for *Theater-Bibliothek: 1988a*, a prompt book for Gotthold Ephraim Lessing's *Nathan der Weise [Nathan the Wise]*; and 18.5 × 23.5 cm for *Theater-Bibliothek: 1379a*, a prompt book for William Shakespeare's *Viel Lärmen um Nichts [Much Ado about Nothing]*. The printed prompt books made by the Stadt-Theater company were generally octavos with dimensions of 10.5 × 16.5 cm.

The visual organisation of the actual writing differs somewhat. Often, everything apart from the actors' lines, i.e., didascalia[7] like information about the character speaking, the setting, and the action taking place, was not written in casual German cursive but in traditional Blackletter/Gothic script. Occasionally, this information was underlined once or twice in the same ink or in a different-coloured one. These distinctions in the visual organisation of the page between didascalia and dialogue ensured that the content of a prompt book was arranged clearly from the outset, as they helped to discern between the different levels of the dramatic text it contained. Changes and updates were added in whatever ink or pencil seems to have been at hand; pages could be cut out or glued over, or additional pages loosely inserted. Since the prompter was part of the process of developing a stage version for a dramatic text (albeit a technical version), prompt books were constantly being modified. They were updated to reflect the changing practical circumstances of a production; each amendment represented the latest state of affairs but was by no means the final one.

---

6 Cf. Chapter 5, section 4, for an example from *Theater-Bibliothek: 571*.

7 For the concept, cf. Issacharoff 1987, 88: "Didascalia are addressed by a *real person* (the author) to other *real people* (director and actors), and […] are intended to be taken non-fictively."

It all started with a fair copy that included the lines that would be spoken by the performers. It is safe to assume that fair copies were set up towards the end of the rehearsal process. Some additional technical cues and annotations that fell within the purview of the user (the prompter or the inspector) were inserted once they had been finally decided. They were changed whenever adjustments needed to be made for a new performance, e.g., when the performance did not have the desired effect on the audience. The changes made with respect to the performers' texts are particularly diverse: additions, corrections, retractions, and comments were made and sometimes altered again when changes were implemented (cf. figure 7).

*Figure 7: Nm, 9v and 10r.*

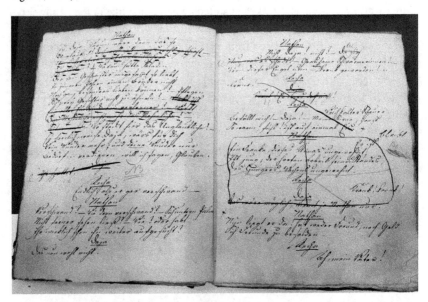

The nature of a prompt book varied depending on who its main user was supposed to be on the night of the performance. In Hamburg, there are often two surviving books for the same performance, both of which were obviously used simultaneously: one with the text version in it and all the technical arrangements the prompter could direct from their fixed position in the box (e.g., some lighting effects), another one with information about additional technical arrangements – everything from remarks about and instructions for the lighting, music, and sound effects to certain positions that the actors were supposed to adopt during the scenes, or indications of where actors were to enter the stage along with stage directions, prop lists, or lists of actors. This latter was used by the inspector, who, during the performance, carried out the tasks of the person who is now called the *stage manager* in the English-speaking world.[8] In the case of Schröder's theatre, there were just as many productions with two versions as there were productions for which one seems to be missing, or the two functions seem to overlap in a single book (the user of which might have changed).

Theatrical practices were (and are) ephemeral in nature: depending on the actors' form on the day or the make-up of the audience, tomorrow night's performance might have come to pass in a different fashion than tonight's. However, these practices were organised by convention, memory, oral arrangements, and not least by the written agreements put down on paper in the prompt books. Thus, the transitory practices of the theatre manifest themselves performatively in the materiality of the prompt book. The various handwritten revisions transform each manuscript (or overwritten printed book) into a unique, multi-layered performative artefact, with each layer expressing a new development in a production. None of these developments were necessarily final, but they were prone to being changed again if deemed necessary. The fundamental incompleteness of prompt books is of great importance for their analysis: the content of a prompt book can never be perceived as final because, as long as it was in use, it was subject to the potentially changing pragmatic requirements of the stage. Therefore, the individual material biography of a prompt book is closely related to the history of the respective theatre production. Prompt books were thus "evolving entities"[9] in a peculiar sense. They did not develop in the way that multi-text manuscripts or composites do[10] as they only contained one play, i.e., one codicological unit. Accordingly, their development and evolution took place on a different level of materiality: they were tied to their functional integration into an artistic process, the dynamics of which they put on display in their own performance. Prompt books never (or hardly ever) remained unchanged once they were in use. Rather, they generally grew with the various additions that sometimes both enriched and enlarged them. The parameters according to which this took place could and did change, as did the prompt book users, even if the context of the prompt book's production and utilisation stayed the same. To this effect, prompt books generally started out as monogenetic entities (fair copies) and, over time, became homogenetic and even allogenetic, for instance, when taken up by a different team decades after the original production.[11] Prompt books were used for long periods of time and sometimes served as the basis for a number of theatre productions. Thus, the dynamics of their material performance were also closely related to what Gumbert has called

---

8  Cf. Düringer/Barthels 1841, 597f. The inspector also assumed overall responsibility for the company that went beyond its performances; cf. Chapter 6.
9  Friedrich/Schwarke 2016, 1.
10  Cf. Friedrich/Schwarke 2016.
11  The terminology we use here is based on Gumbert 2004, 40f.

"continuous enrichment", as it is not always possible to clearly distinguish between the boundaries of the various layers that were added by "one person, or a group of persons […] behind or between the existing text(s) during a prolonged period".[12]

As objects of utility, prompt books were the centrepiece of the text-based theatre developing in the eighteenth-century German-speaking world. On the level of content, they served as the basis for theatrical practices such as rehearsing and staging a play. At the same time, those ephemeral practices and processes materially manifested themselves in – and "interacted" with – a prompt book whenever it was updated. Thus, these manuscripts undermine the traditional distinction between text and performance mentioned at the beginning of this study. Both dimensions become intertwined when we regard prompt books in their material performance.

## II. Adding and Retracting Dialogue and Stage Directions

The texts written in prompt books tended to differ from the text versions circulating in print – sometimes considerably. Stage versions needed to be adapted according to the technical possibilities and requirements of the stage as well as to the tastes and expectations of the audience, and, last but not least, to reflect theatrical conventions. Shakespeare wrote for the London stage around 1600, which, for the most part, was devoid of props, for instance. In such a context, a few words could indicate a change of scenery (a device of which Shakespeare's plays made ample use). In contrast, audiences in eighteenth- and nineteenth-century Hamburg expected to see and admire elaborate stage sets that looked realistic.[13] To avoid constant interruptions when re-arranging sets, the order of the scenes of a Shakespeare play had to be modified and simplified from the outset. However, modifications like these could always be made at a later point as well. The claim that Stephen Nichols first made in relation to mediaeval manuscripts, and which has provided the basis for manuscript studies ever since, also applies to stage adaptations in the European theatre since the early modern period: "No one version, no matter how complete, may be viewed as authoritative."[14]

Evidently, most modifications were retractions or additions, first in the fair copy, then in the added layers of earlier retractions or additions. The material manifestation of these basic operations, however, turns out to be rather complex.[15]

---

12 Gumbert 2004, 31.
13 Cf. Malchow 2022, 138–172.
14 Nichols 1997, 17.
15 For an overview of the different forms and functions of crossing-out as well as the potential positioning of new words, cf. Grésillon 2016, 83–87. Taking Grésillon's differentiations as a

Chapter 3. Writing and Paper Practices    63

Take, for instance, the retraction of a certain part which had been written down at an earlier point in time: a retraction was often indicated by a simple straight line drawn through the respective passage; it was literally crossed out using a writing tool that often clearly differed from the one that had been used to pen the initial content. Sometimes the line seems to have been crossed out hastily or in passing, but in other cases, frames were carefully drawn around the retracted elements, highlighting the act of cancellation. The writing tool used for this purpose may also have been employed to highlight specific elements and thus to underscore the structural organisation of the passage in question. (Cf. figures 8 and 9.)

*Figure 8:* Theater-Bibliothek: 1379a, *86v and 87r.*

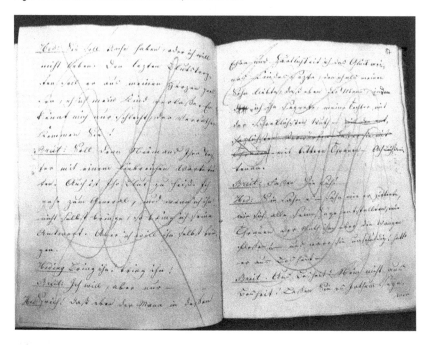

starting point, Uwe Wirth has reflected on the "Logik der Streichung" (Wirth 2011) [logic of the strike-through]. Both authors agree that crossing out writing is an operation that does not simply negate something but materially visualises both the act of negating and what is being negated at the same time. For specific examples, see Chapter 5.

*Figure 9:* Theater-Bibliothek: 215a, 118 and 119.

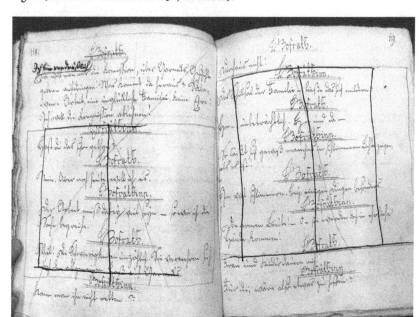

The crossing out of content and the various techniques that went along with it could pertain to anything from a single word to an entire scene. Cancellations of this kind could be made to elements of the plot as well as characters that a respective production had decided to exclude, dialogue that needed to be shortened or condensed, or expressions, phrases, or actions that had been deemed inapt or even inappropriate. The reasons might have been of a pragmatic or aesthetic nature. However, social expectations and norms also influenced the changes: retracting a minor scene could tighten up the storyline; a certain turn of phrase might have been too difficult to articulate properly on stage or might have proven to be simply too explicit or drastic. The standards according to which such qualifications were made often originated at the intersection of aesthetic and social values.[16]

---

16 The most notorious retraction of content in German theatre history, albeit a rather unimposing one, can be found at the Theater-Bibliothek and will be discussed in great detail in Chapter 5. It concerns Friedrich Ludwig Schröder's 1776 adaptation of Shakespeare's *Othello* and consists of six small strokes of black ink that indicate the retraction of three words in the corresponding prompt book *Theater-Bibliothek*: 571. The unobtrusive marks actually indicate a major change in the plot: the stage direction "Er sticht sie" [He stabs her] has been crossed out. The words refer to Desdemona's infamous murder by her husband. After negative reactions from the audience, the six little strokes cancelled out Othello's terrible act: he did not kill her after all.

An equally common practice in prompt book manuscripts that often went hand in hand with a retraction was, of course, the addition of handwritten content such as in straightforward corrections (cf. figure 10).[17]

*Figure 10*: Theater-Bibliothek: 586a, 100.

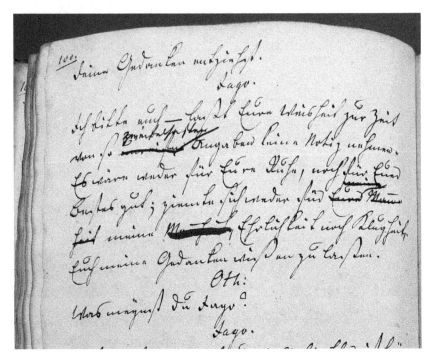

Although this was to be expected, it does not seem to have been taken into account when creating the fair copies as they generally contained too little blank space for extensive additions to be made. Prompt books were also objects of utility, and it had to be possible to handle them easily and effectively; they could not be too voluminous as that would have made them unwieldy. Additions therefore had to be inserted between the lines in many cases. This was easy enough if the addition was a small one, i.e., a change to just a single word, expression, or response, but things became more complicated when more text needed to be added.

Only a minority of prompt books incorporated potential future changes into their visual organisation. In such cases space was left in the margins from the

---

17 These manual operations can be subsumed under what Patrick Andrist, Paul Canard, and Marilena Maniaci have categorised as the "[m]odèle de transformation A2: ajout de contenu sans support matériel" (Andrist/Canard/Maniaci 2013, 64) [A2 model of transformation: adding content without material support].

outset to allow more extensive changes to be made next to the section the changes applied to.[18] It was easier to update prompt books like these because they remained perfectly usable, i.e., they were still arranged clearly and legible (cf. figure 11).

*Figure 11:* Theater-Bibliothek: 1379b, *56 and 57*.

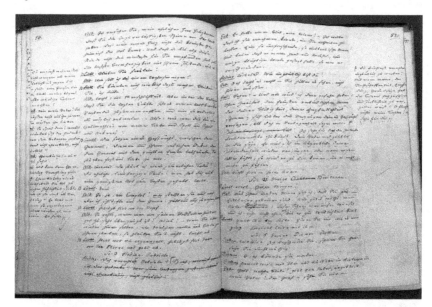

This feature can also be found in prompt books that used printed text, where the uniform, standardised layout allowed for all sorts of handwritten annotations and additions to be made. A rarity among the Theater-Bibliothek prompt books is one of the two prompt books for Friedrich Schiller's *Dom Karlos*, Theater-Bibliothek: *1989b*, where an interleafed copy of the printed book was produced to serve as a prompt book.[19] In the vast majority of cases, saving space and quires seems to have

---

18 The visual organisation bears a resemblance to manuscript practices in certain scholarly or monastic traditions. The main difference, however, is not just contextual but also functional: the margins in a prompt book were not there to accommodate commentary on the text but to update it (or update the respective stage arrangements) according to the requirements of the theatre production. For the monastic tradition, cf. Treharne 2021, 62–87.

19 So far, we have been unable to find any similar formatting in the manuscript-based prompt books that we have reviewed. The Theater-Bibliothek contains two prompt books from the debut production of *Dom Karlos* (now known as *Don Carlos*) in 1787, which have attracted remarkably little attention as material objects. The handwritten 1787 prompt book (*Theater-Bibliothek: 1989a*) was heavily reworked during rehearsals and the first few performances. At some later point, the theatre swapped the manuscript for an interleafed volume of Schiller's first published print version (*Theater-Bibliothek: 1989b*), which was then used and constantly revised until 1813.

been of the utmost priority. As a consequence, the format usually did not easily allow for more extensive amendments to be made. (Cf. figure 12.)

*Figure 12*: Theater-Bibliothek: 1989b, 291.

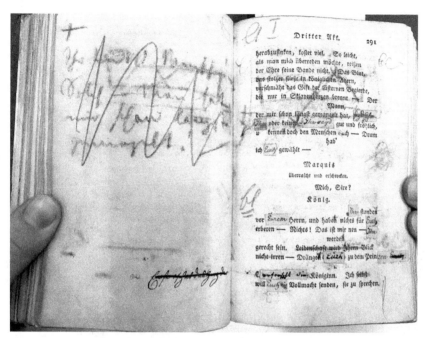

Despite the lack of space, prompt books were irrevocably tied to the changes that took place in the staging of a performance: amendments added up, and additions were sometimes modified or retracted again. Prompt books could also be so extensive that they left no space for any further changes. At some point, the constant revisions made it more difficult for a prompter to find their way through the pages, especially if they had been heavily revised. This was probably the case when productions were staged with a new prompter after a hiatus of several years. The constant use that a prompt book was intended for could eventually impair how it functioned as a tool.

The illegibility of the various layers of the *Dom Karlos* prompt book is a case in point – even though the (orderly) print version was used as a basis and then interleafed. Anyone other than the prompter, who probably remembered what the various layers of pencil and ink stood for and how they related to each other, might not have been able to make use of the prompt book at all. In cases less prominent than Schiller's, the prompt book in question might have been discarded and replaced with a new copy in pristine condition. In that case, there would not have been any need to keep the prompt book in the company's collection.

As the *Dom Karlos* sample shows, each modification used up more of the written artefact's material resources. The same goes for a sample page from the prompt book for Schröder's equally well-known adaptation of *Hamlet*, *Theater-Bibliothek: 1982 (1)*, which was based on a print copy of Schröder's own adaptation (cf. figure 13).[20]

*Figure 13*: Theater-Bibliothek: 1982 (1), 36.

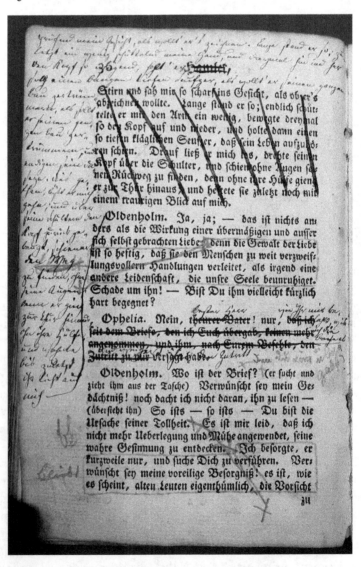

---

20  Cf. Chapter 5, section 2.

Here, Ophelia's response has been crossed out at the top of the page. The amendment takes up the entire top margin and most of the left margin as well, leaving hardly any space for further changes. The legibility of the page decreases significantly where writing has been added on top of the existing changes to Oldenholm's (the Germanised name for Polonius in the production) response. At this point, the different layers enter into a complex interplay; their back-and-forth extends into the margins. The writing is in a faded reddish ink, and one or two pencils have been used as well. The retraction was later cancelled out with the word "bleibt" (meaning "stays") next to the retracted text. However, the cancellation of the retraction was then crossed out again, after which Ophelia's new text was written more or less around the retracted correction. As a consequence, the amendments to her next response in the middle of the page needed to be added in a different way if they were to remain in close proximity to the section they pertained to. The scribe somehow managed to write them between, next to, and even across the retracted lines. The inevitable consequence was that their arrangement and allocation became harder to make out. Thus, the *Hamlet* prompt book sample exemplifies how the usability of the written artefact could quite literally get pushed to its limits by theatrical processes.

The dynamics of the processes in question regularly manifest themselves materially in several layers of handwriting. While the manuscript page (or the printed page with handwritten additions) could come to look like a work of twentieth-century calligraphic – and graffiti-like – European art,[21] the theoretical hierarchy of these changes was always clear: it was only the latest revisions that counted. The last revisions constituted the version of the text that the production had to adhere to until more changes were made and a new layer added. But the material interplay between the layers gets even more complicated, as it is not always clear which was the latest revision. Pencilled notes were sometimes written over ink and vice versa; black, reddish, or brownish ink were used in a sometimes orderly, sometimes random fashion. We have to reconstruct the succession of different layers by looking at a) the point of reference for the respective operations, e.g., a retraction and its subsequent cancellation, or b) the concrete material layering, as in the case of Ophelia's altered text. The dark ink seems to have written over the graphite pencil that previously referred to Oldenholm's text. The extent to which c) ink analysis can be of help differs from prompt book to prompt book. One example of this will be discussed in Chapter 5 in relation to *Theater-Bibliothek: 2029*.

In order to insert the numerous, extensive amendments made during a number of revisions into the limited page space, which was visually organised in a way that was not always conducive to changes, prompters and other users frequently resorted to using further paper tools as well as paper practices: additional layers

---

21 Cf. Greub 2018, for example.

of paper – sometimes even entire pages – were inserted in various ways.[22] In most cases, they were directly pasted over the respective parts with glue. If the amendments were extensive and the sheet of paper required was bigger than the passage it was supposed to cover, it was glued in and then partly folded so that it could be opened out if needed but would still fit inside the book, which we can see here in *Theater-Bibliothek: 1988a*, an inspector's book for Lessing's *Nathan der Weise*, which we will analyse in great detail in a later chapter (cf. figure 14).

*Figure 14: Nm, 45r.*

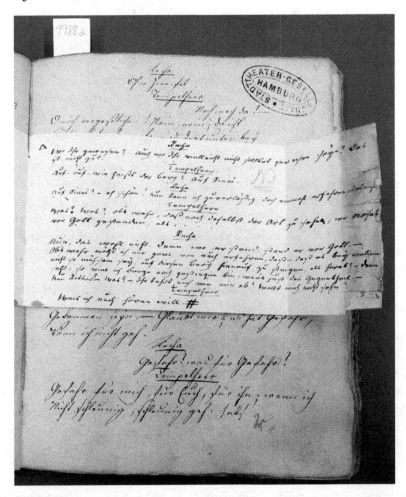

---

22 These cases can be subsumed under what Andrist, Canard, and Maniaci have categorised as the "[m]odèle de transformation A1: ajout de support matériel et de contenu" (Andrist/Canard/Maniaci 2013, 63) [transformation model A1: addition of material support and content].

Chapter 3. Writing and Paper Practices    71

In another sample from the accompanying prompt book *Theater-Bibliothek: 1988b*, we can see how pages were removed right alongside the addition of a new page. Removals appear only infrequently, probably due to their irrevocable character; they did not fit in very well with the "valid until recalled" order of prompt book processes (cf. figure 15).

*Figure 15:* Np, 50 and 57.

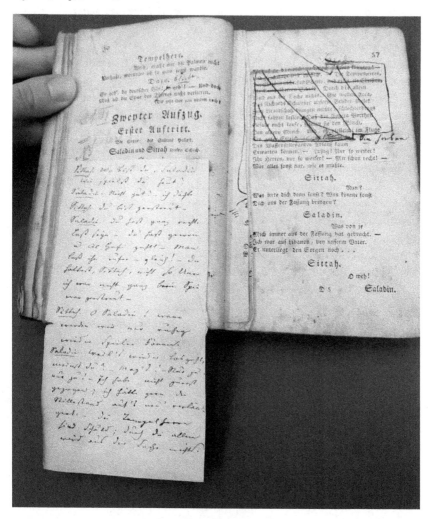

On another occasion in *Theater-Bibliothek: 1988b*, a much less intrusive paper practice was implemented. The pages for a whole scene that has clearly been cut (because it is absent in the complementary inspector's book) was materially retracted by folding over the bottom corner of each page and then folding all the other corners over each other, meaning that the user of the prompt book would naturally skip to the next valid piece of text.[23]

Added sheets, however, were not necessarily pasted in and linked to the book materially; sometimes, they were attached to the page with a pin, e.g., in *Theater-Bibliothek: 1460*, the prompt book for Kotzebue's *Die Sonnen-Jungfrau* [*The Virgin of the Sun*]. We can assume that the pin was actually used at the time of the performance and was not inserted later, as the pin clearly places the amendment at the desired position and incorporates it into the written artefact materially. Conveniently, the extra sheet could easily be swapped for another one or rearranged in the event of another revision.[24]

We will examine in detail what seems to have been a trial copy for the subsequent prompt book of *Die Sonnen-Jungfrau*, *Theater-Bibliothek: 728*, in the next chapter. As we will explain, this manuscript is a particularly relevant example of how a retraction was combined with an addition. In *Theater-Bibliothek: 728*, a whole scene was cut in Act I, Scene 6. But parts of the dialogue were then transferred to Act II, with diacritical signs marking several beginnings and ends to the crossed-out passages that needed to be shifted in Act I. As can be seen on the cover of our own book, an insertion mark on the margins of Act II, Scene 2, indicates that, after another textual addition was made, all the pieces cut beforehand were to be placed here, one by one.

## III. Types and Functions of Other Additions and Retractions

Not all characteristic prompt book amendments were made to the content of the play to be performed. Some applied to timing, others to technical tasks that could be performed from the prompt box or, if it was the inspector's book, that were the duty of the person responsible backstage in the first place. Many of them pertained directly to the technical arrangements on stage during a performance. Another Shakespeare adaptation by Friedrich Ludwig Schröder provides examples of both types. Schröder published his version of *König Lear* [*King Lear*] as a printed book shortly after its premiere in 1778. We will examine in a later chapter how, as in the case of *Hamlet*, the manuscript version of the prompt book was exchanged for a print copy at some point during the play's forty-year performance history in Hamburg,[25] which then served as a foundation that was enriched over time.[26]

---

23 Cf. Chapter 6, section 4.
24 Cf. Chapter 4, section 6.
25 Cf. Chapter 5, section 6.
26 In this case, the production was taken up again in 1812 during the French occupation; cf. Chapter 5.

Chapter 3. Writing and Paper Practices    73

*Figure 16: L, 50.*

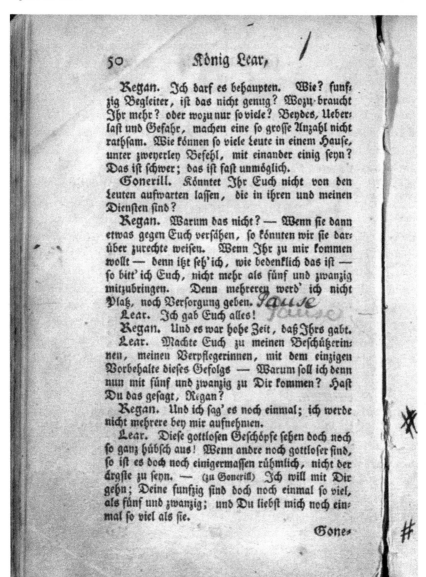

Until 1798, Schröder played the old king himself despite his own young years. As an actor, Schröder worked effectively with the interplay of speech and silence when portraying Lear's inner conflicts and troubles. When the old king is rejected by his two daughters Goneril and Regan, Lear slowly realises their fundamental betrayal. Schröder considered this to be a psychological process and took his time before uttering, "Ich gab Euch alles!" (L, 50) [I gave you everything!] in shocked disappointment.[27] In the respective passage of the prompt book, the word "Pause" [pause] has been inserted twice, once in pencil and again in dark ink – apparently by the same hand and seemingly referring to Lear's line both times. As the pencilled-in addition remains rather ambiguous as to the timing of the pause (before or after Lear's reply), it seems the ink addition was made afterwards so as to leave no doubt. The insertion seems to have served as a reminder to the prompter that the actor, and the other actors that followed in Schröder's footsteps until 1827, would deliberately remain silent for a moment as part of his role, not because he had forgotten his lines. Obviously, the last thing that the company wanted to happen on stage in such a situation was for the audience to hear the prompter's semi-audible whisper. (Cf. figure 16.)

As far as notions of place and atmosphere were concerned, instructions and cues in the prompt book referred to the technical dimensions of the performance. In the prompt book for Schröder's *Lear* adaptation, *Theater-Bibliothek*: 2029, the opening of the third act is littered with technical annotations presumably made by various users at different times. The location changed after the second act: from a setting in front of a castle, the stage became a "Heide mit einer Hütte" [heath with a shack], indicated by the word "Verwandlung" [transformation] written in pencil. Other handwritten insertions refer to the lighting. This can be safely assumed with regard to the word "blau" [blue], which was written in pencil but then crossed out – it probably referred to a specific colour or quality of light. Two additional annotations determined the time and atmosphere for all of the following scenes: "Nacht" [night] was written in pencil and then again in red ink; and "ohne Mondschein" [without any moonlight] was written in a darker ink, apparently by another hand.

The likely reason for the crossing-out of "blau", the initial lighting mood, only becomes apparent at second glance: the header "Dritter Akt" [third act] was crossed out in pencil and the Roman numeral "II" was written next to it in black ink. The first scene in Schröder's third act had originally been taken out of the middle of Shakespeare's second.[28] Despite the obvious dramaturgical dissonances, it seems to have been transferred to the beginning of Act III in Schröder's adaptation because using similar scenery would have eliminated the need to change the set. However, at some point during the long history of Schröder's *Lear* on the Hamburg stage, the scene was reincorporated into the second act – this time as its ending. At that point, there may not have been enough time to change the lighting effect back to "blue" again,

---

27 A particularly detailed description of Schröder's depiction of Lear was published by Johann Friedrich Schink in 1790 and combined with interpretations and assessments he made. Schink worked as a librettist and dramaturge at the Hamburg theatre at that time; cf. Schink 1790, 1087–1142.

28 See *Theater-Bibliothek*: 2029, 54 for Schröder's adaptation. In both Schröder's templates and current editions of Shakespeare's works, this scene is the third one in the second act; cf. Eschenburg 1779, 82.

although there does seem to have been enough time to dim the brightness to the level of a "night without any moonlight". The fall of the curtain and the customary musical interlude were thus delayed for a few minutes in the performance – and shifted to the next page in the prompt book (cf. figures 17 and 18).

Figure 17: L, 54.   Figure 18: L, 55.

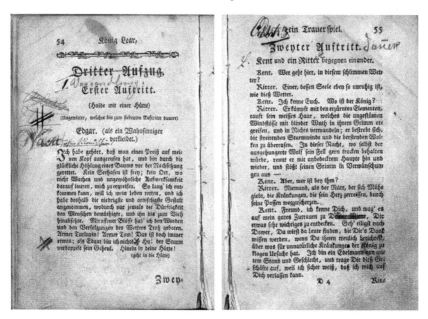

Creating a specific atmosphere or situation, or performing certain actions backstage, called for appropriate sounds and sound effects. These were indicated by cues in some of the prompt books. As we see in the *König Lear* example, a number or diacritical sign was used. On page 54, the cue written in dark ink and the other two cues written in pencil refer to the "Ungewitter" [thunderstorm] that rages during the first seven scenes of the act, or rather, to the claps of thunder that resounded every now and then. Generally, a # symbol was added to the prompt book whenever any kind of sound originating off stage was to be heard that was connected to the actions being shown.

While the use of the # symbol was common in the prompt book manuscripts of the time, the written artefacts also worked with handwritten letters, signs, and icons that are part of the traditional repertoire of Western scholarly manuscript cultures. Time and again, there are cues in the prompt books that did not primarily refer to a certain event that was supposed to take place on stage, but rather addressed those who worked with the manuscript: a "nota bene" ligature ("NB") may have drawn attention to a certain dialogue or to a certain response or action that was likely to happen on stage at that moment. It is not always possible to tell why the prompter or inspector needed to be on their guard on such occasions; however, an actor might have had trouble with their text, or a candle might have been lit on stage that had to be prevented from going out. The need to draw attention to an action could subside again at a later point, of course; the "nota bene" might well have been crossed out again, as can be seen in the prompt book for Lessing's *Nathan der Weise* (cf. figure 19).

*Figure 19: Nm, 15v.*

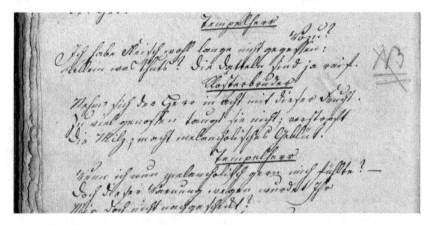

The manicule is another traditional icon of Western manuscript and book practices that can be found in the Hamburg prompt books. In Schröder's *Othello, Theater-Bibliothek: 571*, which we will discuss in a later chapter, a manicule points to a scene that has been added in a blank space on the following page in the course of the prompt book's fundamental revision.[29] It not only reminds the user that the amendment is there but also visually directs them to the continuation of the act that had ended earlier in the fair copy.[30]

---

29  For an overview of the tradition of the manicule, see the chapter "Toward a History of the Manicule" in Sherman 2008, 25–52.

30  Cf. Chapter 5, section 3.

*Figure 20: S2, 98r.*

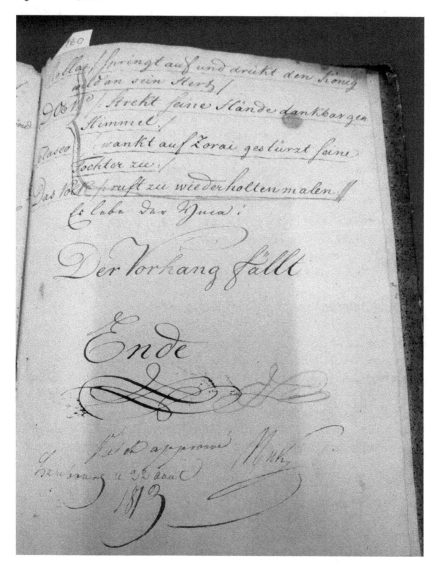

The various phenomena presented so far all relate to the theatrical processes that a prompt book was immersed in. They were the result of decisions made in the theatre context during a production run on the basis of pragmatic assumptions about the feasibility of staging a given dramatic text. Practical matters such as the capabilities of the technical equipment and personnel at hand, as well as aesthetic norms and anticipated public expectations, were taken into account. However, revisions were also made that had nothing to do with these intra-theatrical dynamics. On the contrary, they signified the intrusion of outside factors. This is the case in the plays staged during the latter part of Hamburg's French period (1806–14), when the city was first occupied by the French army and then became part of the French Empire in 1811. After 1810, only plays that had been approved by the censor could be performed. As we will discuss in Chapters 4 and 5, the permission of the censor can be found in various prompt books: on the last page of the text, there is a censor's note that consists of an approving phrase, mostly "vu et approuvé" [seen and approved] along with a date and signature, e.g., in *Theater-Bibliothek: 1460*, the prompt book for Kotzebue's *Die Sonnen-Jungfrau*. Sometimes, a seal of approval of this kind was only granted if parts of the text were changed, mainly unfavourable references to France or the French army, although they could also include negative assessments of the current social or political status quo. Even though they are materially indistinguishable from other corrections and cancellations, these alterations differ completely in terms of their origin: they did not emanate from the internal artistic and pragmatic practices of the theatre. Rather, they represented the influence of extra-theatrical agencies and political power. (Cf. figure 20.)

## IV. The Material Performance of Prompt Books

Judging by the variety of material forms, paper practices and writing operations, and the procedures, techniques, and tools used in conjunction with them, prompt books were clearly intersections between complex material and historical circumstances: aesthetic, pragmatic, social, and even political factors affected the entire process of a theatre production from the outset, and it is this process that manifests itself in the material performance of a prompt book. Each written alteration, each amendment, addition, or retraction of text, each pasting over or cutting out of pages, and each cue or note made about technical matters expresses the individual dynamics of a written artefact that was treated as a means to put on a performance of a specific production – even if the last performance had taken place years ago. These revisions not only transformed the respective manuscript (or hybrid) into a unique, multi-layered written artefact organised by the principle of "latest amendment valid until revoked"; rather, in the way that they emerge, react to one another, and build up layers of writing, these edits also put a specific material performance on display. This material performance is the mode in which the material biography of a prompt book evolved over the course of its use; it must be observed, reconstructed, and analysed. Doing so sheds light on the material biography of a given written artefact while allowing us to gain a more general understanding of the material point of contact that undermines the traditional distinction between a text and its staging. When we regard a prompt book with respect to its material performance, the entanglement between the literary text, its stage performance, and a host of other cultural practices in the theatre manifests itself on a material level. To this end, the full spectrum of manuscript practices must be considered and related to the various intra- and extra-theatrical contexts that motivated them. In doing so, it becomes possible to conceive of prompt books as the centrepiece of a particular manuscript culture. Indeed, by examining and retracing "the milieu in which they were produced, used and transmitted",[31] it is also possible to describe the ways in which that milieu uniquely interacted with the materiality of each prompt book.

The following three chapters set out to do just this. They will present case studies which examine some of the prompt books that we have already introduced from different angles: with respect to their creation and use, their connection to the "age of print" in which they were embedded, their relationship to the paying audience and the censor as an "audience of one", the interdependence of prompting and stage-managing, and not least the status of the literary dramatic text as soon as it was written down as content in a prompt book and then enriched. By writing thick descriptions and conducting analyses of selected prompt books, we will point out the often overlooked but important role they played in the entangled histories of theatre, literature, and (manuscript) culture.

---

31  Quenzer 2014, 2.

# Chapter 4. Creating a Prompt Book, Two at a Time: Scribes and Multi-Layered Revisions for the Hamburg Production of Kotzebue's *Die Sonnen-Jungfrau* (1790–1826)

Prompt book *Theater-Bibliothek: 728* and the related *Theater-Bibliothek: 1460* both come with the spotted, orange-brown cardboard covers typical of Schröder's private collection. Both contain a version of August von Kotzebue's international success *Die Sonnen-Jungfrau* [*The Virgin of the Sun*], which was first performed in Hamburg in April 1790 and published in print the next year.[1] As in so many prompt books, the cluttered layers of writing and enrichments seem incomprehensible, mysterious, and, at best, utterly idiosyncratic at first glance (and, for that matter, at second, third, and fourth glance). With considerable patience, some perseverance, and a little bit of luck, we have ascertained that these layers follow regular patterns. This chapter aims to reconstruct what the two processes of creation might have looked like and how the two written artefacts as well as their respective layers seem to relate to one another.[2]

## I. Doubling Down: Two Prompt Books for *Die Sonnen-Jungfrau* at the Theater-Bibliothek

*Theater-Bibliothek: 728* and *Theater-Bibliothek: 1460* reveal the extent to which the creation of a prompt book's fair copy was already a complex and multifaceted process. The two fair copies are already multi-layered. In addition, these two written artefacts show how prompt books often came in successive pairs. In this case, one was created on the basis of the reworked other. It is the only example we have come across in which a trial draft for the written artefact that later became the actual

---

1 Cf. Kotzebue 1791.
2 Cf. Felser/Funke/Göing/Hussain/Schäfer/Weinstock/Bosch 2024, especially file RFD08[HandwrittenTheatre]_Sonnenjungfrau_TextualComparison-TheaterBibliothek1460_728_print1791.pdf), (http://doi.org/10.25592/uhhfdm.13916).

book used for prompting was also bound and preserved. The reason might be that, at some point, someone had believed *Theater-Bibliothek: 728* might be of use for the prompter or the inspector. (Cf. figure 21.)

*Figure 21: S1 and S2 in front of sheet music for* Die Sonnen-Jungfrau.

The production of *Die Sonnen-Jungfrau* is a special case in that both fair copies were created by more than one scribe, who, apparently by design, worked independently of one another. There were three working on *Theater-Bibliothek: 728* (who we will refer to as 1A, 1B, and 1C in the following) and two working on *Theater-Bibliothek: 1460* (2A and 2B). We have not come across any other examples of this practice at the Theater-Bibliothek. However, we will explain why, in the case of Kotzebue, the most popular, prolific and commercially thriving playwright of the time,[3] there might have been ample reasons for such a division.

The same scribe wrote the first part in both prompt books. (Nevertheless, we will continue to distinguish between 1A and 2A for clarity's sake.) The quires were then brought together in the chronology of the play intended by Kotzebue and stitched together using the usual thick thread. However, one prompt book was made on the basis of the other. *Theater-Bibliothek: 1460* contains a copy of the revised version of *Theater-Bibliothek: 728*, which came into existence when at least one

---

3  Cf. Košenina 2011; cf. Birgfeld/Bohnengel /Košenina 2011.

other hand, 1D, created a second layer of additions and retractions and shifted some passages. The updated version then served as a template for the two scribes who created fair copy *Theater-Bibliothek: 1460*, a written artefact that was then constantly enriched by various hands using different paper technologies over a period of decades. The results are two unique, complex written artefacts whose internal coherence is not immediately discernible, giving rise to the need for thick description and detailed reconstruction.

Some confusion during filing might have been why the two written artefacts, which were clearly created in quick succession, were never indexed side by side. On its cover, *Theater-Bibliothek: 1460* is titled "Sonnenjungfrau", written in one word (in Schröder's own hand), while *Theater-Bibliothek: 728* has "Sonnen" and "Jungfrau" written separately but without the hyphen used in print publication. On their respective front pages, both written artefacts make do without the hyphen again, using two words instead. However, at the Theater-Bibliothek, 1460 is filed with and 728 without the hyphen. The cover of *Theater-Bibliothek: 1460* is identified as a "Soufleur Buch" [prompter book] instead of the more common "Soufflierbuch" [prompt book]. The handwriting is that of Schröder himself. The cover of *Theater-Bibliothek: 728* only states the title (in an unidentified hand) but makes no further specification whatsoever.[4]

When looked at separately, *Theater-Bibliothek: 1460* in particular elicits confusion. Its content closely resembles that of the play that Kotzebue published in print in 1791, but it contains a few completely different scenes and some divergent dialogue arrangements. The transition between the two scribes seems to have taken place randomly in the middle of one central scene. Various hands have added lines that are missing in the first layer and that have clearly been taken from the 1791 print version (or one of the 1797 and 1810 editions of Kotzebue's collected plays with an identical text[5]), sometimes on extra sheets that have then been attached in various ways. There is no discernible pattern to the enrichments made in black or brown ink, red crayon, and graphite pencil. In contrast, *Theater-Bibliothek: 728* is multifaceted because of the three distinct scribes who seem to have worked much more independently of each other. The enrichments are few but complex in nature. This prompt book does not seem to have been put to use in day-to-day performances. The effort required to create a prompt book, i.e., having the play copied and the bifolios bound, seems to have been disproportionate compared with the result. But when taken together, the two written artefacts provide valuable in-

---

4  The Hamburg production of *Die Sonnen-Jungfrau* is one of the few for which almost all the musical scores for the orchestral interludes have survived. As mentioned in a previous chapter, the work of the orchestra and that of the actors took place independently of one another. We will not discuss them in the following.

5  Cf. Kotzebue 1797; cf. Kotzebue 1810.

sights into how prompt books were made, how they evolved, how their materiality interacted with their content, i.e., the literary text, and how they were used in everyday theatre operations.

As a play, the print version of August von Kotzebue's *Die Sonnen-Jungfrau* is an exoticist take on the then-popular *comédies larmoyantes*, i.e., sentimental dramas with ominous plots that dissolve into happy endings. The play features the verbosity and redundancy typical of Kotzebue's successful style, with the characters putting various, but always grand, drawn-out emotions on display. The tone ranges from dramatic and tragic to histrionic and comic; the action switches effortlessly between registers or mixes them with a perfect sense of timing. The (national and international) impact of *Die Sonnen-Jungfrau* was so great that Kotzebue himself wrote a sequel, and both German and international (Western) authors came up with their own adaptations.[6]

The play was inspired by Jean François Marmontel's widely read 1776 novel *Les Incas*. Kotzebue had seen its 1782 opera adaptation by Johann Gottlieb Naumann.[7] Set during Spain's cruel, sixteenth-century conquest of Peru, war hero Alonzo has taken the side of the enlightened Inca king Ataliba, has become his friend, and is now advising Ataliba on his path to reform. As luck would have it, Alonzo and Cora, one of the young priestesses of the Inca sun religion, have secretly fallen in love, and the "virgin of the sun" is pregnant. Having committed the gravest of sins, Alonzo and Cora receive the death penalty: Cora is sentenced to be buried alive; Alonzo is to burn at the stake. However, they receive help from the great Inca warrior Rolla, the hero of Kotzebue's 1796 sequel *Die Spanier in Peru oder Rolla's Tod* [*The Spaniards in Peru or Rolla's Death*]. Rolla's own love for Cora is so great that he would gladly sacrifice himself for her happiness. Thus, the star-crossed lovers receive a last-minute pardon from the imposing King Ataliba, to whom Schröder would later dedicate a play of his own.[8] Ataliba chooses the law of the heart over the brute laws of religion and the state that he is supposed to represent and enact. Kotzebue's *Die Sonnen-Jungfrau* therefore presents the fantasies of the "good colonizer" and the "noble savage" that were prevalent at the time (as well as the respective gender stereotypes). It also serves as a prime example of the literary current of sentimentalism in its critique of both rigid (religious) traditions and the one-sidedness of reason.[9]

---

6 Cf. Kotzebue 1795; for the successful English adaptation, cf. Sheridan 1809; for *Franzesko Pozarro oder Der Schwur im Sonnentempel* cf. Soden 1815.

7 Cf. the preface in Kotzebue 1791, 5–8.

8 For the 1794 play *Ataliba, der Vater seines Volkes*, there are attributions to Kotzebue as to Schröder himself (cf. Zantop 1999, 150). A play of this name was neither included in editions of Kotzebue's collected works nor in the posthumous edition of Schröder's own collected plays; cf. v. Bülow 1831.

9 Cf. M. Schneider 2023, 216–228, 384–392.

## Chapter 4. Creating a Prompt Book, Two at a Time

*Die Sonnen-Jungfrau* premiered in Reval in 1789, at Kotzebue's private amateur theatre (an instance of the then-popular *Liebhabertheater* [fan theatre]), and was published in print by Paul Gotthelf Kummer in Leipzig in 1791. In the intervening period, Kotzebue made money by allowing the play to be performed by professional companies that were not yet able to get their hands on a print copy.[10] The first performance in Hamburg took place on 19 April 1790 as part of the seemingly endless output of Germany's most high-profile playwright of the time. Even though, in Hamburg, Kotzebue's plays did not enjoy the success they had had in, e.g., Berlin, they were still box-office hits. Judging from the playbill collection of the time, Hamburg's Stadt-Theater under Schröder must be reappraised as a Kotzebue stronghold.[11] Although *Die Sonnen-Jungfrau* fell short of the success of Kotzebue's most popular plays in Hamburg (some of which clocked more than fifty performances each over the decades), it proved to be one of his most enduring works. The play was performed thirty-two times overall and was revived on a regular basis until 1826, shortly before the theatre changed hands as well as its location.[12]

As we will argue below, it is highly likely that the prompt book archived as *Theater-Bibiothek: 1460* was in use the entire time, i.e., stored, retrieved, and intermittently enriched. After three performances of the play on 19, 21, and 22 April 1790 (with presumably no production staged at the theatre on 20 April), there were two subsequent performances over the following three weeks, two more during the rest of the year, and then one each in 1791, 1792, and 1793. After a hiatus, *Die Sonnen-Jungfrau* was put on eight times between August 1801 and March 1804 under Schröder's successors. The Hamburg collection contains six corresponding playbills from the nearly eight-year period of French occupation, 1806–14. *Theater-Bibliothek: 1460* includes approval given by the censor in 1813, who had to sign off on productions once Hamburg officially became part of the French Empire in 1810. We have been able to verify three further performances put on until 1816. After a break, the company staged *Die Sonnen-Jungfrau* five more times between 1823 and 1826.

As stated in the previous chapter, and as we will elaborate upon in Chapter 6, the Theater-Bibliothek collection contains several written artefacts that come in pairs comprising a prompt book (in the strict sense for the prompter) and an inspection book (for the inspector backstage). While *Theater-Bibliothek: 1460* has been explicitly designated for use by the prompter, there is no corresponding designation on *Theater-Bibliothek: 728*, nor are there any significant traces of wear and tear. It seems that it was initially a trial version of *Theater-Bibliothek: 1460* and then became a backup copy. While circulation of the prompt book as such was

---

10 Cf. Spoerhase 2018, 134f.
11 Cf. Schröter 2016, 423–425. Axel Schröter counts performances of 112 different plays, operas, farces, burlesques etc. by Kotzebue for the time between 1789 and 1819 alone.
12 Cf. Jahn/Mühle/Eisenhardt/Malchow/M. Schneider (https://www.stadttheater.uni-hamburg.de).

highly restricted, it always made sense to have an additional copy available in the event of loss, severe damage, or theft. For commercial reasons, a theatre company might have had no interest in publishing its successful adaptation or of lending it to a rival company without the latter returning the favour – even if another version of the play was also available in print. Losing a unique prompt book would have meant losing the master copy of the adaptation altogether, e.g., in the event that the inspector's book had not been updated regularly enough. This was even more true of plays that had not yet been published in print: before the advent of copyright licensing, playwrights like Kotzebue were only able to claim payments from a theatre company when it was not yet possible to purchase their plays from a bookseller.[13] Since bootlegs were legion, playwrights had as little interest as the company in having their unpublished works in circulation. An extra prompt book containing the same text served as insurance against losing the exclusive play from the company's repertory.

The content of the primary layer of the prompt book often initially consisted of a fair copy of the print edition of the play or a version that had been sent in by the author or a representative of another theatre company. Most of the times, this layer would then be deliberately enriched.[14] Someone, usually the company director and/or the company's head writer, would make additions and retractions amounting to a secondary layer of revisions. Together, the layers would make up the starting version of the company's stage adaptation, which would be stitched together and then bound into book form. However, this procedure only made sense if the secondary layer was not too dominant and did not affect the overall readability of the written artefact. As we will see in the next chapter, fully reworked stage adaptations such as the Shakespeare productions that Schröder's company staged in Hamburg in the 1770s warranted their own fair copies – presumably because the fundamental changes made to the available German Shakespeare translations and adaptations rendered any revised version impractical to work with. It is safe to assume that heavily revised, unbound quires and sheets of paper like this were either destroyed or remained the private property of the director.

As outlined in Chapters 1 and 2, Schröder's *Laws* stated that the actors' parts were to be written out by at least two different scribes in order to prevent the scribes from copying and bootlegging entire plays. However, a fair copy of the prompt book was usually made in one hand. The scribe in question had to be a trusted figure from inside or outside the company. Having said that, creating a prompt book for a hitherto unpublished and unperformed play by a well-known author seems to have been a different affair altogether. It is clear that *Theater-Bibliothek: 728* and *Theater-Bibliothek: 1460* were divided up between different scribes

---

13  Cf. Spoerhase 2017, 134f.
14  Cf. Chapter 3.

by design. The rule for the actors' parts seems to have been applied to Kotzebue's *Die Sonnen-Jungfrau*: Kotzebue sent the play to principal Schröder himself,[15] and Schröder divided the copying work up into different parts, thereby preventing or at least impeding the possibility of bootlegging.

The written artefact that Kotzebue sent in for the Hamburg production of *Die Sonnen-Jungfrau* has not been preserved at the Theater-Bibliothek. It is well known that Kotzebue had individual print copies made by letterpress – presumably in order to send them to different places at the same time – which he then marked as "Manuskriptdruck" [manuscript print] in order to underline their unique nature.[16] Thus, no recipient could claim that the play, although they had obtained it as a print version, had already been published or was for sale (a practice common until the late twentieth century). Kotzebue's payment and thus his livelihood depended on this. However, as discussed below, there seem to have been obvious errors and undecipherable words in the template for *Theater-Bibliothek: 728*. Scribe 1A in particular left several blanks to be filled in with words. It seems that either the print version was of poor quality or the template was a handwritten manuscript after all.

There was no need on Schröder's part to undertake a large-scale stage adaptation of a Kotzebue play. As a playwright, Kotzebue had many tricks up his sleeve; there was no doubt about the performability and audience impact of his works. In good conscience (and probably after giving it a read), Schröder was able to divide the written artefact that Kotzebue had submitted into parts, have it copied, and come up with possible minor tweaks later. Depending on the arrangement, Kotzebue's initial submission either had to be sent back, was kept by Schröder, or was traded with other companies at a later date.

## II. *Theater-Bibliothek: 728* as a Not-So-Fair Fair Copy

Traditionally, manuscript studies has examined the *syntax* and cohesion (or lack thereof) of written artefacts containing heterogeneous parts, e.g., multi-text manuscripts.[17] *Theater-Bibliothek: 728* and *Theater-Bibliothek: 1460* display a phenomenon of a different kind. While the cohesion of each of the two written artefacts (which, after all, were both stitched together and then bound in book form) is obvious, the fact that the scribes were kept apart meant that the written artefacts were designed to be internally heterogenous. While all three scribes of *Theater-Bibliothek: 728* were evidently by and large free to follow their own distinct style, the written artefact was plainly planned from the outset as a primary layer that would be revised in a

---

15 For some of the preserved correspondence between the two, cf. Schröter 2016, 429–434.
16 Cf. Spoerhase 2017, 134–154.
17 Cf. Friedrich/Schwarke 2016.

second step: the three scribes wrote on similar paper in a similar black ink. (The ink used by scribe 1B has faded more than that of the other two, which makes the already narrowly written lines much harder to read.) The scribes created three distinct visual arrangements, each of which has some kind of margin. Additions, corrections, and comments were then written into these margins in at least one other hand using a pencil as well as a different ink that has yellowed into brown. At the same time, all three original scribes worked in their own style. On the first fifty bifolios used by scribe 1A, approximately one-fifth of each manuscript page has been reserved as a side margin, although there are hardly any margins at the top or bottom. The margin has been created by folding the bifolios and is thus on the right side of the rectos and the left of the versos. On the thirty-two bifolios used by scribe 1B, the significantly narrower margin (of less than approx. one-sixth of the manuscript page) is marked by a straight pencil line drawn with a ruler on the left of each folio. Thus, the margin is located on the inside of each recto and the outside of each verso. In the main section, scribe 1B has hardly left any space between the lines and even less at the top and the bottom than scribe 1A. In contrast, the twenty bifolios used by scribe 1C have healthy margins at the top and bottom due to the generous line spacing. The visual arrangement is similar to that of the plays available in letterpress print: the name of the character speaking the lines is written in an unmarked column on the left that takes up approximately one-sixth of the page. The spoken text and the stage directions have been written down on the right. Although lacking a distinct margin, there is enough space to write, especially in passages with little back-and-forth. However, in scribe 1C's section, the margins were hardly used to enrich the manuscripts at all. The major interventions into the play took place in the parts written by scribes 1A and 1B. (Cf. figures 22, 23, 24.)

As we will demonstrate below, Kotzebue's lost *Die Sonnen-Jungfrau* template seems to have been apportioned partly with respect to content and partly with respect to the format of the writing support at hand: scribe 1A copied Acts I and II of the five-act play and left one folio blank when they had finished. Scribe 1B copied Acts III and IV as well as Act V, Scene 1, after which the quire they were working with was used up. Scribe 1C only copied Scenes 2 to 6 of Act V, which, in terms of its content, seems quite uneconomic. However, when the fair copy was later reworked, Act V, Scene 1, was integrated into the final scene of Act IV. This decision might have been made before the acts were divided up between the scribes. Scribe 1B, the untidiest of the three, introduced Acts III and IV with Roman numerals. However, 1B then switched to Arabic numerals when marking Act V – but made a mistake by writing down "Act 4" instead of "Act 5" (107). Some knowledge of the impending merger may have accounted for this confusion.

*Figure 22: S1, 31v.*

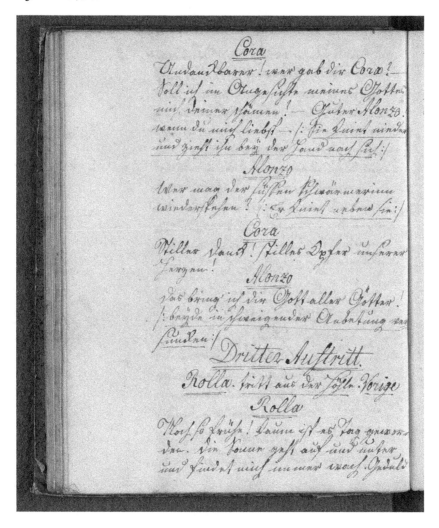

*Figure 23: S1, 77.*

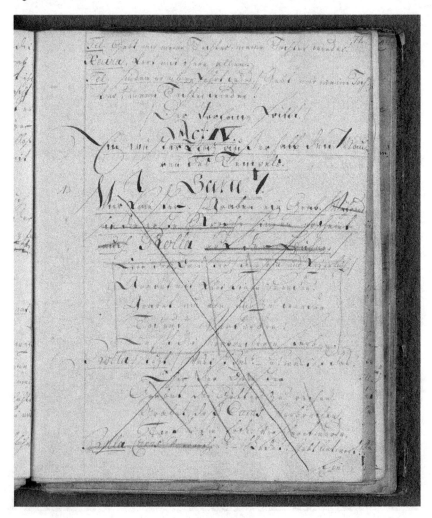

*Figure 24: S1, 118.*

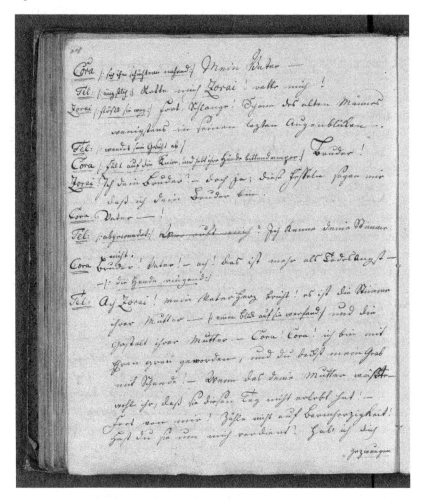

The three parts are independent and yet relate to one another in a complex manner. Scribe 1A used six quires generally consisting of nine bifolios each. The first one includes an empty folio that, in other prompt books, is often used to accommodate additional technical information (e.g., the set and prop lists, cast sheet). Folio 9r, the other half of the book endpaper, has been cut out in a way that still allows its remainder to frame the end of the quire. Quire two contains eight bifolios (with its last folio glued to the first folio of quire three), while quire four has only six. While there is no apparent reason for these minor irregularities, scribe 1A seems to have estimated quite well how many bifolios they would need altogether: "Ende des zweyten Aufzugs" [End of the second act] is written in the middle of 49r. Only 49v and both sides of 50 remain empty. 50v is distinctly more yellowed than the rest of the writing support: 50v was exposed to light for a significant period of time at some point. The quires may have been bundled up but not bound together with the work of the other scribes for some time.

The work of scribe 1B seems to have begun only after that of scribe 1A had finished, but without scribe 1A's work available to consult: someone other than scribe 1A numbered the respective folios in pencil (leaving out the empty first one). In contrast, scribe 1B numbered each side of the folios as if they were book pages, beginning on their first verso with number 49, which seems to have been due to a miscommunication: 49 is also the number of the folio on which scribe 1A's transcription of Act II finishes – well before the end of scribe 1A's last quire, which also includes the empty folio 50. As a result, in *Theater-Bibliothek: 728*, a folio by scribe 1B which is numbered 49 on the recto and 50 on the verso side follows scribe 1A's empty folio, which is numbered 50 on the recto and unnumbered on the verso. Scribe 1B then filled exactly two quires comprising eight bifolios (resembling the book binding format that was established at that point in history and that is still prevalent today[18]). Only the second of those quires was made in one piece, i.e., consists of eight stapled sheets that are folded into sixteen bifolios down the middle. In contrast, scribe 1B's first quire is also framed by one bifolio but combines the other seven bifolios in an irregular fashion.

The various scribes' individual use of format might be the reason for the illogical division of labour. Scribe 1A's task was to copy two acts; they therefore left more than two manuscript pages blank in their last quire. Scribe 1B, on the other hand, seems to have had two quires at hand and stopped when they were filled. It remains a matter of speculation whether scribe 1B was unable to continue, was no longer available, or ran out of paper, or whether there was some other reason to change scribes at that point. As mentioned above, shifting the first scene of the last act to the act before might have taken place beforehand. Getting a third scribe, 1C, to copy the final act (minus the deleted scene) might have seemed entirely reasonable for an endeavour as secretive and economically important as the staging of a Kotzebue play.

Scribe 1C seems to have been able to precisely appraise the space required. They used one quire comprising ten bifolios, with exactly one empty folio remaining before the back cover. "Ende" [The End] has been adorned with an artistic flourish. The apparent effort made gives the impression that *Theater-Bibliothek: 728* was initially planned as more than a correction version for what ultimately became the main prompt book, *Theater-Bibliothek: 1460*. But the scribe might also have been simply following a rather common pattern with respect to ornamental pieces of writing, they might not have been fully informed about the plans the director had for their work, or Schröder might not yet have decided on the final status of *Theater-Bibliothek: 728*. (Cf. figure 25.)

---

18  Cf. Burdett 1975.

*Figure 25: S1, 150.*

In the end, before or after binding the written artefact, the hand that had numbered the first part in pencil got to work again in part three. However, by this point, the hand had adopted the numbering system of scribe 1B: each recto and verso page received its own number, starting with 113 and ending with 150. It can be assumed that either scribe 1B took a superficial look at the work of scribe 1A or that someone aware of the pencil numbering in the work of scribe 1A told scribe 1B to start with number 49. Only afterwards did that person realise that scribe 1B had changed the order, which they then stuck to while working through the quires handed in by scribe 1C.

Thus, even in the pragmatic world of prompt book creation, the primary layer of *Theater-Bibliothek: 728* is hardly what one would normally consider to be a fair copy. Instead, the primary layer of *Theater-Bibliothek: 728* is itself a heterogeneous written artefact in different hands, taking different approaches to the relationship between format and content, producing a different visual organisation, and numbering the folios differently. Due to the tidy layering of scribe 1B's second quire and scribe 1C's only quire, the bound written artefact gives the impression of a multi-text manuscript with three distinct sections: one large pile with irregular quires and two tightly organised piles (cf. figure 26).

*Figure 26: S1, transversal view.*

## III. The Error-Prone Dynamics of Copying: Unintentional Gender Trouble

The primary layer of *Theater-Bibliothek: 728* from 1790 is largely identical with the play that Kotzebue published in 1791. Rather than inconsistencies in the template, the routines that each of the scribes had developed while copying plays might be to blame for formal discrepancies: scribe 1A of *Theater-Bibliothek: 728*, for example, calls scenes "Auftritte" [entrances] like in the 1791 print publication, while scribes 1B and 1C stick to the equally common "Szene" [scene]. However, it is unlikely, though not impossible, that Kotzebue's template itself was inconsistent in this respect.

Minor differences between *Theater-Bibliothek: 728* and the 1791 print publication probably indicate that Kotzebue made slight revisions to certain phrases before publishing the work in print for the book market. Only on very few occasions have changes been made to the content, but these are trivial in nature. The greatest discrepancy is that two other "virgins of the sun" narrating their encounter with two Spaniards use different descriptions: "[D]er meinige hatte einen schönen schwarzen Bart und rothe volle Wangen. / Der Meinige hatte weiche blonde Locken und ein freundliches Auge" (S1, 53) [Mine had a beautiful black beard and full, red cheeks. / Mine had soft blond curls and a kind eye] in the 1790 version became "Der meinige hatte schönes bräunliches Haar und eben solche Augen. / Der Meinige hatte so lockiges schwarzes Haar und einen so freundlichen Blick"[19] [Mine had beautiful brownish hair and eyes the same. / Mine had such curly black hair and such a friendly look] in the 1791 version. Kotzebue might have simply begun with a description of his 1789 actors and then altered the description either for theatrical effect or with other actors in mind.

Overall, Kotzebue also standardised the use of words in the play. The lines uttered by the Inca king Ataliba are always preceded by his proper name in the print version. In contrast, *Theater-Bibliothek: 728* and *Theater-Bibliothek: 1460* both alternate between the proper name and "D. König" for "der König" [the king] (e.g., S1, 72). It is highly unlikely that, in the assembly-line work of putting on new (and old) productions, Schröder would have already inserted such trivial changes into Kotzebue's submission before having it copied.

There are also a few small changes to the content that Kotzebue had written for the print publication to amplify some dramaturgical effects. When, in Act I, the forbidden lovers, sun virgin Cora and the "good coloniser" Alonzo, are confronted by "noble savage" Rolla, who is in love with Cora himself, Cora stops Alonzo from drawing arms. The wording in *Theater-Bibliothek: 728* is, "Sieh in sein Auge, ob er nicht unser Freund ist" (S1, 78r) [See in his eye whether he is not our friend]. The

---

19 Kotzebue 1791, 99.

print version published one year later emphasises the inner nobility of Rolla, to whom Kotzebue would dedicate his sequel (which, in Hamburg, ran up a similar number of performances as *Die Sonnen-Jungfrau*[20]). Cora already knows that selfless Rolla is on the couple's side. Instead of turning to her lover, who is prepared to defend her, she has already seen the unquestionable truth in Rolla's eyes and says to Alonzo, "Sieh in sein Auge, da stehts geschrieben, daß er unser Freund ist"[21] [See in his eye, there it is written that he is our friend]. The minor change makes major dramaturgical sense because, in the prompt book as well as in the published play, the scene quickly goes from being a possible fight to the death to becoming a quarrel of words and emotions. In a sudden shift in alignment, Cora and Rolla have to appease Alonzo, who is now jealous of Cora's longstanding friendship with a potential male rival. The sudden change in register is more convincing when Cora is no longer speaking to Alonzo as her defender but informing him in a self-assured manner of her assessment of Rolla's overall harmlessness. However, in the specific dialogue in question and in the overall play, this kind of tweak hardly changes anything.

Another category of minor differences between the content of *Theater-Bibliothek: 728* and the published version of the play from 1791 could be the result of either copying errors or mistakes in the template that Kotzebue had sent in. At one point in the play, Rolla reminisces about his time as a war hero standing with the Inca against Ataliba's historical competitor Huascar: "als Ataliba's Thron durch Huascar's Macht erschüttert"[22] [when Ataliba's throne was shaken by Huascar's power]. *Theater-Bibliothek: 728* does not name Huascar (who is not mentioned in the play before or after) and leaves some blank space instead. The clause remains grammatically correct but becomes unusually mysterious for a Kotzebue play: "als Ataliba's Thron durch Macht erschüttert" (S1, 5r) [when Ataliba's throne was shaken by power].

In another passage, the high priestess of the sun interrogates two sun virgins called Idali and Amazili about possible interactions they have had with men outside the temple. The two young women cannot keep their stories straight and get tangled up in a comic exchange. When Idali addresses not the high priestess but Amazili, the stage directions emphasise it: "Idali. (zu Amazili) Einfältiges Ding! Du hast auch alles vergessen"[23] [Idali. (to Amazili) You simpleton! You have forgotten everything]. In *Theater-Bibliothek: 728*, the two characters speak in unison: "<u>Id.</u> U. <u>Amaz.</u>". The abridged names are underlined. The "und" is abbreviated with "u.". This could mean that the two sun virgins are deriding each other at the same time. However, on other occasions, the stage directions clearly point out when

---

20 Cf. Schröter 2016, 416.
21 Kotzebue 1791, 73.
22 Kotzebue 1791, 12.
23 Kotzebue 1791, 98.

characters are speaking in unison, which would not make much sense in the context of this scene. The mistake was either in the template sent in by Kotzebue or was made during the copying process, in this case by scribe 1B.

As we will discuss below, the content of the *Theater-Bibliothek: 1460* fair copy is a transcription of the revised *Theater-Bibliothek: 728* – including the latter's minor divergences from the 1791 print publication. The passage concerning the friendship reflected in Rolla's eye has been faithfully copied from handwritten artefact to handwritten artefact, as has the obvious mistake regarding Idali and Amazili. With respect to Rolla's war memories, scribe 2A of *Theater-Bibliothek: 1460* has actually intensified the mistake, possibly by trying to mend it: instead of "als Ataliba's Thron durch Huascar's Macht erschüttert" in the print version and "als Ataliba's Thron durch [blank] Macht erschüttert" in *Theater-Bibliothek: 728*, the wording in *Theater-Bibliothek: 1460* is, "als Ataliba's durch Macht erschüttert" (S2, 4r) [when Ataliba's was shaken by power]. Aside from the grammatically awkward construction, it sounds as if Ataliba as a person (or synecdoche for his kingdom) was shaken. As stated above, scribe 2A of *Theater-Bibliothek: 1460* is scribe 1A of *Theater-Bibliothek: 728*. The fresh mistake was thus made while copying their own handwriting.

However, in the later *Theater-Bibliothek: 1460* transcription, both mistakes were at some point (to be determined below) corrected in black ink and aligned with the published print version. "Id. U. Amaz." Has become "Id. Zu Amaz." [Id. To Amaz.], which now makes perfect sense. The missing "throne" and the missing name "Huascar's" have also been inserted above the line. The hand responsible was that of Schröder himself. Below we will argue that these insertions were probably not immediate corrections but were made when the play was being revised at a later date, when the print version was already available as a point of reference. Only the omission of "throne" in *Theater-Bibliothek: 1460* can be safely identified as a copying error from *Theater-Bibliothek: 728*. The two other examples (as well as other minor divergences from the later print version) could have come from the written artefact sent in by Kotzebue. Judging by the "friendship in Rolla's eye" example, we can thus safely assume that Kotzebue had revised the version he sent in around 1790 before the 1791 print publication.

Abbreviations seem particularly prone to copying errors, which leads to some comic confusion in both *Theater-Bibliothek: 728* and *Theater-Bibliothek: 1460*. The Inca cult of the sun has a high priestess of the sun ("Oberpriesterin") as well as a high priest of the sun ("Oberpriester"), who both remain nameless in *Die Sonnen-Jungfrau*. As seen with Idali and Amazili, who become "Id. U. Amaz.", it was common practice to abridge long character names in prompt books when indicating their share of the dialogue. "Oberpriesterin" and "Oberpriester", however, seem to have been too long for even the 1791 print version: each character's name has been spelled out in the stage directions but then shortened to "Oberpr." in the dialogue. The two characters only meet once, when the high priestess brings the charges against the ill-fated lovers. On this occasion, the print version adds the gendered articles "die" and "der" [the] to indicate which character is about to speak.[24]

In contrast, *Theater-Bibliothek: 728* continuously distinguishes between the two characters. Since the three scribes proceed in different ways, it can be assumed that they were told to shorten the character names even if they were spelled out in the template. Scribe 1A has written "D.Oberpr." for the high priest and has not covered any scenes with his female counterpart. In the crowded folios made by scribe 1B, "Die Oberpriesterin" [the high priestess] has been shortened to "Die.Ob.Pr." and "Der Oberpriester" [the high priest] to "Der.Ob.Pr" in the beginning, then generally "D.Ob. Pr.". Scribe 1C's tidy, elegant handwriting has only dealt with the male variant; nevertheless, it is highly flexible in terms of the abbreviations it doles out: the shorter the high priest's lines, the longer the abbreviation. "D.Ob. Priest" (S1, 141) on a recto is, for instance, followed on a verso by "D.Ob.pr." (S1, 142), as already used by scribe 1A.

A lack of clarity in the template and scribe 1B's general untidiness might have contributed to some gender trouble arising in their part. Even in the scenes in which clearly only the male high priest is on stage, scribe 1B has mixed up male and female abbreviations in a seemingly arbitrary fashion. Since this problem does not occur in scribe 1A's or scribe 1C's parts, the fault does not seem to lie with the template. One scene that is particularly crucial to the melodramatic subplot thus takes on a different meaning– or at least would leave any unsuspecting reader confused. Selfless Rolla, who is willing to sacrifice his own love for Cora in order to fight for her happiness (and, indeed, her and Alonzo's lives), has always considered himself to be an orphan. In Act IV, Scene 3, his uncle, the high priest, reveals that he was once in Alonzo's shoes. He also fathered an illegitimate child with a since deceased virgin of the sun. The child is Rolla himself. Where the son realises that his supposed uncle is actually his father, scribe 1B has run especially wild with their gender abbreviations. In the stage directions, the high priest has been consistently spelled out and identified as a *he*. But when writing down the name of the character about to speak, scribe 1B has mixed up the male and female versions over six folios until, at the end of the scene, where we find the female "Die. Ob.Pr." alternating with the male "D.Ob.Pr.", even though both will be addressed as "Vater" [father] by Rolla later on. It almost seems as if there are three characters on stage instead of just two, with "Die.Ob.Pr." and "D.Ob.Pr." alternately telling Rolla, "Du bist mein Sohn" (S1, 87) [You are my son]. The error is obvious: the high priestess has never even entered the stage in the scene, and it would not make any sense whatsoever for her to be a part of the dialogue. But since the actor playing the high priestess would only have arrived on the actual stage in the event the booklet in which her lines were written out told her to, this kind of mistake is unlikely to have done any harm in the grand scheme of things (cf. figure 27).

---

24  Cf. Kotzebue 1791, 127–133.

*Figure 27: S1, 87.*

When *Theater-Bibliothek: 1460* was copied from *Theater-Bibliothek: 728*, the mistake was only partially recognised. The change in scribes took place shortly after the beginning of the scene in question.[25] In Acts I and II of *Theater-Bibliothek: 1460*, scribe 2A was still using the abbreviation they themselves had established as scribe 1A of *Theater-Bibliothek: 728*, with the high priest referred to as "D.Oberpr." (S1, 2v). Scribe 2A corrected the falsely allocated gender and, for their small part, used "D.Ob.pr." (S2, 67v) (close to the spelling established by scribe 1B in *Theater-Bibliothek: 728*). It is striking, however, that scribe 2A followed their colleague's alternative choices (e.g., "Szene" instead of "Auftritte") to the letter in all other aspects when correcting scribe 1B's misgendering from *Theater-Bibliothek: 728*.

Scribe 2B in *Theater-Bibliothek: 1460* was more organised than their counterpart in *Theater-Bibliothek: 728*. Nevertheless, they picked the wrong one of the two genders on offer in the continuation of the scene. For the rest of Act IV, Scene 3, in *Theater-Bibliothek: 1460*, it is the female "Die Ob P." whom Rolla addresses as "Mein Vater" (S2, 73) [My father]. In fact, the misgendered version now persists throughout the rest of Act IV, which ends with what is supposed to be an all-male assembly of priests! Only once in *Theater-Bibliothek: 1460* is the mistake corrected in red crayon[26] within the scope of what were probably very late revisions in the 1820s (as we will address below). It seems the mistake was either not recognised or, more likely, not corrected until then. At the same time, the stage directions were faithfully copied in the male form only: "Rolla: bebt zurück und sieht den Oberpriester starr an" (S2, 72) [Rolla: shrinks back and stares at the high priest].

The gender trouble with the priestess and the priest in *Theater-Bibliothek: 728* and *Theater-Bibliothek: 1460* indicates the scope of the scribes' work. Their activities oscillated between the faithful, even mechanical reproduction of the letters, a certain

---

25  Cf. S2, 69r.
26  Cf. S2, 78r.

freedom to find the appropriate abbreviations, the power to correct inconsistencies, and the possibility of creating minor (or not so minor) mistakes, which would potentially be carried on through the various copies – and thus through the decades.

## IV. Reshaping *Theater-Bibliothek: 728* – Tweaking a Play for the Stage

A fourth hand in ink, 1D, and a pencil that could be a fifth hand but, in most cases, seems to have been an additional tool used by hand 1D, went through the work of all three scribes who worked on *Theater-Bibliothek: 728*. Pencil and ink worked in close alignment – whether in the same hand or not, whether during the same step in the production process or not: the additions in pencil laid the technical groundwork, made retractions, and checked for accurate numbering (even if it was not always systematic as far as the mixture of Arabic and Roman numerals was concerned). The work done in ink provided the technical and textual additions made necessary by the pencil's interventions. Major retractions have been indicated by rectangular shapes drawn around the respective content in pencil and additionally by vertical lines drawn through the middle (cf. figure 28).

Alongside the pencil, an ink different to the ones used by the three scribes who worked on the fair copy has been used for everything else. Since this ink has faded differently, or had a different consistency to begin with, the brown ink of hand 1D is easily distinguishable. Although it is, for practical reasons, untidier and more crowded than the elegant handwriting of Schröder's letters, 1D seems to be the principal's own hand. Later, the two scribes working on the designated prompt book *Theater-Bibliothek: 1460* adhered to the enriched version when reproducing the play for the fair copy that would be used as the actual prompt book. In all likelihood, *Theater-Bibliothek: 1460* served as the basis of the performances that began in April 1790.

Apart from minor interventions into the content, the revisions carried out by hand 1D in *Theater-Bibliothek: 728* still differ from the wording in the 1791 publication. We can therefore safely assume that their author was unaware of its existence; they are probably from an earlier date, most likely from the period in which the theatre was preparing for the first performance. Many of the enrichments were corrections of obvious errors such as the ones described above: copying errors by the scribe or the errors that had already existed in Kotzebue's faithfully copied template. Examples already abound on the first folios,[27] where hand 1D has crossed

---

27 On some occasions, it was clearly not yet hand 1D but scribe 1A, 1B, or 1C self-correcting their own work. When Alonzo's noble but irritable sidekick Don Juan first enters the stage, he asks Alonzo's weapon bearer Diego a question ("Sind wir sicher, Diego?" [Are we safe, Diego?]). But when

out an aimless syllable left behind by scribe 1A. In Rolla's opening soliloquy, where he calls on "das Gewimmelsel eurer Schöpfung" (S1, 2v) [your teeminging creation] of his pagan gods, scribe 1A had added a superfluous syllable with no meaning ("sel" [the second "ing"] at the end of "Gewimmel"), which has been crossed out by hand 1D. On the next folio, scribe 1A had left a little space where the meaning of Rolla's self-pity seems to have been unclear in the template: "laßt sie Rollas An sehen, wie er auf feuchtem, kalten Boden, sein liebesiches Leben ausgehaucht" (S1, 3r) [let her Rollas look how he exhales his lovesick life onto cold, humid ground]. A lowercase "ansehen" [look at] would have made more sense, but scribe 1A was apparently not able to decipher a word placed between "An" and "sehen". Hand 1D has struck through the "An", amended the misleading "liebesiches" to the more obvious spelling "liebessieches", and filled in the gap with "Überrest" [let her see how Rolla's remains exhale...]. "Überrest"[28] would also be used in the 1791 print, which otherwise used slightly different phrasing. It is thus a matter of speculation whether the word was already in the template sent in by Kotzebue and could not be identified by scribe 1A, whether the template had already been tampered with, or whether this was an honest mistake. For more profound enrichments, hand 1D sometimes used the margins (of varying sizes) that had been left by the scribes. The purpose of this was apparently to make space for alternative lines and correction marks wherever these could not be conveniently placed between or next to existing ones. The margin was not intended for discussions between hands but did sometimes include comments. Generally speaking, however, revisions were placed between the lines of the main content as was common in prompt books without margins. Overall, only very few prompt books with margins can be found at the Theater-Bibliothek. Either correction versions such as *Theater-Bibliothek: 728* were not usually deemed worth keeping (if they were not repurposed as prompt books or inspection books at a later point)[29] or the creation of distinct correction copies was itself unusual. In some instances, a commercially available print may have been used[30] or the template for the respective fair copy might not have been

---

scribe 1A mistakenly wrote down the character uttering the line down as the addressee Diego, they then swiftly crossed out "Diego" and wrote "D. Juan" (S1, 9r) next to it.

28 Kotzebue 1791, 11.

29 *Theater-Bibliothek*: 728 is the only example of a bound and preserved correction version that we know of in the collection. There are many prompt and inspection books for the other Kotzebues staged in Hamburg during the time, some of them based on commercially available print copies. Either the respective correction versions were lost, *Die Sonnen-Jungfrau* was an exception, or Schröder and the company had had other plans for the written artefact in the beginning. Given the sheer number of written artefacts with Kotzebue-plays in the Theater-Bibliothek collection (292), there is no way to rule out other fascinating entanglements between the respective pairs.

30 This was sometimes the case for other Kotzebue plays. The use of print copies will be discussed in greater detail in Chapters 5 and 6.

as organised as *Theater-Bibliothek: 728* (or it might not have been, for that matter, arranged into a book format during or after the copying process). But then, Kotzebue was the most successful contemporary author, at least commercially speaking. His plays might have deserved special attention, and – as we see in the dividing-up of the manuscripts between three and two scribes respectively – extra caution. But Kotzebue knew his trade: the play seems nearly stage-ready; hand 1D only made use of the margin twelve times altogether. Nevertheless, the existing retractions, additions, and rearrangements are telling manifestations of both the manuscript practices employed in the creation of prompt books and the business of adapting plays to the stage.

*Figure 28: S1, 21v.*

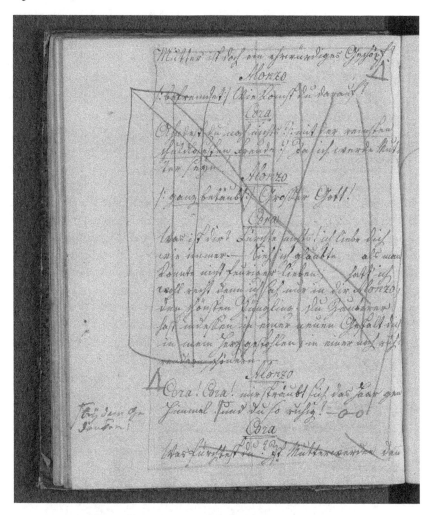

## Replacing an Offensive Scene with Comedy

Schröder greatly appreciated Kotzebue as an author. Although there was no copyright at the time, he did not intervene much into Kotzebue's submissions.[31] However, as we will discuss in the following, Schröder took the liberty of making dramaturgical tweaks when he deemed it necessary. He also made suggestions in order to avoid brushes with the authorities wherever Kotzebue's plays came across as too politically or morally frank. While some of Schröder's letters to Kotzebue about other plays are housed in the Hamburg Staatsbibliothek collection, we do not know of any letters regarding *Die Sonnen-Jungfrau*.[32] If there were any, Schröder's suggestions would have been made in the same vein: the minor changes to the text for the Hamburg production related to the practicalities of its theatrical realisation, but above all to the morals of the play. Even though very little in Kotzebue's play seems derisive or ostentatious, it was probably best to not overtly emphasise potentially delicate topics that were obvious enough in the exoticist outlines of the play.[33] Therefore, Schröder made some efforts to cushion the blow of the play's action. The Hamburg adaptation would, of course, rely on the central element, Cora's pregnancy out of wedlock (which was, moreover, punishable by death in the theatrical diegesis), but Schröder's changes would put much less emphasis on it. It was during the editing process that the margins left by the scribes in *Theater-Bibliothek: 728* came into play.

In the 1791 print edition, Act I is set at dusk, some of it in front of, some of it inside a wall surrounding the temple of the sun. In Act I, Scene 4, Alonzo's side-kick Juan talks him into breaking up with the virgin of the sun – for her own safety and for that of his own political and personal friendship with the Sun King. After the two men squabble about the precautions they should take, Diego, Alonzo' fearful weapon bearer, brings some comic relief in Act I, Scene 5. The audience then meets Cora for the first time in Act I, Scene 6. In a long, melodramatic exchange that runs for twelve pages in the print edition, Cora reveals that she is pregnant and conveys her steadfast belief in the purity and innocence of the love she shares with Alonzo. She then takes leave of Alonzo, promising to return the next day to watch the sunrise with him. Cora believes that the sunrise will be a test of her god's benevolence towards the fruit of their love. In Act I, Scene 7, Alonzo confesses to Juan

---

31   Cf. Schröter 2016, 429ff.
32   The letters concerning Kotzebue's sequel, *Rolla's Death*, state that negative comments about the Spaniards had to be cut. Due to its commercial interests, the city of Hamburg wanted to be on good terms with the Spanish ambassador. Cf. Schröder's respective letters to Kotzebue, LA 49–50, LA 51–52.
33   For instance, a 1791 Viennese production of *Die Sonnen-Jungfrau* failed to win over the local censors and could only be staged in a heavily redacted version. Cf. Höyng 2007, 112.

that the worst imaginable thing has happened. The curtain falls with Alonzo agonizing and his companions sleeping. Act II returns to a tragicomic mode with said companions refusing to be woken up by an ever-more desperate Alonzo in Scene 1. He then greets the sun virgin alone in Scene 2. The drawn-out back-and-forth between his infatuated anguish and her loving innocence resumes as the sun comes up – before Juan and Diego wake up and Rolla arrives (mourning his unrequited love for Cora by living a hermit's life in a cave right next to the Spaniards' camp), setting the almost fateful chain of events in motion.

As described above, the Kotzebue template used as the basis for *Theater-Bibliothek: 728* in 1790 seems to be nearly identical to the content of the print version that went on sale the next year. Scribe 1A faithfully copied it into *Theater-Bibliothek: 728*. Remarkably, Act I, Scene 6, was then unceremoniously retracted in the Hamburg revisions by means of a rectangular frame in graphite pencil, with a vertical pencil line or slash at the approximate centre of the two rectos and two versos as well. Any such line is missing in the smaller frame around the beginning of Act I, Scene 6, at the bottom of 18r (which only presents stage directions). The frame at the top of 20v, however, has been filled in with several pencil graphite strike-throughs in the form of an X in order to give special emphasis to the retraction. The retraction of Scene 6 has removed the revelation of Cora's pregnancy, her extended delight, and Alonzo's horror.

Curiously, hand 1D has also made several changes to the text in the passages that it had itself retracted (if we assume that the ink enrichments were working in concert with the pencil ones). In addition, hand 1D has drawn some diacritical signs, which we will discuss below. For now, it is important to note that, instead of the retracted scene, a loose sheet in a smaller format (not organised by any ruled lines) has been folded over on the left-hand side and glued in between 17v and 18r as an additional manuscript page numbered 18a by the hand of scribe 1D. Whereas the verso remains empty, hand 1D, Schröder, has untidily scribbled an alternative Scene 6 on the recto without any margins in densely packed lines, some of them slanted. Some self-corrections seem to have taken place during the writing of the lines, with apparently no need to create a cleaner version of 18a. (Cf. figure 29.)

Act I, Scene 5, had ended with Juan and Diego arranging to go on rounds to keep guard. In the new Scene 6, Diego doubles down on the comic servant character which was so well known to audiences of the time. He delivers a self-referential monologue about his fear of the dark. If played by the book, a drop curtain would have probably come down immediately to show Alonzo and Cora meeting inside the wall. But now, the content of the additional sheet has cheeky Diego returning to the set of Scene 5, which he had just vacated with everybody else: "[...] ich bleibe hier. Hier giebts doch ~~Gest~~ noch Gesträuche hinter die man sich dukken kann, wenn was passirt" [I'm staying here. Here are bushes where you can take cover if anything happens]. Diego's extemporisation on fear is as funny as it is pointless. He chooses the darkness of his closed eyes in the hope of escaping not only the darkness of the night but also the terror of his imagination. However, he keeps moving about the stage, squinting – probably still afraid, probably making comic gestures: "[...] ich muß die Augen zudrükken oder der ganze Busch hier verwandelt sich in einen Kirchhof. / er geht mit geschloßenen Augen auf und ab" (S1, 18a) [I have to close my eyes or the whole bush will transform into a graveyard. / he walks up and down with his eyes closed]. While this was intended to have a hilarious effect on the audience, the punchline that Diego is covering his eyes in the same way that loose sheet 18a covers some unwanted dialogue remains lost on everyone – except for perhaps its originator, hand 1D, which did the writing and presumably the covering as well.

*Figure 29: S1, 17v and 18a r.*

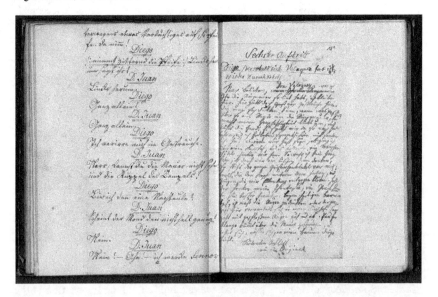

Diego's extra solo number is just like the scenes that the proponents of eighteenth-century German theatre reform (who generally came up with their theories from outside the theatre) tried to marginalise in favour of the inner logic of a well-made play.[34] Although here, the addition serves a purpose: the end of 18a proclaims the return of Diego's master. "Alonzo kommt über die Mauer gesprungen" [Alonzo comes jumping over the wall]. Depending on how long Diego's antics have been entertaining the audience, it is likely that Alonzo has been meeting with his beloved and will now report back to his companions. Diego's interlude also fits in perfectly with the beginning of Act I, Scene 7, in which he is scared by the entrances

---

34  Cf. Weinstock 2019, 70–93; cf. Malchow 2022, 261–265.

of both Alonzo and Juan. "Siebenter Auftritt / wie im Original" [Seventh scene / as in the original] (S1, 18a) has been written at the bottom right of the recto of the loose sheet by the same hand, 1D, but is somewhat removed from Diego's lines.

The dramaturgical effect is striking: Schröder can now keep the text of Act I, Scene 7, *ad verbatim*. Thus, the pregnancy is rather hastily introduced instead of being verbosely elaborated upon throughout Scene 6 as in the template (and later in the print version): "Deine Warnung kam zu spät! [...] Sie ist Mutter!" (S1, 25v) [Your warning has come too late! [...] She is a mother!]. Instead of Cora's drawn-out excitement and unshakable belief in the innocence of her love, the audience would have only seen the men's perspective – their despair and their implicit assessment that a pregnancy out of wedlock would be a catastrophe. Without sacrificing the core element of the play, the revised version shrewdly aligned it with the prevailing morals of the time.

## Shifting the Lovers' Passion Using Diacritical Signs

The introduction of Cora and Alonzo's love as it had been portrayed in the former Scene 6 had to be integrated into the dialogue at a later point. The same went for some pieces of information provided there. To this end, hand 1D made use of the margin of 26v: in ink, it added twenty densely scribbled, scarcely legible, and sometimes self-corrected lines of two to four words each, in which Alonzo gives his companions notice that Cora will return the next morning: "in ihrer liebenswürdigen Einfalt, will sie die Sonne zur Schiedsrichterinn über unsre Liebe machen" [in her charming naivety, she wants to make the sun the judge of our love]. At what was probably a later point in time, a rather generous bracket was drawn in pencil to point out the position of the insertion (cf. figure 30).

While the second insertion sums up the gist of the conversation that has been cut, Diego's comic scene is a seemingly redundant addition to Kotzebue's text, even though it elaborates on the already established theme of his cowardice. Both insertions were made in line with Kotzebue's overall style. Schröder, who had modelled his own style as a playwright (of comedies and sentimental drama) on Kotzebue's,[35] would have had no problem coming up with additional lines like these. However, because another extra scene with comic lines for Diego was inserted later on (in Act IV, Scene 2), it is also possible that he told Kotzebue about his plans and asked for additional dialogue. Having said that, it seems likely for practical reasons that the actual shifts and rearrangements of the text were carried out on site in Hamburg.

---

35  Cf. Hoffmann 1939, 35–74.

*Figure 30: S1, 26v.*

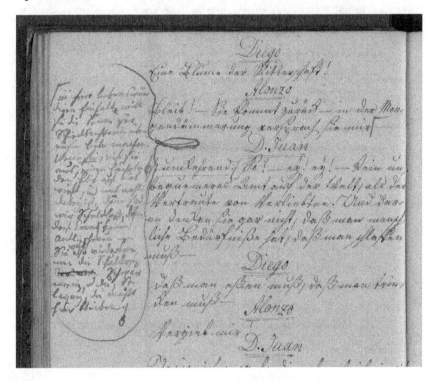

Particularly effective parts of Cora and Alonzo's dialogue in the revelation scene, Scene 6, were bundled together and moved to the sun trial scene in Act II, Scene 2, affecting the content of approximately two and a half of the twelve folios of Act I, Scene 6, in total. In Act II, Scene 2, Schröder kept Cora's entrance, in which she voices her disappointment about her plans to lovingly wake Alonzo being laid to waste by his insomnia. Then, an insertion mark follows, and Alonzo's next reply has been retracted. In the left margin, on the same level as the beginning of the scene, rather than the end of Cora's last line, hand 1D has placed the related insertion mark and eight lines beneath it, starting with the beginning of an alternative reply: "Alonzo. Wie könnt ich? Sieh die ganze Nacht stand ich–" [How could I? See, the whole night I was up –]. Hand 1D has continued in the same style with comments in the next two lines: "NB" for *nota bene* and then "Siehe den 6ten Auftritt in vorigem akt von Zeichen Θ bis zu #" (S1, 29v) [See the 6th scene in the last act from signs Θ to #]. If we turn back the pages, we do indeed find the horizontally crossed out circle and the # symbol in the previously cut Act I, Scene 6, on 19v and 20r! The text inside the pencil rectangle indicating the retraction has itself been revised with minor strike-throughs and one small addition: the comment on 29v in Act II, Scene 2, instructs the scribe of *Theater-Bibliothek: 1460* (or any user of *Theater-Bi-*

*bliothek: 728* for that matter) to transfer the passage between "ϴ and "#" to the respective position in Act 2, Scene 2. Thus, after it was copied into *Theater-Bibliothek: 1460*, the now displaced dialogue continued to introduce the audience to the lovers' extended assurances of their mutual longing, which would have otherwise gone missing with the cancellation of the original Act I, Scene 6 (cf. figures 31, 32, 33).

*Figure 31: S1, 29v.*

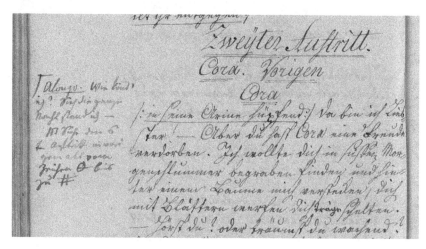

*Figure 32: S1, 19v.*

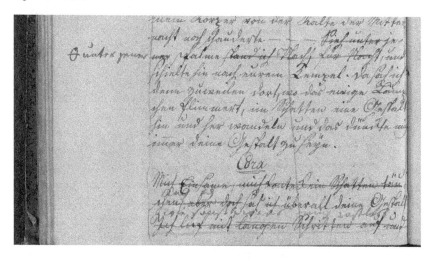

*Figure 33: S1, 20r.*

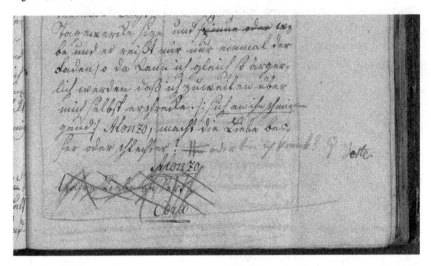

A second transfer from Act I, Scene 6, to Act II, Scene 2, is more complicated and, to the uninitiated, less comprehensible. On the top of 30r, right after Alonzo's first, now crossed-out speech, the fourth hand has drawn a peculiar symbol: in the middle of the writing is a triangle on top of a vertically crossed out circle. This symbol can also be found earlier in Act I, Scene 6, on 23v. Here, the vertical line only goes halfway through the circle; the symbol thus gives the impression of an arrow pointing to the passages above. Scribbled to the right of it (and thus leaving the margins empty), an insertion mark has been placed. Under it, there is nothing to be inserted but an instruction: "Siehe S 2. Act 2." [See s 2. Act 2.] – where the same symbol can indeed be found. However, any implicit instructions are far from obvious. Either Schröder conveyed them verbally to the scribe of *Theater-Bibliothek: 1460* or they had a working relationship where his emending marks were well known (cf. figures 34 and 35).

Only when comparing *Theater-Bibliothek: 728* with *Theater-Bibliothek: 1460* does the function of the symbol become apparent. Some parts of the writing after the # symbol between the bottom of 20r and the arrow on 22v were to be transferred to Act II, Scene 2. Right next to the # symbol on 20r, hand 1D has written "verte", a common Latin phrase for "turn [the page]" in European manuscript cultures. Afterwards, until the symbol in the middle of 22v, not only has most of the text been crossed out like the rest of Act I, Scene 6, but in addition to the rectangular enclosure and the continuous vertical strike-through, more strike-throughs have also been added in pencil and sometimes in ink as well. At some points, the additional strike-throughs amount to three traverse lines in one direction, at others up to eleven in both directions. Thus, on the four and a half manuscript pages in question, some passages give the impression that they have somehow been retracted with more emphasis than others. The reason for this becomes apparent when we take a look at *Theater-Bibliothek: 1460*. Here, the "less heavily retracted" passages have been reassembled as a coherent dialogue in Act II, Scene 2, at the very place the arrow symbol was positioned in *Theater-Bibliothek: 728*. These passages portray Cora as being so joyful in anticipation of motherhood that she ignores Alonzo's horror about having to become her "Mörder" (S1, 22v) [murderer].

*Figure 34: S1, 22v.*

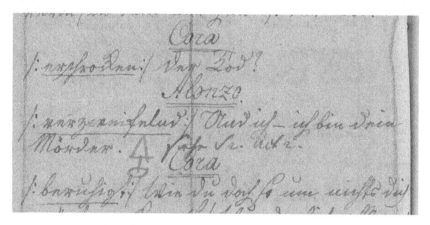

*Figure 35: S1, 30r.*

Hand 1D has marked the beginning and the end of the "more heavily retracted" passages with seemingly random and idiosyncratic correction marks, mostly in ink, generally in the margins, but sometimes in the writing itself. On 20v, there is a vertical line with a circle on top of it next to "verte" and before Cora's reply (that hand 1D has heavily revised). There is a first "B" after Cora's lines and, after a longer passage from Cora, on the next manuscript page as well. There is also triangle near the top and close to the bottom of 21v. Moreover, a horizontal line with a circle to the left and right of it appears after a quick reply from Alonzo (with a short insert) and again on 22r (now in pencil). Finally, we find the same shape, albeit rotated by ninety degrees, after an even shorter comment by Alonzo (which is connected to the previous one by a pencil line) and its partner near the top of 22v – with some dialogue on half a manuscript page to come before the arrow and the accompanying instruction, "See s[cene] 2. Act 2." (cf. figure 36).

*Figure 36: S1, 21v and 22r.*

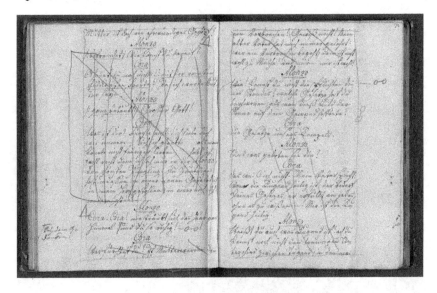

Without deciphering the instructions behind the signs in Act I, Scene 6, and Act II, Scene 2, the respective folios seem enigmatic and even arbitrary: the pattern of revision is irregular; the diacritical signs are unusual. Only in hindsight does the overall idea behind hand 1D's revision become clear. In Act I, the whole of Scene 6 has been cut. A longer passage ("from signs Θ to #") and some scattered shorter passages have been taken up in Act II, Scene 2, instead. Passages that have been retracted altogether have been crossed out twice and sometimes three times. The beginning and the end of those passages are marked with these curious diacritical signs – as if to make sure the scribe would know what, in the midst of all the cancelled writing, was in and what was out.

## Accelerating the Dramatic Pace

Apart from the significant changes relating to the pregnancy, the modifications in *Theater-Bibliothek: 728* mostly comprise minor interjections and corrections as well as several strike-throughs of the many redundancies and repetitions in Kotzebue's text. It was not until the beginning of Act IV and at the transition between Acts IV and V that hand 1D intervened in a major fashion once more: by first shortening Act IV and then shifting the first scene from Act V into Act IV.

Act IV, Scene 1, in which Rolla encounters a chorus of priests digging a grave for soon-to-be-sentenced Cora, has been cut altogether, with a huge ink cross over manuscript pages seventy-seven and seventy-eight. An unretracted four-line insertion in the margins, "für Priester" [for priests] (S1, 78), suggests an alternative version of the scene. As we will discuss below, the content of Act IV, Scene 1, in *Theater-Bibliothek: 1460* is in fact largely similar but appears in a structurally completely altered form. It includes a different use of music and an altered version of Rolla's interaction with the priests. However, except for an "NB" for "nota bene" at the beginning of the next scene, of which the first dialogue part has also been crossed out by means of a pencil square containing three horizontal strokes, and a retracted # symbol with no apparent point of reference, nothing indicates that any of the content of *Theater-Bibliothek: 728* has been added or changed.

A quick look at *Theater-Bibliothek: 1460* reveals that a loose sheet with alternative content (such as for Act I, Scene 6) was in all probability lost: another additional scene was indeed inserted at this point. Once more, it is the comic character of Diego who makes an additional major appearance. In Kotzebue's original template (and later print publication), Diego runs into the horrified Rolla in Act IV, Scene 2, says that he knows nothing about the turn of events, and refers him to Alonzo's friend Don Juan instead. In the respective scene in fair copy *Theater-Bibliothek: 1460*, however, Rolla's horror and sense of urgency is counteracted by Diego's funny inability to give a straight answer. Their back-and-forth now drags on for as long as the preceding gravedigging scene, providing some comic relief for those who have been overwhelmed by Rolla's horror.[36] As we will demonstrate below, this additional scene was retracted once more at some point, probably in an 1820s revision.

The last change that takes place in the transition from Acts IV to V is a matter of dramaturgical condensation and simplification. Kotzebue's template (as well as the 1791 print version) draws out the discussion of Alonzo and Cora's guilty verdict (that the gravedigging priests anticipate in Act IV, Scene 1) before and after their interrogation. Act IV, Scene 6, in which a group of priests are waiting for a consultation between the high priest and the Inca king to end, takes up two pages without adding much to the plot. Except for the information about the setting and

---

36 Cf. S2, 65v–67r.

characters, it has been cut altogether by means of a pencil square and two vertical pencil lines, followed by the addition of four lines on manuscript page ninety. There, the heading "Szene 7" [Scene 7] has also been crossed out (albeit horizontally) in ink. Thus, the former Act IV, Scene 7, has become the new Act IV, Scene 6: the high priest discusses the upcoming verdict with his second in command, who rudely rejects his superior's and the Inca king's implied wish for leniency.

In the *Theater-Bibliothek: 728* fair copy, the act had ended after the interrogation in Act IV, Scene 8, which has now been changed to "Scene 7". The priests of the sun withdraw inside the temple to discuss the sentencing. In *Theater-Bibliothek: 728*, the call to depart has been crossed out using the usual pencil square, as has the subsequent stage direction, "Der Vorhang fällt" [The curtain falls], the heading "Act V" (S1, 107) as well as the following short description of the interior setting. Thus, it is still the new version of Act IV, Scene 7, outside the temple. The high priest takes his second in command aside and implores him to let mercy prevail, before the priests reach their joint judgement. Some finer points of their lengthy discussion have been cast aside using the customary rectangular pencil shape on the following folios; the end of the scene thus concludes the fourth act with a small, but underlined "Vorhang fällt" (S1, 112) [curtain falls], which has been inserted in ink. The act of shortening and simultaneously bringing forward a scene that largely repeats the content and tone of the previous ones has accelerated the dramatic pace of the Hamburg stage version.

The beginning of the new Act V is also the beginning of the work of scribe 1C. "Szene 2" is still faithfully written at the top of the page and has been underlined twice. What was presumably hand 1D has scribbled over the Arabic "2" in pencil and put a Latin numeral "I" next to it on the right. "Act 5" (S1, 113) has also been written in pencil further to the left. An ink addition informs us that the setting is the one that had been crossed out at the beginning of the previous scene. Except for a few retractions made in pencil as well as square and vertical pencil lines, the work of scribe 1C remains undisturbed. As we have just outlined, this also applies to the content of *Theater-Bibliothek: 728* as a whole. The overall tweaks made to the content of the fair copy are minor – even though the material performance of the cut-and-paste work sometimes comes across as the most dramatic of interventions. The fair copy of the unknown template remains largely intact, except for the discussion of the pregnancy in Act I and Act II, the changed arrangement of Rolla's confrontation with the priests in Act IV, the transition between the last two acts, and a few minor changes and some retractions to Kotzebue's many repetitions and redundancies.

Conspicuously, the main changes just outlined were not carried out in a manner that would have rendered the written artefact suitable for use as a prompt book – it just would not have been practical for a prompter doing their work from the prompt box to flip back and forth within the written artefact, to assess the changes, and at the same time help out the actors in the event of an emergency on stage. Therefore, the new version of *Die Sonnen-Jungfrau* that developed in *Theater-Bibliothek: 728* was copied again in order to produce the prompt book that would be employed from the prompter's box during the performance: *Theater-Bibliothek: 1460*.

## V. Going It Alone: Fair Copy *Theater-Bibliothek: 1460*, Assisted Reading, Technical Instructions

*Theater-Bibliothek: 1460* has "Soufleur Buch" [prompter book] written on its cover in Schröder's tidy hand. It has been neatly bound from twelve quires of irregular size. Three of them consist of three bifolios, three of four, two of five, two of six, and one, as we will discuss below, of only two. The last quire originally consisted of three bifolios with the last folio having been cut – presumably since it would have otherwise remained empty. Half a centimetre protrudes, meaning that the quire as a whole remains stable. Some writing on the front endpaper is illegible and does not seem to have been involved in the production process or the use of the prompt book in a narrow sense. A note on the last verso seems to be a reminder that one of the actors has also to help out with one of the scene changes in Act IV.[37]

The main content of *Theater-Bibliothek: 1460* comprises several different forms of writing: 1) the text of *Die Sonnen-Jungfrau* as updated in *Theater-Bibliothek: 728* has been copied in black ink by two different scribes, 2A and 2B; 2) some secondary texts (such as stage directions) have been highlighted in a different brown (or faded) ink, helping to orient the prompter within the text; 3) a very small number of technical instructions of the kind the prompter usually carried out from the box have been written down in graphite pencil, probably by different hands and during different revision periods; 4) there are extensive enrichments that have sometimes been written on extra writing supports and then pasted over other passages using glue or tucked in using a needle. These enrichments have been made in black ink, brown (or faded) ink, graphite pencil, and red crayon. The ink enrichments were made by three or four different hands: 2C (again Schröder and thus identical with 1D), 2D, plus the hand of the French censor giving his approval at the end, and possibly another additional hand. The pencil enrichments have been made by different hands but can sometimes be seen working in concert with hands 2C and 2D (just like the pencil additions do in *Theater-Bibliothek: 728*). Below we will argue that the highlighting in brown ink seems to have also been part of the revision stage that 2C was responsible for.

Altogether, the enrichments suggest that *Theater-Bibliothek: 1460* was in use for as long as *Die Sonnen-Jungfrau* was being performed in Hamburg, i.e., until the mid-1820s. Hand 2D can be attributed to a prompter who had been active in Ham-

---

37  Cf. S2, 98v.

burg since 1821, as we will show below. It is, in fact, certain that the prompt book was being used in the 1810s: the French censor signed off on the text on August 22, 1813, on the day of the first of two performances of *Die Sonnen-Jungfrau* during the French censorship period (1811–1814).[38] Since scribes 1A and 2A were the same person, *Theater-Bibliothek: 1460* was probably created soon after the underlying written artefact, but definitely before Kotzebue published his play in print in 1791. After publication, there would have been no need to divide the text between two scribes anymore. Due to the theatre's considerable output, the creation of prompt books obeyed economic criteria. It thus seems safe to assume that *Theater-Bibliothek: 1460* was already in use on the opening night of the Hamburg production in 1790; at least some of the technical instructions may have been included as part of the original process as they had already been necessary for the first performance.

First of all, the work of the two scribes 2A and 2B warrants examination. The two main scribes of *Theater-Bibliothek: 1460* created a largely faithful reproduction of the final version of the enriched and updated *Theater-Bibliothek: 728*. Scribe 2A accurately copied the word "Auftritt" that they had used in *Theater-Bibliothek: 728* for each "scene", but then adopted it (probably in the name of standardisation) for the parts of Acts III and IV that they had also copied for *Theater-Bibliothek: 1460*. In contrast, scribe 2B followed the divergent template (from scribes 1B and 1C) and changed the wording to "Szene" again.

As far as the plot and the action are concerned, Act I, Scene 6, has now indeed been replaced by Diego's new monologue and the extemporisations that had been added to *Theater-Bibliothek: 728* on a loose sheet. The replaced lines have been taken up in Act II, Scene 2, as prescribed by Schröder's intervention in *Theater-Bibliothek: 728*. In the same vein, the original ending of Act IV and the beginning of Act V have now neatly been folded into one; the numbering of the scenes (and acts) has accordingly been adjusted from the start. As indicated above, Rolla's confrontation with the gravedigging priests in Act IV, Scene 1, which was retracted in *Theater-Bibliothek: 728*, has now been replaced with an alternative altercation.

Similarly, Rolla's retracted exchange with Diego in Act IV, Scene 2, has been swapped for a dialogue providing comic relief. While a loose sheet in *Theater-Bibliothek: 728* might have gone missing, the new lines are brief enough to fit onto one piece of paper, and the song at the beginning of Act IV is no longer part of the prompt book. The mention of "Musick" in the graphite pencil used for technical details could mean that it or some other music was being played during the transition between acts (although no songs of this kind have survived as part of the musical material for *Die Sonnen-Jungfrau*). It is also possible that, in Act IV, Scene 1, Schröder considered the song written out in *Theater-Bibliothek: 728* to be too gruesome for the stage, as it describes in some detail the priests digging a grave in

---

38  For a more detailed discussion of this time, cf. Chapter 5, sections 5 and 7.

which to bury Cora alive for breaking her vows. In the *Theater-Bibliothek: 728* fair copy (as well as in the 1791 print version), the horrified Rolla learns about this when priests respond to his interjections with their song.[39] In contrast, the updated version seems short and painless. In *Theater-Bibliothek: 1460*, the scene opens with the four priests digging; the first utterance from their lips is "Es ist vollendet" [It is finished]. Rolla's question as to their purpose, which is by now a few words shorter than it had been in the *Theater-Bibliothek: 728* fair copy (and the 1791 print version), receives a brutal reply: "das Grab der Tempelentweiherin" [the tomb of the temple deconsecrator] (S2, 65r). In the *Theater-Bibliothek: 1460* fair copy, the confrontation draws to a close quickly with a shortened variation on the dialogue in front of the temple. (However, this part of the folio was enriched at a later stage while the prompt book was in use.)

The partitioning of the text between the two scribes 2A and 2B seems to have taken place randomly in the subsequent scene. The aforementioned identification of the high priest and Rolla as father and son in Act IV, Scene 3, was interrupted in full swing, i.e., after scribe 2A had already copied out two-thirds of *Theater-Bibliothek: 728* (including their own work as 1A and some, but not all, of scribe 1B's work). Scribe 2A stops working randomly at the end of the ninth of the twelve quires that make up *Theater-Bibliothek: 1460*. At this point in the play, Rolla has just started working himself into a frenzy. The high priest of the sun shares in his misery by exclaiming, "Um aller Götter willen! – Rolla –!" (S2, 68r) [For the sake of all gods! – Rolla –!]. In the subsequent lengthy exchange, he will reveal that he is Rolla's father. But at this point, scribe 2A's work stops abruptly. The scribe leaves the rest of 68r and the whole of 68v empty.[40]

The ninth quire consisted of only two bifolios to begin with. Either scribe 2A ran out of paper or, as we will argue below, they knew beforehand where they would be stopping and were aware that they definitely would not need any more. Scribe 2B then started on a new folio, 69r, and a fresh quire, and continued the dialogue (including the mix-up between the high priest and the high priestess as discussed above) (cf. figure 37).

---

39   Cf. S1, 78; cf. Kotzebue 1791, 135.
40   For reasons that we will discuss below, a third hand first crossed out the dialogue on 68r but then added a longer version from a print copy to the rest of 68r and the top of 69v.

*Figure 37: S2, 68v and 69r.*

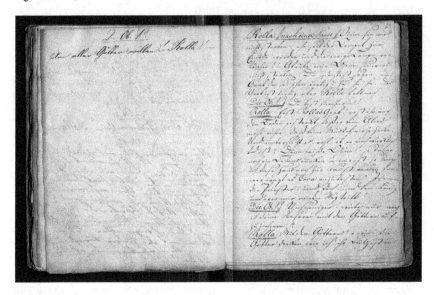

At second glance, the allocation of content to the two scribes with the abrupt interruption was not carried out on the basis on Kotzebue's play at all, but clearly had to do with the technical arrangement of *Theater-Bibliothek: 728*. As described above, the first seven untidy quires of *Theater-Bibliothek: 728* (six by scribe 1A and the first created by scribe 1B) are followed by two neatly folded ones (the second copied by scribe 1B and scribe 1C's only quire). The scribes in *Theater-Bibliothek: 1460* switched between the untidy and the tidy quires! One bundle, up to quire seven of *Theater-Bibliothek: 728*, went to scribe 2A and one bundle, from quire eight onwards, went to scribe 2B. The differences in the organisation of the quires seem to have caused an arbitrary division of the text, which is nevertheless clearly visible at a material level – hence the rough transition between scribes in the middle of a scene.

Act IV, Scene 3, is thus interrupted right after "D.Ob.Pr" exclaims, "Um aller Götter willen! – Rolla! –" (S1, 80)! It is likely that, after reworking the content of *Theater-Bibliothek: 728*, but before it was bound, scribes 2A and 2B of *Theater-Bibliothek: 1460* received their respective portions to copy: the untidy one went to scribe 2A, the tidy one to scribe 2B. The two written artefacts were then probably stitched together and bound at a similar time: *Theater-Bibliothek: 1460* for use by the prompter, *Theater-Bibliothek: 728* perhaps for an undesignated purpose at first (e.g., as a backup for the principal or initially planned as the inspector's version).

In contrast to *Theater-Bibliothek: 728*, the scribes of *Theater-Bibliothek: 1460* seem to have had specific instructions regarding the visual organisation of their folios. Both scribes wrote in a tidy fashion, with letters of similar heights and similarly generous spacing between the lines. Both placed the characters' speech next to a slight margin of a similar size on the left of each folio. For scribe 2A, the margin seems to have been for the sake of clarity rather than for possible corrections. Thus, scribe 2A's work differed slightly from their own work as scribe 1A in *Theater-Bibliothek: 728*, where the spacing was more crowded. However, scribe 2A stuck to their established pattern of placing the twice underlined name of the speaking character in the middle of the line above the respective portion of the dialogue.

Scribe 2B seems to have worked more in line with the possibilities afforded by the small margin – and the visual organisation of a dramatic text in print: the name of the character speaking has been underlined once and placed in the left margin. Thus, the spacing between the speech of two characters has become smaller. Perhaps this is why, at some point during a later revision stage, someone went through scribe 2B's part and underlined the speaking characters' names once more using a thicker quill and brown ink. In contrast, the twofold underlining in scribe 2A's part clearly belongs to their original work. Both scribes had put the speaking characters' names in Latin instead of German cursive to create a contrast. But due to the additional underlining, both arrangements allowed the prompter to see more clearly where and when a new cue might be needed as far as the actors' lines were concerned.

*Figure 38: S2, 91v and 92r.*

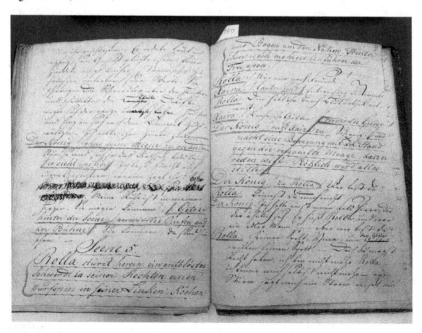

Throughout the written artefact, this form of reading assistance provided to the prompter has been adapted to most other secondary texts as well. This can be observed for most of *Theater-Bibliothek: 1460*, although scribe 2B had already written the stage directions and other didascalia in Latin cursive (which scribe 2A had not). The brown ink underlines some secondary texts, such as shorter stage directions, while accentuating the ending, quite often the beginning, and sometimes even internal punctuation with vertical lines (cf. figure 38).

*Figure 39: S2, 28r.*

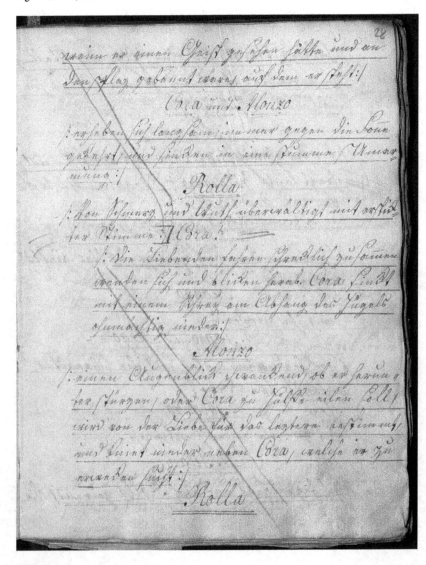

## Chapter 4. Creating a Prompt Book, Two at a Time 119

In other instances, where stage directions have been placed within a longer portion of one character's text (such as a characterisation of their changed state of mind), the brown ink has not been used to underline them, but to cross them out instead, horizontally for shorter injections, transversally when they span multiple lines. This was in no way a retraction of content; rather, it simply signalled to the prompter that the passage was of no or little concern to them in their work. In one particularly striking case, nearly two pages of silent interaction have been crossed out in brown ink. Rolla steps out of his cave, happening upon the Spaniards, with Cora sleeping in their midst. Rolla, who believes she has been kidnapped, and his counterparts, who fear that their cover has been blown, draw swords and launch into a heated exchange of threats. Except for one exclamation ("Cora!"), the whole passage has been crossed out with slashes in the brown ink, which at this point was also being supported by a graphite pencil.[41] (Cf. figure 39.)

In other cases, curly brackets on the side drew attention to longer passages of stage directions. Sometimes, they did so without considering the beginning or ending of a scene, which quite often consisted of stage directions but was not always of interest to the prompter. At one point the word "Verwandlung" (S2, 55r) [transformation] has been written next to a curly bracket at the beginning of a scene. This indicated that, in this case, Kotzebue's secondary text not only contained some of his usual verbose descriptions of the characters' intense feelings, but that the prompter also needed to be aware of an actual change of stage set. (Cf. figure 40.)

The initial scribes had faithfully copied Kotzebue's lengthy stage directions, such as descriptions of the stage setting and portrayals of the characters' changing tones and moods, first into *Theater-Bibliothek: 728* and then into *Theater-Bibliothek: 1460*. Going through them one by one and cutting the descriptions no prompter would ever take a second look at would have cost them additional effort. (However, it was always good to have the full version of a play in the safe hands of the prompter, who was, after all, also the librarian at that time.) In practice, an excessive number of secondary texts interrupted the prompter's focus during the performance. In a situation where they always needed to be two steps ahead, they would no longer lose precious seconds while figuring out which were and were not the lines the actors needed to utter on stage. This was especially true when, after years or perhaps even decades, the play was performed again. By that point, a new prompter might have taken over, and they would have had to familiarise themselves with the prompt book and perhaps rework it in a manner conducive to their own work habits.[42]

---

41  Cf. S2, 27v–28v.
42  In this vein, we will argue below that the brown ink belongs to a revision of *Theater-Bibliothek: 1460*, which was carried out more than two decades after the initial creation of the two prompt books.

*Figure 40: S2, 55r.*

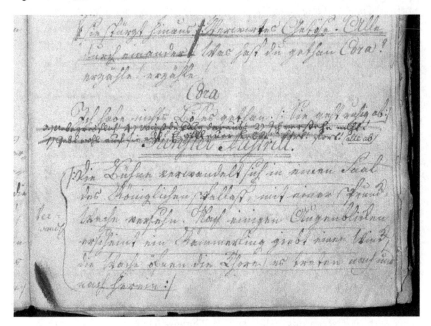

In any case, each prompter needed to be aware of possible internal contradictions in their writing system. Here, the same operation, i.e., highlighting in different inks, was intended to both draw attention (to the speaking characters' names) and divert attention (from the secondary text) at the same time. But since the characters names were set apart visually, which the secondary text was not, this might not have mattered too much in practice. It was probably less disruptive to the prompter's concentration than performing yet another writing operation to distinguish between the names of the speaking characters and stage directions.

*Theater-Bibliothek: 1460* has also had some technical information added to it in pencil. Interestingly, it contains some peculiar lighting instructions, which are a common occurrence in prompt books. From their box, the prompter had access to candles or tallow lights at the front edge of the stage. The instructions generally refer to changes that fell within the prompter's purview. This also applies to a few notes in Acts I and II, which have been added in pencil in a different hand to that of all the scribes of the main text. The additional information pertained to the part of the set-up that was supposed to be illuminated, to the lighting mood, and, due to its position on the folio, to when the lighting was supposed to start.

Where night sets in at the end of Act I, Scene 5, shortly before Don Juan leaves to meet Cora, a small horizontal box has been added rather untidily one-quarter of the way into the folio space. It makes use of the area that has opened up between the end of one of Diego's speeches, which does not take up the whole line, and the name "D. Juan", which indicates the next speaker in the middle of the next line. "1 Seite Nacht" (S2, 17v) [1 side night] has been written into the box. At the top of the next folio, Diego's fear-filled monologue, which now fills Scene 6, has already started. In the space left open by the end of a paragraph, the same hand has added "2 Seite Nacht" (S2, 18r) [2 side night] in a similar box. It appears that the prompter was responsible for creating the effect of nightfall on the stage: first on one side, then on the other. Accordingly, a few folios later, the heading "Nacht" (S2, 22r) [night] has been added in a box next to the header of the second act in order to underline that the lighting would not change when the curtain fell and rose again. In Act II, Scene 2, during the conversation between Don Juan and the sun virgin, the sunrise was then represented by gradually reilluminating the stage. On 27r, the respective cues can be found that materially correspond to the process they indicate: first, top right, and then, a little later, further down on the left, "1 Seite Tag" [1 side day] and "2 Seite Tag" [2 side day] has been crammed into the blank space within the space of half a folio: the sun has come full circle. Apparently, the prompter dimmed or extinguished and then relit the lights within their reach in order to give the impression of dusk and dawn. The additions have the character of a personal reminder. There is no hint of whether stage left or stage right was the first side of the stage to be lit. The prompter just knew, perhaps from other productions. The hand adding the notes (which most likely was the prompter's) simply noted down a short reminder for themselves in order to use as little space as possible (cf. figure 41).

At least one pencil is active throughout *Theater-Bibliothek: 1460*, but the pencil insertions and strike-throughs were probably made during distinct revision stages and have thus been made by different hands. While, as mentioned above, the appearance of a chorus at the beginning of Act IV in the print publication and in *Theater-Bibliothek: 728* has largely been cut in fair copy *Theater-Bibliothek: 1460*, the word "Chor" [chorus] has been added in Latin cursive in graphite pencil, as has the word "Music", once with only one "c", once further down as "Musick" (S2, 65r). One of the two deployments of music seems to have been added at a later stage because some of the pencil enrichments are clearly thicker than others. Different hands, although barely legible, seem to have been at work here as well. Only a few of the other enrichments provide further technical information, e.g., about the earlier onset of Act II before a retraction. The lowering of the curtain has been marked with the addition of "actus" (S2, 44r) right before the crossed-out passage starts. If it were not for that note, the prompter would have either missed their cue to signal the lowering of the curtain to a stagehand or would have had to turn the page to realise that no mistake was being made and that the curtain was indeed supposed to come down at this point.

*Figure 41: S2, 27r.*

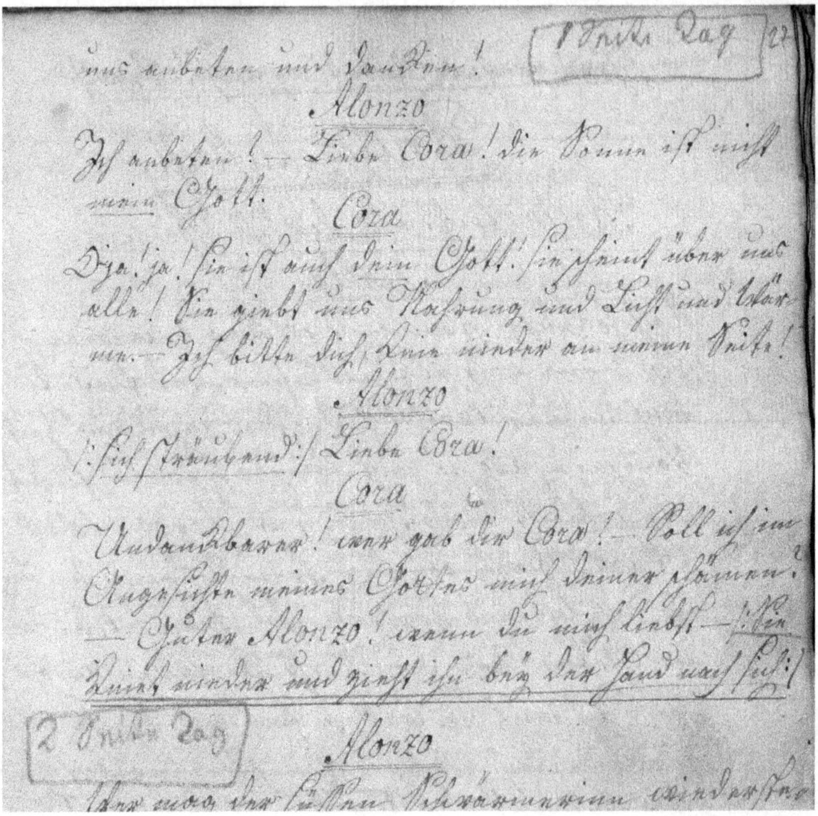

So far, we have covered several types of writing in *Theater-Bibliothek: 1460*: the fair copy with text copied from *Theater-Bibliothek: 728*, the highlighting of character names and secondary text in a thicker quill and another ink, and the technical instructions given in graphite pencil (especially with respect to the lighting of dusk and dawn). The following considerations will examine textual additions and retractions, reconstructing when they were made. We will also examine another kind of paper practice in *Theater-Bibliothek: 1460*, namely the adding of content by appending extra sheets.

## VI. Reworking the Play, Reshaping *Theater-Bibliothek: 1460* I: Political Pressure in 1813

Besides the two scribes, there were at least three, probably four hands enriching *Theater-Bibliothek: 1460* with textual additions in black ink: two (hands 2C and 2D) are especially prominent. The only text insertion that can be clearly attributed to the French censor is the comment, "Vu et approuvé", accompanied by his signature, dated, "Hambourg, 22 août 1813" (S1, 98r). There is one longer enrichment, which seems to have been written rather hastily and was not necessarily made by the censor, 2C, or 2D – although none can be ruled out. Of the two more prominent ones, one (2C) is clearly Schröder's own neat handwriting, the other (2D) that of one Christian Friedrich Zimmermann, who was a prompter in the 1820s (perhaps starting after Barlow's death). Oddly enough, both 2C and 2D have added lines from the versions of Kotzebue's play that were published in print in 1791, 1797, and 1810. For reasons that we will discuss further on, Kotzebue's redundancies and repetitions that had been cut for the Hamburg debut of the play made their way back into the Hamburg adaptation over time. As we will show below, this probably first occurred nearly a quarter of a century later, and then after yet another decade. Most often, it concerned text that had been part of *Theater-Bibliothek: 728* but was then retracted. In most instances, text has been added from the slightly different print version that had never been part of *Theater-Bibliothek: 728* to begin with.

The brown ink used to highlight the secondary text has sometimes also been used to cross out text or draw attention to other sections. This could very well have been performed by one and the same hand and might have occurred during the revision stages associated with scribes 2C and 2D. The same goes for a red crayon that performed various tasks. As mentioned, graphite pencil enrichments run throughout the written artefact and have clearly been made by more than one hand. While it is impossible to identify how many hands there were, we can often attribute their work to a particular revision stage. It is also impossible to come to a definitive conclusion as to whether the same hand may have used black, red, or graphite grey to organise their own working process or might have been trying to visually organise the written artefact in a manner more suitable for the actual work carried out from the prompt box. However, many enrichments can be attributed to specific revision stages with high probability.

The most striking additions are extra pieces of paper. Altogether, seven formerly loose sheets have been integrated into *Theater-Bibliothek: 1460*: five as paste-ins, two attached by needle. Two have been written in Schröder's hand (2C) on a white sheet of paper (S2, 48r, 70r); four on scrappily cut, (now) greenish paper, likely in hand 2D, which was also active during the transition between the work of scribe 2A and that of scribe 2B (S2, 31r, 65v, 79r, 92v); and one possibly by an extra hand (S2, 73v). Additions such as these were either made when the intervention into the initial text was so far-reaching that it could not have been achieved by means of writing alone or when previous interventions were so complex that the prompter could no longer immediately recognize which text was valid.

It was only possible to cut two of the paste-ins in *Theater-Bibliothek: 1460* to the size of the passage they were to replace (S2, 31r, 65v). One that contained an insertion for which there was no room on the recto (S2, 70r) had a margin glued to it, meaning that the additional sheet could be folded outwards over 69v once the prompter had reached that point in the play. An insertion mark on folio 70r then led them to the extra sheet and from there straight back to 70r. Two paste-ins with additional text from the print version take up more space than the text they replace. Since the initial passage was situated towards the bottom of the folio, in both cases only an upper margin has been glued on from the loose sheet; the rest could be folded back into the written artefact whenever it was not in use and folded out again whenever it was.[43] Two loose sheets have been pinned in with a needle. The needle used for the one in the unidentifiable hand has been lost, but its puncture marks are still visible. Since the insert is nearly half the same size as the whole verso, it has been folded twice, and had to be folded in and out as the prompter followed the action.[44] The other pinned-in insert[45] extends over both the bottom of the folio and its right edge onto the next recto. It seems it was tidily folded in from both sides whenever it was not in use (cf. figures 42 and 43).

*Figure 42: S2, 70r and inlay.*

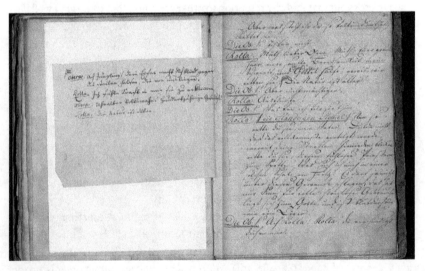

---

43  Cf. S2, 48r, 79r.
44  Cf. S2, 73v.
45  Cf. S2, 92v.

*Figure 43: S2, 92v.*

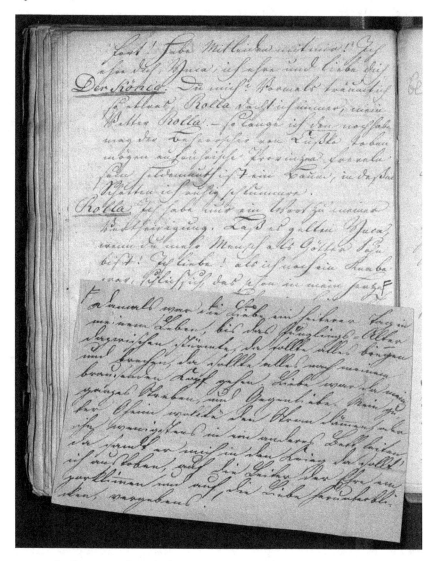

Prompt books were reshaped when circumstances changed. A new prompter might have gone through the book and made it their own by clarifying the visual arrangements and cues; the dramatic text might have needed to be adapted due to outside pressure from the audience or the authorities. As we will discuss in the next chapter, a significant amount of pressure was required to have an effect. During the pragmatic work of everyday operations, a prompt book would only be reworked if really necessary.

The initially confusing multitude of hands and writing tools responsible for the enrichments can, upon closer inspection, be attributed to two coherent stages of revision. Schröder, whose handwriting is all over these updates, had returned to the Stadt-Theater in 1811 and left on March 31 in 1812, among other things after a conflict with the French authorities concerning several successful performances of August von Kotzebue's musical play *Das Dorf im Gebirge* [*The Village in the Mountains*].[46] While still in charge, or perhaps later from behind the scenes, Schröder seems to have reworked *Theater-Bibliothek: 1460*, another work by Kotzebue, for the French censor. The other revision stage has the handwriting of C. J. Zimmermann at its centre; the enrichments thus seem to have been made for the performances that began in 1823, shortly after Zimmermann took up his post. Of course, revisions and updates might have been made at any other point in time, too. However, due to the inner coherence and coordination of the 1813 and 1823 enrichments, this seems doubtful.

As stated above, *Die Sonnen-Jungfrau* playbills from Hamburg Stadt-Theater have survived for ten performances that were staged between 1790 and 1793, during which it seems unlikely that there was any urgent need for changes. Eight performances took place in the early 1800s, for which Schröder was not at the helm and had no business scribbling in the prompt books, which he still technically owned but had leased to the theatre. At that time, there might not have been much pressure to make changes. Then, there are leaflets with playbills for six performances put on during the French occupation period, although the censor only signed off on the two 1813 performances. On the one hand, Kotzebue's play was based on a popular French novel and was as such unlikely to have been suspected of being overtly anti-French. On the other hand, the elements of revolt and political upheaval in *Die Sonnen-Jungfrau* might have caused the theatre company to tread lightly, especially for as long as an official censor was in office. Just a few months after the French left town, the play was put on once more in 1814 and then again in 1815 and 1816 respectively. There are additional playbills for four performances that took place between 1823 and 1826. We might speculate that any concessions to the censor had been long withdrawn by that point. However, the play might by now have seemed historically so far removed that the company felt inclined to review the text's suitability anyway. But these are all speculations. All we can do is take a closer look at *Theater-Bibliothek: 1460*, try to declutter the various layers, and examine the ways in which they do or do not interact with each other. If we assume there were outside pressures such as demands from the censor, we can also watch out for possible clues about related interventions into the content.

We will be paying special attention to the French censor in the next chapter. In general, the Stadt-Theater company did not rewrite plays for him, nor does he seem to have intervened directly into the written artefacts on a large scale except

---

46 Cf. Meyer 1819b, 317–322.

by way of his signature. Possible revisions seem to have been done in-house. It was mostly unproblematic plays or those in which minor cuts and tweaks would ensure a positive judgement that reached his desk. In the years that Hamburg spent under French rule but was not an official part of the empire, procedures had been less formal. But the company had to be careful not to run afoul of the authorities and might have changed texts proactively (like it did with the original Hamburg authorities in 1790 regarding Cora's pregnancy). At first glance, very few of the enrichments in *Theater-Bibliothek: 1460* seem to have been censorship-related. The revolt incited by Rolla against the death sentences might not have been considered particularly threatening, as Kotzebue allowed it to fizzle out in the face of the Inca king's moral authority. Only the king's line "wer seinem Volke Gutes that, der darf sein Volk nicht scheuen" (S2, 91v) [he who did good to his people must not be afraid of his people] might have been seen as inviting the audience to apply the same maxim to the occupying forces. Consequently, the respective one and a half lines have been rendered illegible by dense black ink scribbles.

It is only at second glance that it becomes apparent that many small details hinting at political struggles of any kind have been retracted, generally by means of strike-throughs or rectangular frames, sometimes in black ink, sometimes in the faded brown ink, sometimes in graphite pencil. The brown ink in a strikingly similar hand was also responsible for highlighting the secondary texts discussed above. The highlighting seems to have been a new kind of mark-up carried out by the prompter to get a grip on the text they needed to be able to prompt – or that of somebody else who feared the prompter might get side-tracked by the extensive secondary texts. However, a similar hand working in brown ink was also active in preparing *Theater-Bibliothek: 1460* for the censor. At the very beginning, the ink was used to make several slanted lines retracting the complicated, nearly two-page-long, sometimes violent political backstory which the characters relate to each other – and thus to the audience. First and foremost, the retracted passage raves about Alonzo, the ideal humanitarian and teacher of the "savages" – such praise for the Spanish enemy may have been deemed out of place in 1813.

Several dynamic instances of "bl" for "bleibt" (S2, 11v–12r) [remains] have been scrawled in black ink in the margins. As we will demonstrate below, these lines were made by a hand from a later revision stage, i.e., the stage when many of the censorship changes were being reversed. While the hand working in brown ink was in charge, however, the dramatic conflict was depoliticised at the very beginning of the play. The plot was now solely based on the clash between love and religion. The tool that, at some point, provided reading assistance to the prompter in the work of scribe 2B also seems to have been working in concert with hand 2C to prepare the play for the censor. It might have been the same hand, but there is also a chance it was a different one. The same goes for the enrichments made in graphite pencil that support this revision stage. (Cf. figure 44.)

*Figure 44: S2, 11v and 12r.*

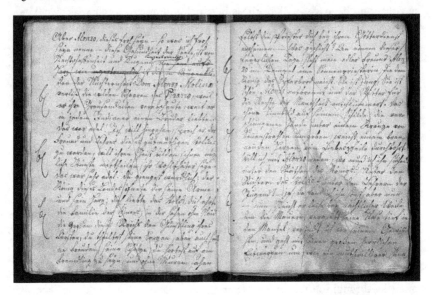

In a similar revision, the early end to Act II (as described above) retracts a speculation made by Don Juan about the possibility of Rolla overthrowing the king.[47] The different timing of the curtain fall, which the pencil reminds the prompter of, might simply have been the technical outcome of a change to the play that was deemed politically necessary. In contrast, the messenger's report of Rolla's sedition at the stirring end of Act V has remained surprisingly intact. It was only when the description became vividly specific that a couple of lines were crossed out in thick graphite pencil: "Trommeln und Hörner tönen. Waffen klirren, ein Wald von Lanzen zieht herauf, alles läuft und schreit durcheinander" (S2, 91r) [Drums and horns sound. Weapons clang, a forest of lances advances, everything runs and shouts in confusion].

Further down on the same folio, it is Schröder's own hand, 2C, that has provided some alternative lines in black ink. Both prompt books and the print publication have the king defending his former general with an assured, "Rolla und Aufruhr. Nein, du irrst" [Rolla and sedition. No, you're wrong]. The black ink has been used to cross out this writing, except for the name, by means of a horizontal line and to add a tiny but clearly legible alternative that is nowhere to be found in either of the two prompt books or the print version: "Rolla weiß das Aufruhr Verbrechen ist und Rolla wird kein Verbrecher seyn" (S2, 91r) [Rolla knows that sedition is a crime and Rolla will not be a criminal]. While the text in the print edition and both handwritten artefacts present the hero rebelling against authority, Schröder's addition

---

47 Cf. S2, 44r.

has the king (who, throughout the play, has also been introduced as an authority figure) stressing what ought to be held of such rebellion – and what will await the perpetrator. Any potential audience would now view Rolla's actions in a far less benevolent light – as would the censor as an audience of one.

In the 1790s, Schröder would have had no reason to make this kind of addition. In the 1800s (including the beginning of the occupation), he was not around. It was only once French control began to tighten in 1811 that he came out of retirement to support the theatre with his international standing.[48] It can therefore be assumed that Schröder's change was aimed at the censor with a possible upcoming performance in mind – and that it was Schröder personally who undertook and directed the reshaping of *Theater-Bibliothek: 1460* (although quite a while before the actual performance). Indeed, his handwriting as 2C not only worked in tandem with the graphite pencil retractions at the end; sometimes the writing in pencil, however hard it is to read, seems to be in Schröder's hand as well.[49] More strikingly, Schröder's hand, using black ink (2C), also worked together with the hand retracting the political backstory at the beginning in brown ink. On 11v, it shifted one word ("unzertrennlich" [inseparable]) to the place immediately before the strike-through begins; Schröder's hand then crossed it out in black ink right before the brown ink was used to retract several folios. All Schröder did here was align the wording of *Theater-Bibliothek: 1460* (which, again, faithfully followed *Theater-Bibliothek: 728*) with that of the wording in the available print editions. Therefore, Schröder likely corrected "unzertrennlich" and nothing more because he had the strike-through of the next passage in mind – or perhaps because he was the one behind the brown ink himself.

Nearly all of Schröder's textual changes as 2C, which are mostly miniscule and hardly ever more than a few sentences long, are identical with the print editions, whether ostensibly for the censor or not. While hand 2C did not systematically check for discrepancies, it seems to have corrected some of the ones it came across. One of these unrelated changes is particularly interesting because the retracted text has been crossed out in the dense black ink scribbling that was clearly done to please the censor. They can thus be safely attributed to Schröder himself. In the scene where the high priest confesses his fatal love for Rolla's mother, saying, "Da gingen wir beyde von Kummer und Liebe gefoltert [...] umher" [There, we both walked around tortured by sorrow and love [...]], the "gingen" copied from *Theater-Bibliothek: 728* has become the arguably more emphatic and effective "schlichen" [crept] (S2, 71v[50]) in the print edition.

---

48   Cf. Meyer 1819b, 111; cf. Wollrabe 1847, 132.
49   Cf. S2, 70r.
50   Cf. Kotzebue 1791, 145.

On other occasions, Schröder might have planned to adapt the play to contemporary tastes. His hand revised his own 1790 revision of Kotzebue's template in *Theater-Bibliothek: 728*. With a straight, vertical black ink line, it cut the comic exchange between the distressed Rolla and the hapless Diego that had been added in Act IV, Scene 2, and instead inserted the much shorter print text at the beginning and ending.[51] Since the 1770s, Schröder had been known not only for his temperate, restrained dramaturgical approach but also as a principal with a feel for the disposition of his audience.[52] While, in 1790, he seems to have seen a need to balance Rolla's agony about Cora's future suffering with Diego's comic inaptitude, in the 1810s, cultural tastes had changed. Rolla's exaggerated agony could now easily be brought in line with the sombre, macabre atmosphere of Dark Romanticism. In fact, the play was advertised as a "romantisches Schauspiel" [romantic play] in 1813 instead of a mere "Schauspiel" as it had been before.[53] This billing was probably also due to the censorship context. It placed emphasis on the star-crossed lovers instead of on the political dimension of the plot. The eerily beautiful horror that Rolla feels about Cora's penalty fitted in nicely with the mitigation of the political. Similarly, on neither occasion in 1813 did the evening end with the swift, happy resolution of the play, i.e., the Inca king's pardon. In addition to the subsequent musical finale, one-act, comic pantomime ballets were performed (*Der glückliche Morgen* [*The Happy Morning*] on 22 August, *Der Schornsteinfeger* [*The Chimney Sweeper*] on 9 September).[54] Framing the politically problematic play as "romantic" and easy-going – not only for the censor but also for the general public – seems to have been a successful strategy for getting *Die Sonnen-Jungfrau* staged. After French occupation, however, the playbills swiftly dropped any mention of it being "romantic", and the amusing epilogue was cut.[55] (Cf. figure 45.)

In most cases, Schröder's hand intervened when the passage at stake was potentially interesting from a censorship point of view. Nevertheless, at some points, deviations from the print attracted his attention in passing as he worked on the censorship revisions. Before the graphite pencil retracted the potentially provocative lines at the end of Act II, Schröder's hand intervened in a completely unrelated matter. In the print edition, Rolla offers to go drinking with Alonzo ("zechen"[56]).

---

51 Cf. S2, 65v–67r.
52 Cf. Hoffmann 1939, 237–246.
53 Cf. the 1813 playbills for August 22 and September 9 on Jahn/Mühle/Eisenhardt/Malchow/M. Schneider (https://www.stadttheater.uni-hamburg.de).
54 Cf. the 1813 playbills for August 22 and September 9 on Jahn/Mühle/Eisenhardt/Malchow/M. Schneider (https://www.stadttheater.uni-hamburg.de).
55 Cf. the playbill for September 19, 1814, on Jahn/Mühle/Eisenhardt/Malchow/M. Schneider (https://www.stadttheater.uni-hamburg.de).
56 Cf. Kotzebue 1791, 100.

As in the *Theater-Bibliothek: 728* correction version, *Theater-Bibliothek: 1460* only had them taking a walk ("gehen" (S2 44r)) and was later realigned with the print version.

*Figure 45: playbill 22 August 1813.*

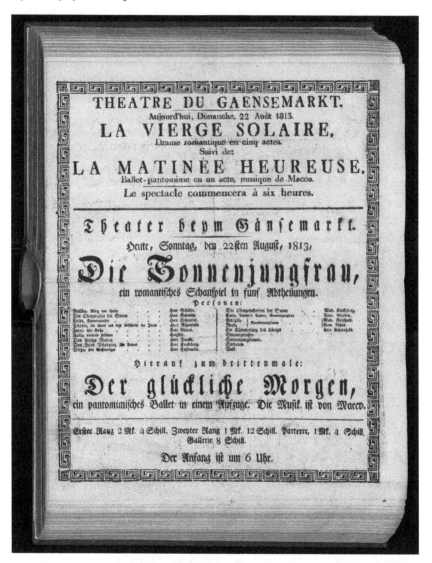

It is thus safe to say that Schröder had a print copy in hand as he was working his way through the 1790 prompt book in 1811 or 1812. Some inserted parts are thus also identical with the original *Theater-Bibliothek: 728* fair copy (such as Act IV, Scene 2), but were cut when it was revised for *Theater-Bibliothek: 1460*. Since the text of *Theater-Bibliothek: 728*, and presumably that of its original template, sometimes differed from the print publication, it is obvious that Schröder did not make use of the earlier version preserved in his collection.

Schröder's hand only deviated from the print edition and from *Theater-Bibliothek: 728* on a very small number of other occasions aside – and frequently only marginally. The play was de-Catholicised at a time when Spain was an enemy of France: the excommunicated Napoleon had the Pope in chains, and references to Rome might have seen as antagonistic towards the (Catholic) occupiers of Protestant Hamburg. A Spanish character's exclamation of "Gott sey Dank!" (S1, 30[57]) [Thank God!], has been changed by Schröder's hand into "Himmel sey Dank!" (S2, 13r) [Thank heaven!]. It has also replaced "Bei allen Heiligen!" (S1, 80[58]) [By the saints!] with "Beym Himmel!" (S2, 37r) [Heavens!]. In a similar manner, implorations such as "beym heiligen Ritter Georg" (S1, 36[59]) [by George, the holy knight] have been reduced to "beim Ritter Georg" (S2, 15v) – written in a black ink like the one Schröder used for his other revisions. While Kotzebue presented members of the Inca as monotheistic (and thus as thinly veiled representatives of his own times), a hand that might have been that of Schröder changed the singular "Gott" [God] into "Götter" (S2, 70r) [gods] in graphite pencil. Where Don Juan worries about Cora's "Aussichten auf Seligkeit" [prospects of redemption], which could be read in a religious sense, Schröder's hand has crossed out "Seligkeit" and added the similar sounding but semantically distinct "eine seelige Zukunft" [a blessed future] (S2, 14r).[60]

As we have pointed out, Schröder corrected some of the obscurities that had made it from *Theater-Bibliothek: 728* into *Theater-Bibliothek: 1460* – that is, wherever they occurred in proximity to a passage that needed to be revised for the censor. It was his hand that clarified who was speaking with or about whom where the two additional sun virgins show up and *Theater-Bibliothek: 728* becomes a bit untidy.[61]

---

57  Cf. Kotzebue 1791, 40.

58  Cf. Kotzebue 1791, 89.

59  Cf. Kotzebue 1791, 44.

60  Schröder's hand also deviated from both the print edition and *Theater-Bibliothek: 728* when it came to weapons: Rolla's troops are described as "schütteln die Lanzen" [shaking the spears], which is changed into a nearly nonsensical but perhaps less menacing "schütteln die Pfeile" [shaking the arrows] (S2, 91v). In the same vein, Rolla's "lance", which is referred to as such in *Theater-Bibliothek: 728* and faithfully transcribed into *Theater-Bibliothek: 1460*, has been changed into a "Wurfspieß" [javelin] when talked about on stage. The related stage direction, however, still mentions the "Lanze" (S2, 95v). "Wurfspieß" sounded a bit more archaic and thus further removed from the reality of French soldiers patrolling the streets – or, and perhaps more likely, Schröder knew that the censor was highly critical of mentions of contemporary weapons or spears on stage.

61  Cf. S2, 45r–48r, see above.

We have already mentioned the two instances when Schröder did not have enough space for the text he inserted from the print edition: two of the paste-ins have been written in his hand.[62] Both follow the same pattern: they contain dialogue that had been cut from *Theater-Bibiothek: 728* and the print editions. Both passages might have been retracted from *Theater-Bibliothek: 728* because they did not contain any new information or contribute anything new to the plot. Both, however, bolstered the authority figure's standing in the face of the rebellious youth. The first is a comic interlude in which the high priestess catches two sun virgins in their lie about having left the premises. In the second, the riotous Rolla is brought back to earth by the high priest. Either Schröder wanted to rid the text of the impression that the authorities could be challenged for no reason, or the conspicuous positioning of his paste-ins was to demonstrate how attentive the theatre company was to any perceived challenges to authority. The fact that the censor only signed off on the very day of the performance (after it had probably already been advertised) indicates that there were some complications or that there was at least some back-and-forth. But if the performance announced on the playbill did indeed go ahead, then the revisions had served their purpose after all.

## VII. Reworking the Play, Reshaping *Theater-Bibliothek: 1460* II: Discovering the Heroic Dreamer in 1823

At some point during the use of *Theater-Bibliothek: 1460*, some of the bigger changes Schröder had made to get the censor's approval were retracted. This might have happened in anticipation of the September 1814 performance, soon after the withdrawal of the French troops. Since none of the changes genuinely impaired the functioning of the play as a piece of dramatic literature, it is more likely that the new revisions were made when *Die Sonnen-Jungfrau* was taken up again in the 1820s after a longer hiatus. The hand of Zimmermann, the 1820s prompter (2D), clearly speaks for the latter hypothesis.

Most of the time, hand 2D, which wrote in black ink on green paper inserts, seems to have been undertaking a joint effort with a hand writing in red crayon – perhaps in two stages, perhaps for the sake of clearer visual organisation; perhaps it was hand 2D itself, perhaps a colleague working as a partner. This becomes evident during the climactic finale, i.e., the showdown between Ataliba and his former general Rolla. When the Inca king orders Rolla's entourage to arrest him, the Inca warrior's lengthy retort makes appeals to their shared memories of battle. Except for "Ihr mich greifen? Ihr mich fesseln?" [You seize me? You bind me?], a graphite pencil had previously censored everything with a sweeping slash, starting

---

62 Cf. S2 48r, 70r.

with the defiant "welcher unter euch?" [who among you?], going all the way through to the aggressive "Ha, du vielleicht?" (S2, 94v) [Ha, perhaps you?]. Retracting the retraction, hand 2D has written a vertical "bleibt" [remains] in neat, elegant black ink letters next to the whole passage. "Bleibt" has been underlined in red crayon. The audience would now once again witness Rolla in full swing. On other occasions that we will analyse below, passages have been struck through in red crayon, with hand 2D filling in the substitute lines. Together, the two writing tools were clearly out to reverse some of the earlier taming of the action (cf. figure 46).

*Figure 46: S2, 94v.*

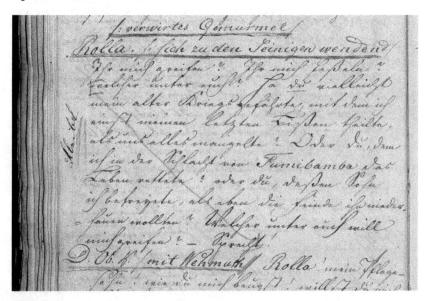

The hand of the vertical "bleibt" on 94v can be clearly identified as that of Christian Friedrich Zimmermann, whose work as a prompter at the Stadt-Theater can be traced back to 1821, i.e., before the 1823 revival of the play. Zimmermann signed his name in some other prompt books in the same elegant penmanship.[63] It seems to be identical with some of the other additions and likely the same as the lines jotted down on the green paper inserts. For those, however, Zimmermann seems to have used a different quill that produced a thinner line. (Cf. figure 47.)

---

63 The earliest example from Theater-Bibliothek is an 1821 production of Ernst von Houwald's one-act play *Die Heimkehr* (*The Homecoming*). Apart from his signatures, there is no record of Zimmermann. The official prompter of the company was a "Herr Haring" in 1821. Cf. *Theater-Bibliothek*: 374b, 93; cf. Klingemann 1822, 410; cf. Zimmermann's DNB entry https://d-nb.info/gnd/1243915552.

*Figure 47*: Theater-Bibliothek: 1428b, 235.

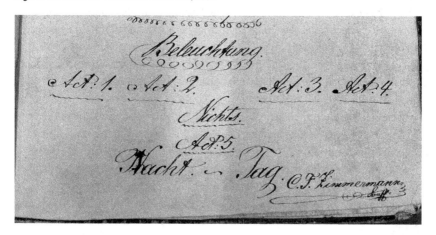

As described above, hand 2D also seems to have been responsible for adding several sweeping instances of "bl" (short for "bleibt" [remains]) where Don Juan's report had given a full picture of the backstory at the beginning – only to then be cut by Schröder for the censor. Now, the Hamburg audience would once again get an overview of the political backdrop to the plot unfolding on stage – not just the sensational story of forbidden love.

On occasions, the black ink used by hand 2D was also working together with a graphite pencil (which could also have been, but was not necessarily being, used by the same hand). At the end of Act III, the priests of the sun take the prisoners away, including, in an act of wanton psychological cruelty, Cora's elderly father. The accompanying turmoil – which might have been deemed a little too similar to what the authorities feared would happen on the streets of Hamburg under French occupation – had been cut for the censor. Hand 2D now added a casual "bleibt" (S2, 64r) using a quill that seems to have been running low on ink. The addition of "bl" in graphite pencil on the verso could also have been made by hand 2D. Three additional instances of "bleibt" in graphite pencil on the recto and one (S2, 64v) on the verso might or might not have been made by the same hand: like Schröder's/hand 2C's black ink, hand 2D also seems to have worked in tandem with someone using a grey writing tool alongside the red crayon – whether applied by a different hand or not.

However, in the case of hand 2D, it is far less obvious whether this layer of black, red, and grey was applied during the same revision stage or whether it can itself be divided into sublayers that might each emphasise a certain operation at a different point in time. While the graphite pencil enrichments in the written artefacts of the Theater-Bibliothek are almost impossible to attribute to a certain hand or revision stage, some interventions by the crayon might already have occurred in tandem with Schröder's 1813 revision. Like Schröder's hand 2C, the wax crayon has casually aligned the text copied from *Theater-Bibliothek: 728* for no apparent reason with the one circulating in various print editions. In the passage where Rolla laments that "ich ein Mädchen liebe, das ihrem Dienst geweiht ist" [I love a girl who is dedicated to their [the gods'] service], the writing tool has cut the relative clause down to a more elegant participle apposition: "ein Mädchen liebe, ihrem Dienst geweiht" (S2, 5v[64]) [I love a girl, dedicated to her service]. The wax crayon was also at work at the beginning, suggesting it might have been part of Schröder's 1813 revisions. Where Rolla is frequently addressed as "Jüngling" [youth] by the high priest, the writing tool has consistently crossed out the appellation and replaced it with "Rolla" (S2, 3r, 4v, 6r). These slight changes would have indeed made sense for the 1813 performances. Up until 1815, Rolla was played by former director Herzfeld, who was in his forties by that point.[65] As the famous role of Rolla was now coveted by prominent (and thus mostly older) actors, there would have been no need to change the appellation back to emphasise the Inca warrior's youth when, in 1816 as well as in the 1820s, guest actors were playing the part. On the other hand, audiences tended to excuse differences in age between their favourites and the parts they played. After all, Schröder himself had achieved stardom in 1778 by playing the aged King Lear just before he turned thirty-four.[66] In 1790, he then played Kotzebue's geriatric high priest at the age of forty-nine. There is consequently no certainty as to when the red crayon got rid of Rolla's youth. Where, at a later point, Don Juan addresses Rolla as "junger Mensch" (S2, 29v) [young person], the "junger" has been crossed out in black ink, which could have been carried out by Schröder's quill in 1813 or by Zimmermann's in 1823. Where the high priest calls Rolla "junger Mann" (S2, 4r) [young man] at the beginning, the red crayon has crossed out "junger", which has then been added again in the margin in Zimmermann's black ink, thereby potentially indicating a later revision. This might also have occurred simply due to the age difference between father and son (as revealed during that scene): the older priest is clearly addressing a younger man. Since a red crayon was evidently assisting Zimmermann's quill (2D), the revision was probably made in the 1820s if the crayon was in fact only used for a single revision stage, but this is by no means certain.

When reworking *Theater-Bibliothek: 1460* in 1813, Schröder's hand, 2C, accentuated the power of authority, cut back on the political backstory, and trimmed Rolla's sometimes bellicose mood to size. Zimmermann's hand, 2D, not only walked many of these decisions back but also gave more emphasis to some aspects of the

---

64  Kotzebue 1791, 16.
65  Cf. the respective playbill for February 17, 1815, on Jahn/Mühle/Eisenhardt/Malchow/M. Schneider (https://www.stadttheater.uni-hamburg.de).
66  Cf. Chapter 5, section 7.

play that we have just mentioned. "Noble savage" Rolla was such a popular character with actors because he had also found such favour with the (theatre-going and reading) audience. His brooding nature fit in with popular Romantic tastes, as did his passion. In 1823, Zimmermann's hand, 2D, working in black ink, and the hand working in red crayon set out to expand Rolla's part once again. In this spirit, other characters' lines were occasionally cut or reduced to give Rolla's part more weight. When he first encounters Rolla, Don Juan defends his friend's Alonzo's passion only to be surprised by the former general and now hermit's confession of his own love for the sun virgin. In 1813, Schröder had aligned the passage with the print version. In 1823, the wax crayon cut it altogether,[67] lending Rolla's feelings more significance. Conversely, in the dramatic finale, one of the green paper inserts has given much more space and assigned more importance to Cora's declaration of her absolute and innocent love for Alonzo than in the pared-down versions in *Theater-Bibliothek: 1460* and *Theater-Bibliothek: 728*.[68] While this shifts the attention from Rolla's revolt to the ill-fated lovers, Cora's purity now gives more weight to Rolla's anger against the powers that be – a righteous anger in defence of truth, virtue, and beauty.

Several times, hand 2D has filled in lines spoken by Rolla that had been cut during the revision of *Theater-Bibliothek: 728* in 1790. Like Schröder before him, Zimmermann also used a print copy as a point of reference. This has created the curious overall impression that redundant lines with no importance for the overall plot were cut from *Theater-Bibliothek: 728* and therefore left out in *Theater-Bibliothek: 1460* only to be put back in again later. At second glance, it is possible to discern the slight re-accentuation of the mood effected by these minor changes. Clearly, Schröder's 1790 impulse to sober up Kotzebue's ebullient style was no longer the order of the day by the 1820s. On the contrary, parts thrown out thirty years earlier had now become suitable or even fashionable.

This is most prominent at the seemingly random transition between the two scribes of *Theater-Bibliothek: 1460* in the middle of Act IV, Scene 3. The red crayon has crossed out the text in the upper half of 64r by making four slashes in the form of two large X's. The lower half and the completely empty 64v have been left for the new text before the first quire of scribe 2B begins. The retracted lines that were copied from the revised *Theater-Bibliothek: 728* into *Theater-Bibliothek: 1460* are emotionally charged to begin with: "Nun so zertrümmre Erde, daß alles untergehe! – Auf ihr Schrecken der Natur! Donnergebrüll und Sturmgeheul! Umgebt mich daß ich frey athme! Daß meine Stimme mit der eurigen kämpfe und mein Arm schneller morde als eure Blize!" [Now smash the earth so that everything perishes! – Here's to the terrors of nature! Roar of thunder and howl of storm! Surround me so that

---

67 Cf. S2, 30r.
68 Cf. S2, 79r.

I may breathe freely! That my voice may fight with yours and my arm may murder faster than your lightning!]. The high priest can only retort with, "Um aller Götter willen! – Rolla! –" [For all the gods' sake! – Rolla! –]. In the printed text however, Rolla's part is nearly twice as long and includes an additional, over-the-top, "Nun so schaudere, Erde, und verschlinge Deine ganze Oberfläche! Murret ihr Gebürge rings umher! Feuer! Feuer aus euren Eingeweiden in die Thäler! Daß Alles untergehe! Kein Gras mehr wachse! Und die Welt aussehe, wie eine große Brandstäte!" (S2, 64r) [Now, shudder, earth, and devour all your surface! Murmur you mountains all around! Fire! Fire from your bowels into the valleys! That all may perish! That no grass may grow! And that the world may appear as a great conflagration!].[69] On the bottom of the recto, hand 2D has inserted this passage into *Theater-Bibliothek: 1460* in its entirety. "Um aller Götter willen! – Rolla! –" [For all the gods' sake! – Rolla! –] then follows at the top of the verso. In his alarm about Cora's fate, Rolla (who is about to find out that his counterpart is his father in an even more dramatic next step) makes a scene in the literal sense of the word. The character had done so in Schröder's slightly subdued 1790s version; however, the work of the red crayon and Zimmermann's black ink quill turned the volume all the way back up in the 1820s. Due to the half-empty recto and the empty verso, *Theater-Bibliothek: 1460* seems to invite such excess: there is indeed space to add more text.

In other instances, the prompt book does not afford space for enrichments. This is where the inserts on additional sheets such as the one with Cora's extra text make their entrance. In one case, only a minor amount of Rolla text has been added. But the red crayon disavowal of Schröder's revisions looks so convoluted that it might have seemed necessary to insert the slightly longer text.[70]

Hand 2D also incorporated Rolla's greater emotional bandwidth into Act IV, Scene 2 – the scene that was entirely reworked in *Theater-Bibliothek: 728* and then realigned with the print version in 1813. Back then, Schröder had not added all of the text from the print edition, instead leaving out the part where Rolla reveals himself to be not only desperate but also emotional and weak – even vis-à-vis the cowardly Diego. Re-adding this side of Rolla in the 1820s now made for a fuller character, whose love and desperation lead him to humiliate himself: "Redet! Es ist Rolla der euch bittet. Rolla bittet so gut ists euch noch nie geworden. Redet was ist vorgefallen?" (S2, 66v) [Talk! It is Rolla who asks you. Rolla pleads[,] you've never had it this good. Talk, what has happened?].

The one insert which is in neither Schröder's nor Zimmermann's (or the censor's) hand was clearly added in line with the spirit of the 1820s revisions. It was pinned-in using a (since lost) needle at the end of scene Act IV, Scene 3, on 73v and replaces only two and a half lines. The insert has been folded twice and thus had

---

69 Kotzebue 1791, 138.
70 Cf. S2, 31r.

to be folded in and out to first follow the additional text and then slide back onto the verso for the reader to continue reading. The lines around the passage that the insert replaced had already been aligned by Schröder with the print version during the 1813 revision. Since this passage has been crossed out in the red crayon, it seems to have been made during the Zimmermann revision stage. In the sober 1790 version copied from the revised *Theater-Bibliothek: 728*, Rolla has regained his balance and gets back to business: "Ja, ich bin wieder ausgesöhnt mit der Welt. Und nun mein Vater, laßt uns Alonzo und Cora retten, ihr müßt sie retten" [Yes, I am reconciled with the world once more. And now, my father, let us save Alonzo and Cora, you must save them]. In the print version and on the insert, the text is nearly six times as long. Rolla's mind goes on a flight of fancy in envisioning how to engineer the lovers' escape: "Hört, wie meine Phantasie sich das frohe Bild träumt" (S2, 73v) [Hear how my imagination dreams the happy picture]. There was clearly no room for the verbose breadth of such "Phantasie" in the 1790 version, certainly not with respect to the heroic Rolla. The 1820s revisions situate the character quite differently but with a remarkable (and pragmatic) fealty to Kotzebue's original publication. Rolla is now a hero because he is also a dreamer. As far as the character is concerned, this is a complete turnaround. On a material level, however, the insert clearly remains a foreign body which is always in danger of falling or fluttering out of the prompt book.

The reshaped *Theater-Bibliothek: 1460* was probably in action five times between 1823 and 1826. Since enrichments like this were rather common, it was nothing worthy of greater attention in the pragmatic work of prompting or in the handwritten artefact. However, the content of the pinned-in insert had come a long way: it had been part of Kotzebue's original submission and had been crossed out in Schröder's 1790 trial version, i.e., in *Theater-Bibliothek: 728*. It was excluded from the production for over thirty years, spanning more than twenty performances under different principals, with different actors, and at least two different prompters. But six years after Schröder's death, Rolla's fanciful side made it back into the written artefact – as part of the life of its own that *Theater-Bibliothek: 1460* had taken on.

Initially, two written artefacts had had to be created to make one prompt book for the original production of *Die Sonnen-Jungfrau* in 1790. One (*Theater-Bibliothek: 728*) was decisive for the make-up of the other but was then left by the wayside. The other (*Theater-Bibliothek: 1460*) went with the historic tides and would be blown about by the shifting political and cultural winds for the next thirty-six years. The seemingly incomprehensible layers of writing bear witness to this history and follow fairly regular patterns. For their part, these patterns were tied to the internal and external circumstances, conditions, and urgencies of the Stadt-Theater as they influenced everyday work in and around the prompt box.

Reconstructing the eventful history of the two prompt books and their entangled relationship calls various well-established notions of literature and theatre into question. The unity of a dramatic text and the authority of the print version published by an author were, on the one hand, treated as self-evident ideas in the world of the Stadt-Theater around 1800. But in practice, they were only ideas. Texts have been materially dismembered and put together again in different ways, sometimes with new ingredients. The many hands of different agents (the principal, the prompter, the impartial scribes) as well as the various styles, tools, and paper practices have contributed to an intrinsically complicated result. It was only by arriving at this result that another play from the ceaselessly productive assembly line of August von Kotzebue, the German-speaking world's most prolific and successful playwright, could grace the stage every now and then for several decades.

# Chapter 5. Prompt Book Practices in Context: The "Hamburg Shakespeare" between Handwriting and Print, the Audience and Censorship Demands (1770s–1810s and beyond)

In the 1770s, the young Friedrich Ludwig Schröder and his company were renowned in the German-speaking world and beyond for their pioneering productions of William Shakespeare's plays on the German stage. The prompt books for the company's Shakespeare adaptations are of particular interest for this study. The multi-handed, multi-layered internal Hamburg Stadt-Theater prompt books hold versions of Shakespeare's plays that markedly differ from the ones attributed to a writer who was about to become the epitome of individual authorship and creation, notions that still widely persist in the popular imagination of the twenty-first century. German versions of Shakespeare's plays (as well as adaptations of them) circulated widely in the 1770s – as printed books – as did Shakespeare criticism (the emerging German strain as well as translations of English writers) in journals and other publications.[1] Shakespeare in print shaped both the popular imagination and intellectual discussions. With respect to the Hamburg Shakespeare of the 1770s, this chapter will examine the relationship between the handwriting of prompt book production and upkeep on the one hand and, on the other, the multitude of printed books that they were related to and that made them possible. The by definition unfinished character of prompt books was what allowed them to be used flexibly in the theatrical context. Handwriting could be added as long as a folio provided enough blank space for it and as long as the valid text remained legible. Handwriting made theatre companies more flexible to outside demands – whether commercial because aspects of a play were not to the audience's liking or political because the authorities objected or were feared likely to object to particular passages. While Shakespearean texts began flourishing in print, their occasionally bumpy introduction to and establishment on the German-speaking stage manifested themselves in print's interaction with handwrit-

---

1 Cf. Paulin 2003, 62–132.

ing. The following considerations focus on two prompt book examples: the hasty transformation of the failing 1776 production of *Othello, Theater-Bibliothek: 571*, and the longevity of the 1778 production of *König Lear [King Lear]*, which was reworked for the French censor's approval in 1812 as *Theater-Bibliothek: 2029*. To set the scene, we will situate the most influential of the company's Hamburg Shakespeare productions, its 1776 version of *Hamlet*, at the intersection between the realm of print media and the practicalities of running a theatre business.

## I. The German Shakespeare in Print and Its Relationship to Theatre

When Shakespeare was introduced to the wider, German-reading public in the 1760s through Christoph Martin Wieland's prose translations, the affiliation between Shakespeare's now printed texts and London's vibrant early modern theatre culture had been seen as a rather unlucky coincidence.[2] It had been thought that currying favour with the "Pöbel"[3] [rabble] of the low-income groundlings who crowded before Shakespeare's London stage had been to blame for Shakespeare's use of foul language and for quite a few "Fehler" [mistakes] in the plot that competed with the many "Schönheiten"[4] [beauties] of his plays. In the theatre district of contemporary eighteenth-century London, Shakespeare's name had been attributed to plays that had been somewhat freely adapted from his works or only loosely inspired by them. "In the present case the publick has decided,"[5] as master critic Samuel Johnson put it with respect to the success of the adaptations. Shakespeare's plays were there to be read, not performed. It was only slowly that David Garrick reintroduced passages taken from various Shakespeare print editions into his productions.[6] Overall, Shakespeare's plays were well known and relatively widely read because they circulated in print. These print editions were themselves notoriously derived from printed works, i.e., the famous Shakespeare folio and quarto editions which provided different semblances of what the actual text that had been handwritten by Shakespeare and then copied out in parts for the actors might have looked like. It has been well established that these print editions (full of variations, inconsistencies, typographical errors, and multiple more or less obviously corrupted passages) gave rise to the unending task of editing the suppos-

---

2 Wieland's translation "imported" this prejudice by including Alexander Pope's introduction to his own 1723–1725 Shakespeare edition in the first book of his translations. Cf. Pope/Wieland 1762, 3–28.
3 Pope/Wieland 1762, 4.
4 Pope/Wieland 1762, 2.
5 Wimsatt 1960, 98.
6 Cf. Tatspaugh 2003, 538; cf. Hoffmeier 1964, 40f.

edly "real" but ever-absent text of Shakespeare's plays – an undertaking already in full swing in eighteenth-century Britain.[7]

After a few scattered appearances on the stage and in print, the German-reading world encountered Shakespeare on a larger scale as an eighteenth-century print phenomenon. At first, this mainly took place in excerpts in journals, and then through the German translations of twenty-two of Shakespeare's plays published by Christoph Martin Wieland between 1762 and 1766 in volumes of two plays each.[8] His prose versions often cut potentially offensive parts, sometimes with and sometimes without comment. This was a successful strategy, if not entirely without controversy. While the linguistic errors and overall misconceptions of the translation were widely noted,[9] hardly anyone took issue with the way that Wieland ignored Shakespeare's free blank verse in its many variations.[10] The (mostly implicit) contemporary conception of translation still considered linguistic form to be a vessel used to transport the spirit of the letter, which could also be placed in a different vessel without friction or loss. Moreover, Wieland's prose fit in perfectly with the rise of the aesthetics of sentimentality and the aim of presenting "natural" characters in literature. During the 1770s, scholar Johann Joachim Eschenburg not only corrected and completed Wieland's efforts but also produced a compendium of everything that was known about Shakespeare and his plays in the English-speaking world and beyond. Shakespeare in German was indeed a figure of letters – and thus of printed books.[11]

Schröder had collaborators but was ultimately in charge of the adaptations produced at Stadt-Theater during his tenure.[12] We can assume that Schröder, who took over the Stadt-Theater in 1771 (at first together with his mother), was reasonably well informed about the goings-on of the London stage due to his interactions with Hamburg merchants, some of whom had extensive trade relations with London. The local Hamburg news reported on what was taking place in London theatres[13]; some merchants were members of the Gesellschaft der Theaterfreunde [Society of Theatre Friends] and relayed what they had seen.[14] But Schröder

---

7 Cf. Colins 1991.
8 Cf. Wieland 2003.
9 Cf. Kob 2000; cf. Stadler 1910.
10 At the same time, there could still be little appreciation of how Wieland's prose captured surprising nuances of "the Bard's" language and how it seems to have introduced a whole array of linguistic creations (such as "Steckenpferde" for Hamlet's "hobby-horses") into common usage. Cf. Itkonen 1971; cf. Kob 2000, 21.
11 Cf. Eschenburg 1787.
12 Cf. Hoffmann 1939, 18–21; cf. Malchow 2022, 99.
13 Cf. Hoffmeier 1964, 41.
14 Cf. Häublein 2005, 59.

also had ready access to Wieland's and then Eschenburg's translations as printed books. He could also read the many, sometimes very liberal Shakespeare adaptations that began cropping up in print before or immediately after they had been performed in theatres. Christian Felix Weiße's *Richard III.* (1765) and *Romeo und Julia* (1767) – which used Shakespeare's plots but were based on more contemporary adaptations – Franz Heufeld's *Hamlet* (1771), and Christian Heinrich Schmid's and Johann Heinrich Steffen's respective transformations of *Othello* (1769, 1770)[15] all customised Shakespeare's bewildering forms and plots to Enlightenment circumstances and prevalent tastes – dampening the impact of or omitting Shakespeare's obscenities and wordplay to comply with contemporary standards of *decorum* by decomplicating the language and generally furnishing the plays with happy or at least happier endings. All of them took for granted what was a well-established fact in London: that Shakespeare's puzzling plays needed to be adapted if they were to come across as presentable for the German stage.[16] Notions of translation and adaptation overlapped in the practices of the time; the two words were sometimes used interchangeably. Even among scholars, a "successful" translation would leave out or amend what was deemed wrong or inappropriate in the original.[17]

Schröder was known to be an avid reader of the journals and criticism circulating in print. In the early 1770s, Shakespeare started to be seen less as the somewhat tawdry and highly irregular (albeit fascinating) curiosity that European Enlightenment critics had made him out to be earlier in the eighteenth century. Instead, Shakespeare's plays began to be viewed as an alternative model to the normative poetics that had long governed what was considered "good taste" among critics – though not necessarily by the public or the theatre companies. The reception of Edward Young's *Conjectures on Original Composition* (1759)[18] allowed writers such as Johann Gottfried Herder to fawn over Shakespeare as a "Genie"[19] [genius] and "Weltschöpfer"[20] [creator of worlds]. At the beginning of Herder's fervent 1773 essay on the Bard, a "Sterblicher mit Götterkraft begabt"[21] [mortal gifted with the power of the gods] sits somewhere high up in the mountains, alone on a throne of rocks, untouched by the "Sturm, Ungewitter und d[em] Brausen des Meeres"[22] [storm, tempest, and the roar of the sea] that rage at his feet but that seem to have

---

15 Cf. Weiße 1836; cf. Weiße 1776; cf. Weilen 1914; cf. Schmid 1772; cf. Steffens 1770.
16 Cf. Dobson 1992; cf. Habicht 1994b, 50–55.
17 For example, cf. Huber 1968, 6–15.
18 Cf. Young 1966.
19 erder 1993, 499.
20 Herder 1993, 509.
21 Herder 1993, 508.
22 Herder 1993, 498.

been summoned at his will. In this vein, Herder saw Shakespeare's plays as quasi-organic formations, the heterogeneous parts of which had been assembled "zu einem Wunderganzen zusammen"[23] [into a miraculous whole]. Nothing was to be removed from or added to such "miraculous wholes". To Herder, every detail seemed "so zu diesem Ganzen [zu] gehören, daß ich nichts verändern, versetzen, aus andern Stücken hieher oder hieraus in andre Stücke bringen könnte"[24] [to belong to this whole in such a way that I would not change anything, move anything, add anything from other plays to this one or from this one to other plays]. Thus, Herder conceived of his reading of a Shakespearean play as a portal into an original, self-sufficient world: "Mir ist, wenn Ich ihn lese, Theater, Akteur, Kulisse verschwunden!"[25] [For me, when I read him, theatre, actor, scenery disappear!] This Shakespeare was for and of the mind, not the artifice of theatre. Herder did not even have to point out that his reading of Shakespeare seemed to make the material printed books containing the letters of the plays disappear together with the material infrastructure of theatre. In the New Testament tradition, Herder took for granted the written word's ability to transcend itself into the spirit. As an individual author, Shakespeare became a divine creator and even transcended the status of the supposedly flawless writer who, according to London contemporaries, "in his writing (whatsoever he penned) [...] never blotted out a line".[26] While the material conditions of writing are skipped entirely in Herder's reading, the assumed essence of Shakespeare needed to be removed from its ties to the theatre and its practical conditions. But such an essence was not impaired by publications in print.

It was this printed Shakespeare as an individualised author who, from today's point of view, received less than respectful treatment when he was adapted for Schröder's stage. Here, the printed Shakespeare was brought into the world of handwritten prompt book creation and enrichment. In prompt book creation and use, lines were "blotted out" on a regular basis – albeit for technical rather than creative reasons. "Changing" and "moving" parts, the sacrilege that Herder foreswore, was more often than not precisely what adapting a play for the stage and creating a handwritten prompt book was all about. As seen in the previous chapter, this was hardly the effort of one creative "genius" but took place over various stages and with the involvement of multiple participants. While the creation and use of prompt books (and the booklets for the actors' parts) were a theatre company's internal affair, they heavily depended on and interacted with the circulation of plays (and reviews, criticism, etc.) in print.

---

23 Herder 1993, 508.
24 Herder 1993, 511.
25 Herder 1993, 509.
26 Jonson 1975, 394.

## II. The 1776 *Hamlet* and Its Relationship to Print

The newly fashionable veneration of the "creative power" of an individual author had little influence on the practicalities of running a theatre business – although Schröder took note of and championed the new reading of Shakespeare that Herder (who was of the exact same age) and younger authors in Herder's circle were putting forward.[27] In 1774, Schröder successfully staged *Götz von Berlichingen*, the young Goethe's homage to the more open form of Shakespeare's plays (albeit in an abridged version that could actually be performed instead of spending the majority of the time carrying out scene changes).[28] Even more than Herder's point of view, Schröder held Lenz's appraisal of Shakespeare's tragedies as "character plays" in high regard.[29] But like the historical Shakespeare, Schröder was dependent on the commercial success of his theatre operation. However sympathetic he was to the Enlightenment programme of turning the theatre into a public place of education in matters of morality, taste, and the overall improvement of humanity (especially in Lessing's version, which had failed in Hamburg in the late 1760s), or to the new notion of literature being put forward by Herder, the seats needed to be filled with paying customers. Schröder had opened his principalship with a performance of Lessing's *Emilia Galotti* to signal the continuity of artistic standards and social aspirations.[30] Intellectual propositions such as Lenz's emphasis on Louis-Sébastien Mercier's call to adapt plays to the audience's intellectual capacity in his 1773 *Du théâtre ou Nouvel essai sur l'art dramatique* [*On the Theatre or New Essay on Dramatic Art*] fitted in well with Schröder's overall undertaking.[31] Schröder might have heartily agreed with Lessing's emphasis on the emancipation and formation of "an educated people",[32] but he also needed to keep the lights on and make a living for himself and his company.

Schröder's audience expected recognisable novelty: new plays, stage sets, and musical scores were always welcome, but they were not to break with well-known patterns. Schröder imported and adapted what had been effective elsewhere (including translations of contemporary plays from France, Italy, and Great Britain). His source materials were often available as print copies, though most of them were not widely read; notions of "fidelity" to an "original" were lenient (to non-existent). The audience preferred comedies and was used to prologues and epilogues, e.g., ballets and musical interludes. Musical comedies and operas were also popu-

---

27 Cf. Hoffmann 1939, 74–91, 152–158.
28 Cf. Hoffmann 1939, 74–91.
29 Cf. Hoffmeier 1964, 129f.
30 Cf. Häublein 2005, 68f.
31 Cf. Hoffmeier 1964, 130.
32 Cf., for example, Haider-Pregler 1980.

lar main acts.³³ A happy ending was in no way mandatory as far as the authorities were concerned (unlike the "Wiener Schluß" [Vienna ending], which had been decreed in Vienna in 1776).³⁴ But if a play did not have a happy ending, it had better have had an uplifting one. If that was not the case, at the very least the closing music needed to elate the audience.³⁵

Schröder prided himself on trying to "educate" his audience on many of these matters (and on taking risks in doing so). But practical circumstances only allowed so much. The work of Schröder's company drew its inspiration from the dramaturgical programmes that had been implemented in the spirit of Diderot's mid-century writings, which had been translated by Lessing into German and then advanced by a host of critics.³⁶ Plays and performances were ideally conceived of as self-contained illusions behind a fourth wall. Actors were to avoid pandering to the audience so as not to interrupt the aesthetic illusion. Diderot hoped that spectators would thus be absorbed by the performance as if they were looking at a picture.³⁷ Lessing added that watching a play could train spectators' capacity for compassion.³⁸ In this vein, Schröder came to consider Lessing's *Miss Sara Sampson* as a model tragedy, and he put it on regularly despite its lack of commercial success.³⁹ He restricted extemporisation on stage and introduced regular rehearsals, preventing the performance from being split up into individualised acting showcases. But there was not much point in trying to mould the audience into a state of Diderotian discipline (although he did prohibit them from visiting actors backstage in their dressing rooms or entering the stage itself).⁴⁰ It was not possible to completely dim the auditorium by technical means, nor was this desired by an audience who was used to seeing and being seen – and to reacting cheerfully or rowdily to whatever happened on stage. Therefore, the audience's devout absorption in the performance remained unattainable.⁴¹ The audience remained interested in comedy, music, and ballet. However, Schröder managed to regularly deprive its members of prologues and epilogues, and simply focussed on the main play (with the usual musical interludes between acts once the curtain had been lowered and

---

33 Cf. Chapter 1.
34 Cf. Roger 2007.
35 Cf. Kramer 2016.
36 Cf. J. F. Lehmann 2000; cf. Weinstock 2019, 140–164.
37 Cf. Diderot 1936; cf. J. F. Lehmann 2000, 97–102.
38 Cf. Weinstock 2019, 61–69.
39 Cf. Hoffmann 1939, 74f.
40 A significant amount of recent research has shown that the disciplined audience was more of an ideal constructed by critics of the time than a reality. Cf. Korte/Jakob 2012; cf. Korte/Jakob/Dewenter 2014.
41 Cf. Malchow 2022, 109–124, 164–172.

before it was raised again). His 1776 production of *Hamlet* (in collaboration with in-house author Johann Christian Bock[42]) was a case in point: at that time, his concentration on the main play alone was still rather unusual.[43]

At the same time, Schröder needed to keep the tastes and expectations of his audience in mind. The paying audience was vital to the commercial success of the company. As seen in the previous chapter, Schröder also had to consider the watchful eye of the authorities.[44] In the case of *Hamlet*, it was obvious that neither the authorities nor large parts the audience – or probably even most members of the theatre company themselves – would have appreciated Shakespeare's exuberant play with its frequent use of foul language and obscenities (of which Wieland's 1760s translation had already left many out). But it was three other aspects above all that seem to have led Schröder to rework the play that was available in print translations. The lack of set design in Shakespeare's theatre, where every change of scenery could be implied by the actors' words, contrasted with the eighteenth-century aesthetics of elaborate stage sets. In order to avoid having to take breaks for scene changes, the number of fast-changing locations in Shakespeare's play had to be reduced and separate parts fused together.[45] Such practical necessities aligned well with Schröder's own Enlightenment temperament and tastes. Following Lessing, he considered the open form of Shakespeare's plays to be a welcome antidote to the limitations that critics like Gottsched had tried to impose on the German stage. But he also agreed with Lessing that English plays were too episodic. Aside from the relaxing of such exaggerated restrictions, a great amount of order needed to be maintained for a play to work.[46]

Most importantly, Schröder's letters and conversations (related by his contemporaries) bear witness to the extent to which he felt the need to pander to the audience (or to address it at a level that was immediately comprehensible) when introducing Shakespeare.[47] Always on the lookout for new material, Schröder was well aware of the impact that David Garrick had had on the London stage as the title character of a (heavily adapted) *Hamlet* from 1742.[48] In Prague in 1776, Schröder watched a guest performance by the Vienna-based Theatre at Kärntnertor, which had been performing Franz Heufeld's trimmed-down, six-character adaptation

---

42  Cf. Malchow 2022, 98f.
43  Cf. Eigenmann 1994, 27–34.
44  Later parts of this chapter will take a closer look at the relationship between print, handwriting, and censorship.
45  Cf. Häublein 2005, 70–76; cf. Birkner 2007.
46  Cf. Hoffmann 1939, 91–106.
47  Cf. Hoffmeier 1964, 46–53.
48  Cf. Hoffmeier 1964, 28.

since 1773 to little effect.[49] On 20 September 1776, *Hamlet* debuted at Schröder's Hamburg company, possibly in Heufeld's version, which had been readily available in print since 1771.[50] The respective prompt book has not survived; it may very well have consisted of the printed Heufeld book with a few handwritten annotations.

Whether the first performances were based on Heufeld or not, Schröder and his company quickly created their own version that was largely based on Wieland's printed translation, which debuted in November.[51] The details of the adaptation are well known as Schröder had it published as an octavo print in 1777, titled *Hamlet, Prinz von Dännemark. Ein Trauerspiel in sechs Aufzügen. Zum Behuf des Hamburgischen Theaters*[52] [*Hamlet, Prince of Denmark. A Mourning Play*[53] *in Six Acts. For the Benefit of the Hamburg Theatre*]. The adaptation needed six acts instead of Shakespeare's (and Heufeld's) five to organise the set changes. Conspicuously, the name of the author, Shakespeare, who was soon to become the "author of authors", was missing. Instead, a later 1779 edition included a copperplate image of Schröder's lead actor Johann Brockmann, who had already been a local star before he got involved with the production, as frontispiece and mentioned it beneath the title: *Nebst Brockmann's Bildniß als Hamlet* [*Besides a Portrait of Brockmann as Hamlet*].[54] When re-adapting *Hamlet* from the theatre into print, it was thus the virtuosic actor rather than the unknown author who was to draw attention to the Hamburg stage (and, at the same time, to sell copies). Schröder might have been trying to emulate a practice that was common in London (and in Paris). Printed books with the content of prompt books were all the rage – and were confusingly also called "prompt books".[55] While the practice continued well into the nineteenth century (and still occurs sporadically in twenty-first-century "Western" theatre), using the leading actor as a selling point did not catch on. In print, and increasingly in general culture, theatrical plays were a matter of the authors who wrote them, not the actors who performed them (and rarely the practitioners who adapted the texts for the stage).

Schröder's actual adaptation of the play differed from approaches such as the one taken by Weiße in that he did not change the main plot – only the ending. When shortening a play, Schröder would generally try to streamline and simplify the overall structure but then intensify the main elements.[56] He had a new respect for

---

49 Cf. Häublein 2005, 70; cf. Malchow 2022, 84; cf. Hoffmeier 1964, 27–31; cf. Weilen 1914.
50 Cf. Hoffmeier 1964, 36.
51 Cf. Häublein 2005, 72.
52 Schröder/Shakespeare 1777.
53 In practice, not much of a distinction was made between the "Trauerspiel" and the "tragedy" around 1800.
54 Cf. Schröder/Shakespeare 1779. There were reissues in 1780, 1781, 1784, 1789, and 1795.
55 Cf. Stone Peters 2000, 129–145.
56 Cf. Hoffmann 1939, 74; cf. Marx 2011.

the content of the adapted text available in print. Unlike in Heufeld's adaptation of *Hamlet* (which had not intervened into the sequence of events before the conclusion either), Schröder's version now included subplots and minor parts such as Laertes and the gravediggers, while Ophelia's status was upgraded to a level similar to the one she had had in the original. But, like Heufeld, Schröder still made do without the Norway plot in the background and got rid of the play's political urgency. The conflict between Hamlet and the court was boiled down to a family drama. The plot line of the comic duo of Rosencrantz and Guildenstern was incorporated but conflated into a single part. Perhaps due to Hamburg's location near areas under Danish administration, Schröder retained the changes that Heufeld had made to the characters' names, which made them sound more Scandinavian: Polonius became Oldenholm; Horatio became Gustav. Most importantly, Schröder took his cue from Heufeld in transforming the ending according to the standards of poetic justice.[57] In the final duel, Hamlet's mother and stepfather died, as Ophelia had before them, but the hero Hamlet survived to become king. In Schröder's version, Hamlet is more energetic than the procrastinator later made famous by Romanticism. Hamlet reconciles with Laertes and is the obvious king in waiting. Schröder, who had voiced his "Furcht"[58] [fear] of the Hamburg audience's reaction, gave his spectators an adequate ending. Perhaps Schröder did not need to square such pandering with his own artistic ambitions: the published opinions of contemporary critics, which he could read in print generally considered *Hamlet's* fatal finale to be one of Shakespeare's "Fehler" [mistakes] (except for the reviews written in the Herderian mould).[59]

The production was a success (with eleven known performances staged over the next two and a half months in 1776 alone). But when the production's lead actor, Brockmann, left for a better-paid position in Vienna, he spent the winter of 1777/78 in Berlin and performed the part of Hamlet in Schröder's adaptation with members of Karl Döbbelin's local theatre company (which was deemed to be much inferior to Schröder's[60]). The reception was so enthusiastic that it led to the creation of fan merchandise such as a coin with Brockmann's face on it and etchings of his performance by well-known artists.[61] Brockmann's guest performance launched the persistent German fascination with *Hamlet* as a play and contributed to the reputation of Schröder and his actors in the German-speaking world and beyond.[62] Schröder's adaptation would be taken up by various other German-speaking companies, which had the print publication to rely on.

---

57  Cf. Malchow 2022, 106–108.
58  Schröder 1978a, V.
59  Cf. Häublein 2005, 76.
60  Cf. Häublein 2005, 118.
61  Cf. Schink 1778; cf. Weilen 1914, 41; cf. Häublein 2005, 83; cf. Birkner 2007, 21.
62  Cf. Häublein 2005, 79–93.

Soon they were spoiled for choice. It was perhaps due to Brockmann's departure that Schröder reworked his own adaptation in 1778. Eschenburg's revision of Wieland's translation had appeared in print in 1777 and was generally viewed as an improvement. Schröder himself had criticised the stiffness of his own adaptation and aimed for a more fluid line delivery.[63] This also applied to the overall structure, which Schröder cut back to five acts. He also got rid of some lines and reexcluded the comedy of the gravediggers (which might have seemed inappropriate), but also added even more complexity to the Shakespearean characters.[64] Before the year 1778 was out, Schröder had had his revised version published in print as well. It was included in a book series called *Hamburger Theater* [Hamburg Theatre] which Schröder himself had established to promote trendsetting plays (including his own work and that of his ensemble) as models for a future "Nationaltheater" [national theatre] in the spirit of Lessing.[65] This print version did point out that it had been adapted but only included an attribution to the author, not the adapter: *Hamlet, Prinz von Dännemark: Ein Trauerspiel in fünf Akten; Nach Shakespear* [Hamlet, Prince of Denmark: A Mourning Play in Five Acts; After Shakespear].[66]

Both editions were reprinted numerous times (including in a number of bootlegs) and were widely available. After Brockmann's departure, Schröder offered the Hamburg audience the choice of three possible Hamlet successors, before graduating from the role of the ghost to playing Hamlet himself.[67] Locally, Schröder's 1778 version was (infrequently) performed until well into the 1840s[68] – and thus until a time when, at least in critical discourse, Schröder's undertaking had been replaced by the Romantic ideal of the metric Shakespeare translation that conformed to the poetic shape of the original.[69] However, Schröder's radical interventions, which had merely seemed pragmatic in the 1770s, had inaugurated a tradition that had been imported from England, was upheld by the older Goethe and then advanced by the proponents of the Deutsche Shakespeare-Gesellschaft [German Shakespeare Society] (founded in 1864), which would endure at least until the end of the nineteenth century: as a text (for reading from a printed book) Shakespeare was sacrosanct; as a text adapted for the stage, experimentation was allowed – even if the tradition of loose Shakespeare adaptations slowly faded

---

63 Cf. Schröder 1778a, VI.
64 Cf. Hoffmeier 1964, 51–55; cf. Marx 2011, 518–523.
65 Cf. Hoffmann 1939, 237–246; cf. Häublein 2005, 57f.
66 Cf. Schröder 1778b.
67 Cf. Malchow 2022, 317–322.
68 Cf. Jahn/Mühle/Eisenhardt/Malchow/Schneider (https://www.stadttheater.uni-hamburg.de).
69 Cf. Paulin 2003, 253–255, 304–308.

away.[70] The point of reference for the text spoken on stage would increasingly be the text by the "author of authors" circulating in print copies.

While the printed books of Schröder's adaptations played no little part in the reception of *Hamlet* and Shakespeare in the German-speaking world, day-to-day theatre operations were carried out in handwriting. As stated above, it was only in a minority of cases that a printed book would form the basis of a prompt book, usually when a printed book contained a version of the text that was not too far removed from the text that was to be performed by the company. That was the case for the Hamburg *Hamlet* – and for many of the other Shakespeare adaptations staged by Schröder as well. As we will explain below, when Schröder's company started preparing their Shakespeare prompt books for the French imperial censor in 1811, it used the self-published prints from the *Hamburger Theater* series as a basis, which were then enriched by hand. Schröder's *Hamlet* seems to have been an exception in that the company started using a print copy of its own 1778 adaptation much earlier. Although no handwritten manuscript of the prompt book has survived in the Theater-Bibliothek collection, a heavily enriched copy of the 1778 printed book has been preserved as the written artefact *Theater-Bibliothek: 1982 (1)*. The prompt book does bear the French censor's signature, but it is clearly from an earlier date: Brockmann's name is spelled out as the performer next to the name of Hamlet.[71] In 1785, Brockmann actually returned to Hamburg for a guest performance. While the surviving playbill of 4 March names different actors to the ones written down in *Theater-Bibliothek: 1982 (1)* for the other parts, it could very well be from that time or even earlier. The revisions are extensive and sometimes run counter to the core of Schröder's principle of adaptation, e.g., cut or heavily reduced scenes have been reintroduced. Altogether, the written artefact is so worn out that it might indeed have been used until the 1840s. The manuscripts might have been thrown away at that point, or someone might have sold them or taken them home as souvenirs at one time or another. When it came to introducing *Hamlet*, first to Hamburg and then to the German-speaking world, printed books supported the amplification and proliferation of *Hamlet* euphoria. But in the *Hamlet* prompt book, print also merged with handwriting, creating a hybrid written artefact at the very centre of the *Hamlet* performances: in the prompter's box on stage.

Because the extensively researched[72] *Hamlet* prompt book *Theater-Bibliothek: 1982 (1)* was used for many decades, the entanglement between print and handwriting is not always easy to declutter or contextualise. For the purposes of this study, it is more feasible to demonstrate the crucial points with respect to more

---

70  Cf. Habicht 1994b, 50–55.
71  Cf. *Theater-Bibliothek*: 1982 (1), 3.
72  Cf. Häublein 2005, 70–91; cf. Malchow 2022, 284–333.

clear-cut cases: firstly, a handwritten Shakespeare prompt book in both its print and theatrical contexts (*Theater-Bibliothek: 571*); secondly a printed Shakespeare copy that was converted into a prompt book and enriched by hand for a specific occasion (*Theater-Bibliothek: 2029*).

## III. The 1776 *Othello*: Adapting *Theater-Bibliothek: 571* from Various Printed Sources

*Theater-Bibliothek: 571* is a prompt book that was handwritten by an unidentified scribe for Schröder's 1776 *Othello* production. It premiered on 26 November to build on the overwhelming success of *Hamlet*. In contrast to the *Hamlet* prompt book, hardly any traces of wear and tear are visible at first glance; instead, the prompt book displays just a few enrichments in Schröder's and the original scribe's hands. The prompt book was probably only put to use six times or less: for four performances in Hamburg in 1776 and for two guest performances in Hannover in January 1777.[73] While a production with more than one or two performances hardly qualified as a failure in the hustle and bustle of the Hamburg Stadt-Theater, its comparative lack of success meant that it differed markedly from *Hamlet*. There was no reason whatsoever to have a permanent version of the Hamburg adaptation published as a printed book in Schröder's own series. However, the manuscript can be examined with respect to the ways in which the production and upkeep of prompt books were situated at the intersection between the print culture of the time and the practicalities of running a theatre, especially meeting the demands of a live audience. There are extensive indications that the written artefact was reworked rather hectically at some point, probably after the second performance, but to little avail. Audience feedback was negative; attendance was dwindling.[74] The first impression had been as unfavourable as could be. Moreover, the use of *Theater-Bibliothek: 571* became tied to the most notorious scandal, i.e., audience upset, of Schröder's career when his *Othello* premiered in late November 1776.

Schröder's company staged *Othello* just five weeks after *Hamlet* and an even shorter time after it started performing Schröder's own adaptation of *Hamlet*, which still took some liberties. This time, however, Schröder would confront his audience with Shakespeare's unhappy ending. Together with *Hamlet*, *Lear*, and *Macbeth*, Shakespeare's tragedy *Othello* had been made out by Herder to be one of the bard's four most significant plays (in accordance with the English critics)[75]; it was also the nearest a Shakespeare tragedy came to a regular play reflecting

---

73 Cf. Häublein 2005, 129.
74 Cf. Schütze 1794, 453f.; cf. Häublein 2005, 132–141.
75 Cf. Herder 1993, 504–511.

eighteenth-century norms[76]: there were few changes of scenery; the plotline did not have to be altered drastically to avoid lengthy set conversions. An announcement of "neuer Kleidungen, neuer Theaterverzierungen"[77] [new clothes, new stage designs] indicated that the company had been investing heavily and planned to build on its success with the newly introduced author. Lawyer, critic, and author Christian H. Schmid had categorised *Othello* as a "bürgerliche Tragödie"[78] [bourgeois tragedy] in 1768, meaning that the play fitted in perfectly with Lessing's contemporary avantgarde plays, which Schröder wanted his audience to get used to.

It has so far been overlooked by research that, at a later point, while frantically revising the play, Schröder (or a collaborator) surprisingly seems to have consulted the English original – i.e., a printed book containing one of the contemporary English editions – on some minor points. But as in the case of *Hamlet*, Schröder started out working with, building on, or rejecting existing German adaptations in print, two of the latter in the case of *Othello*. Both of these German adaptations had received poor reviews, had had little influence so far, and were hardly ever staged.[79] They were still interesting starting points for Schröder since both presented themselves as modifications of Shakespeare's play, not as complete makeovers, and both freely made use of Wieland's translation, which they transformed into simpler sentences and fewer lines. Johann Heinrich Steffens's 1770 version, *Das Schnupftuch oder der Mohr von Venedig, Othello* [*The Handkerchief or the Moor of Venice, Othello*], focussed on the external action, deprived Othello of his dramatic fall from grace, and suggested that the brutishness of the foreign "Mohr" [Moor] was to blame for his unnecessary jealousy. According to the principle of poetic justice, which had already saved Heufeld's and Schröder's Hamlets, the innocent Desdemona was rescued before the mortified Othello committed suicide and died in Desdemona's (still) loving arms.[80] In contrast, the aforementioned 1769 adaptation by Christian H. Schmid aimed to make the tragedy playable with regard to the conditions of the German stage (i.e., its scene changes, linguistic standards, etc.) instead of amending it. His adaptation (which was published in a second 1772 edition and was bootlegged in 1769 and 1775) focussed on the internal action of Othello's jealousy. It reduced the number of locations, cut down on characters and subplots, and trimmed down the dialogue to pointed exchanges. Schmid's Othello did not hit Desdemona; her erotically charged strangulation became the more straightforward stabbing that German audiences were used to on stage. Critics largely panned Schmid's work because its reductions distorted the inner logic of

---

76 Cf. Häublein 2005, 95f.
77 Schütze 1794, 453.
78 Schmid 1768, 311.
79 Cf. Häublein 2005, 98–120.
80 Cf. Steffens 1770, 105–108.

the play. He prominently left out the pigment of Othello's skin and his foreign cultural background as the reasons for Othello being treated an outsider. He instead became a "bürgerliche[r] Kerl"[81] [bourgeois fellow] "von geringer Herkunft"[82] [from humble origins] in contrast to Shakespeare's noble "Moor". Othello thus had much less reason to fall for his ensign's seduction. The novelty of having a non-white character being something other than an exotic foil[83] had completely vanished.

To state the obvious, Schröder was immersed in a culture of printed books and journals. As he hastily adapted *Othello*, he was probably well aware of these two unsuccessful publications and their reception. That is how the two adaptations had come about within the context of printed Shakespeare books in German in the first place. Schröder therefore already had some notion of the problems that would need to be solved or avoided as he frantically put together his *Othello*. None of Schröder's notes or any trial version (such as those that exist for *Die Sonnen-Jungfrau*) have survived. But the version he came up with has been neatly written down in *Theater-Bibliothek: 571*. In the absence of an Eschenburg translation, Schröder largely relied on the language of Wieland's 1766 translation, with its in part streamlined and tightened-up dialogue. As for adapting the 1603 or 1604 play for the 1776 Hamburg stage, Schröder's fair copy steered clear of Steffens's semi-happy ending altogether. However, the sequencing of scenes relied relatively heavily on the way that Schmid had organised the play around the protagonist's inner turmoil. Schröder staged Wieland's text but generally followed Schmid's reorganisation of it, i.e., his omission of scenes and characters. Nevertheless, on the occasions when Schmid's cuts hindered understanding of the action or the characters, Schröder stuck with Wieland. Othello is a "Moor"; his initial authority and dignity are emphasised; the audience actually sees him slapping Desdemona, which now comes as a great shock, etc. But Schröder mitigated the provocative impact of Shakespeare's language in a fashion similar to Schmid's and also substituted Desdemona's death by strangulation with the stabbing proposed in Schmid's adaptation.

The ways in which Schröder's version merged the two printed book templates of Wieland and Schmid have been analysed elsewhere in great detail.[84] In the context of this study, it is the material dynamics of *Theater-Bibliothek: 571* that are of relevance. *Theater-Bibliothek: 571* consists of ninety-three folios stitched together using rough thread, mostly in quires of four bifolios. These are still in the original small quarto size, measuring 16.5 x 20.5 cm, with the inexpensive cardboard binding intact. The sprinkled yellowish-brown of the cardboard indicates that this written artefact was part of Schröder's personal collection. However, the num-

---

81 Schmid 1772, 161.
82 Schmid 1772, 154.
83 Cf. Sadji 1992, 117, 153–160.
84 Cf. Häublein 2005, 122–132.

ber of pages varies wherever one act ends and another begins. Since each new act begins at the start of a new quire, the final quire of the preceding act can differ in length. The final quire of the first act consists of three bifolios, but that of the third act of only two. At the end of the second and fourth acts, a single bifolio has been added. The folios were numbered later. Each character's dialogue has been written in *Kurrent* script (German cursive) in black ink, while all other parts of the text, such as the character names and the details of the act, scene, and plot, have been written in the blackletter script *of German Fraktur*, a standard practice to distinguish between the "primary text" and "secondary text". References to acts, entrances, locations, and the plot as well as the speaking characters' names have been twice underlined in reddish ink. Two vertical pencil lines to the left and right delineate the part of the page that was to be written on, and it is quite likely that the very orderly and easily readable text was written with the help of line marking.

While the overall organisation of what can be assumed to be the original fair copy of *Theater-Bibliothek: 571* before any revisions were made comes across as very neat, there is also some evidence that the creators were either pressed for time or were affected by some technical mishap. At the beginning of Act V, Scene 5, the scene with the grisly murder, the bifolio containing 82r to 83v has been written on in a different hand on darker, rougher paper. Here, the characters' lines are in German cursive as in the rest of the prompt book; the characters' names, however, are in Latin cursive instead of blackletter. On these pages, horizontal pencil lines are visible in addition to the vertical lines that delineated the margins and apparently served as a writing aid. Although this section looks like it was a later revision, an analysis of the stitching has shown that it was probably part of the book's original binding. It has been bound into the book in the usual manner, as the fourth of four bifolios in the quire. However, the handwriting is much untidier. There is no evidence whatsoever that the written artefact was first unbound and then rebound at some point, which would have been highly impractical and not worth the effort.[85] The bifolio either replaced one the other scribe had written on, or, for some reason, a replacement scribe filled in at the beginning of Act V, Scene 5. The latter seems more likely since the main scribe's transition to the next quire was as neat as could be. In both scribes' work, Schröder's original version of Act V, Scene 5, sticks closely to the text of Wieland's translation but mixes it with Schmid, e.g., by adopting the less formal "du" [thou] instead of Wieland's "Sie" [you]. It is on occasions like this that the fissures within a fair copy become visible: it is not a monolith but has been put together from heterogenous parts, which form a unit because they are bound together within one cover. (Cf. figure 48.)

---

85 Häublein assumes that the bifolio was part of the subsequent revision process. Cf. Häublein 2005, 122–124.

*Figure 48: O, 83v and 84r.*

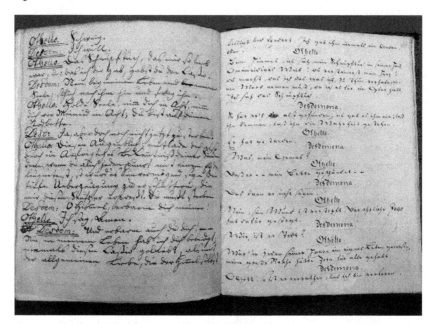

The fair copy had soon been enriched by numerous interventions: corrections, cuts, additions, sometimes written into, sometimes glued over the existing handwriting. These enrichments might have been part of the fine tuning carried out before the actors' parts were copied out or even during the rehearsal process. However, it seems more likely that they were part of hasty revisions made shortly after the premiere (and perhaps also after the repeat performance the following night). It is well known from historical sources that, shortly after its premiere, Schröder's *Othello* underwent fundamental changes. It is obvious in the case of some changes whether they were done before or after the disastrous first night. For some, this question cannot be answered. To take one example, Desdemona and Iago's quarrel about the nature of womanhood in Act II, Scene III, has been pasted over with new text. Wieland's translation has been replaced with a German version, in which Iago's lines come across as somehow more vernacular but also much coarser.[86] Since Schröder still included bits and pieces of the original translation in the revision after the premiere, and because some of it was glued in as well, the new song might also be part of the later revisions. But the update does not seem as dramaturgically necessary as other revisions.

---

86 Cf. O, 25r and v; cf. http://doi.org/10.25592/uhhfdm.13916 (Felser/Funke/Göing/Hussain/Schäfer/Weinstock/Bosch 2024, especially RFD08[HandwrittenTheatre]_Theater-Bibliothek571_OTHELLO_Masterdatei_xls.xlsx).

The opening night of the *Othello* production did not go to plan at all. What ensued was one of the most notorious scandals in German spoken-word theatre history. However, Schröder's *Othello* may have owed a great deal of its subsequent impact to the bombastic style in which Johann Heinrich Schütze reported on the first night in his *Hamburger Theater-Geschichte* [*Hamburg Theatre History*] some eighteen years after the fact:

> Ohnmachten über Ohnmachten erfolgten während der Graussszenen dieser ersten Vorstellung. Die Logenthüren klappten auf und zu, man gieng davon oder ward nothfalls davon getragen, und (beglaubten Nachrichten zu Folge) war die frühzeitige misglückte Niederkunft dieser und jener namhaften Hamburgerin Folge der Ansicht und Anhörung des übertragischen Trauerspiels.[87] [Faints upon faints occurred during the horrific scenes of that first performance. The doors of the boxes were flung open and slammed shut, people walked out or were carried out if necessary, and (according to certified reports) some notable Hamburg woman or other went into premature and unsuccessful childbirth as a result of viewing and hearing the tragic play.]

The veracity of the details notwithstanding, all contemporary sources agree with Schütze's account that the action had been too crass and too hopelessly negative. It was commonplace for the next day's playbill to be announced after the performance,[88] which would have given the audience a direct chance to complain. An additional performance the next day did not draw the expected crowd.[89] Afterwards, pointed rewrites took place in a very short space of time to save the *Othello* production from economic failure. New performances were scheduled for the next week.[90] As seems to have been customary, the creation of a new prompt book was avoided if the enrichment of the existing one was feasible. Thus, additional sheets and pieces of paper were glued into the existing prompt book; words, phrases, and complete scenes were crossed out and added; the plot was changed, and dialogue rewritten. All these material changes resulted in a "new" version of the play with a single goal: to give the rather gloomy play a happy ending by preventing Othello from tragically murdering his wife Desdemona in a jealous rage. Perhaps because he was pressed for time, Schröder surprisingly turned towards a print of the Steffens adaptation he had originally avoided.[91]

---

87 Schütze 1794, 454.
88 Cf. Malchow 2022, 113f.
89 Cf. Schütze 1794, 454.
90 Cf. Schütze 1794, 455; cf. Jahn/Mühle/Eisenhardt/Malchow/ Schneider (https://www.stadttheater.uni-hamburg.de).
91 Cf. Häublein 2005, 133f.

## IV. In Search of an Audience: Hasty Prompt Book Revisions in *Theater-Bibliothek: 571*

*Theater-Bibliothek: 571* is full of revisions until Act 5, Scene 5. But the prompt book does not contain the new (happier) ending that Schütze and all the other sources reported on. It can be safely assumed that the actors received their parts while the updated text was being inserted into the prompt book in the form of loose sheets – which was a common practice, traces of which can still occasionally be found at the Theater-Bibliothek.[92] While only the last scenes of the revised version seem to be missing, in the four and a half acts leading up to the murder, the folios contain significant elements of "an amending revision"[93] (in the words of Uwe Wirth). A "new" *Othello* was created with the help of glued-in, retracted, and newly added scenes that effected the rewriting of events and dialogue in the prompt book. These enrichments did not take place because the "old" *Othello* prompt book had been corrupted as a transcript or dramatic text, but because the production had not met the expectations of an audience that was consequently refusing to attend the theatre (and therefore not paying for tickets). The amendments correspond to what Uwe Wirth calls "late corrections" and "late cancellations"[94]: they were "strategic interventions" that were made locally but carried out in relation to an already existing textual whole, in reference to which "the validity of individual sections and parts of the text [was] decided".[95] In the case of *Othello*, these decisions were attempting to meet a twofold requirement: they had to take the expectations of the audience into account but also the norms of theatre aesthetics. The happier outcome of the play could not simply be proclaimed; it had to be motivated by preceding events. Therefore, the interventions not only had to change the action that would allow Desdemona to be rescued but also had to coherently pave the way for her rescue.

One example of a significantly changed scene can be found in Act IV, Scene 10, where a complete page has been glued over. Theoretically, a revision like this could have been part of the preparation process for the first night of the production. However, the content of the enrichment is clearly in line with the overall preparations for Desdemona's rescue. The handwriting can also be clearly attributed to Schröder himself, making it likelier that he was dealing with an emergency.[96]

---

92 Cf. Häublein 2005, 123.
93 "eines korrigierenden Überarbeitens", Wirth 2011, 23.
94 "Spätkorrekturen" and "Spätstreichungen", Wirth 2011, 32.
95 "strategische Eingriffe", "über die Geltung von einzelnen Abschnitten und Textteilen [entschieden] wird", Wirth 2011, 32.
96 We agree with Häublein 2005, 122f. However, the revisions in prompt books from the time under principal Schröder are often from his hand, emergency or not.

Restoration work carried out by the Staats- und Universitätsbibliothek Hamburg has revealed that the emphasis of the original transitional scene between Desdemona and her chambermaid Aemilia (Wieland's version of Shakespeare's Emilia) was lengthened and pasted over twice. In this minor transitional scene, Desdemona reproaches herself for having brought about her husband's increasingly threatening, jealous behaviour – without knowing exactly how: "Es ist billig, daß mir so mitgespielt wird, sehr billig; warum hab ich mich so aufgeführt, das er nur den Schatten eines Grundes zum allerkleinsten Mißtrauen gefunden hat!" (O, 71v) [It serves me right that I am mistreated in this fashion, very right; why have I acted in such a way that he has found only the shadow of a reason for the slightest mistrust!]. In the initial underlying version, Schröder had merged Schmid's template with Wieland's. The latter had used "billig" for Shakespeare's "'Tis meet I should be used." But Shakespearean Desdemona's open question as to "how" she had acted to provoke her husband becomes a self-reproach in Schmid's determinative "warum" [why][97]. (Cf. figure 49.)

*Figure 49: O, 71v, primary layer.*

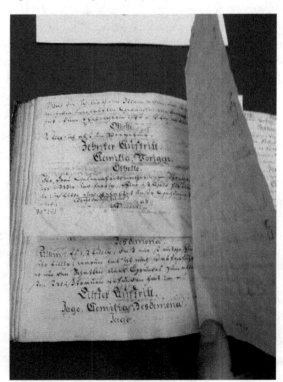

---

97  Wieland 2003, 750; Shakespeare 2016, 2141; Schmid 1772, 251.

Chapter 5. Prompt Book Practices in Context   161

In the course of the revisions, this scene was extended and re-accentuated: first, a narrow, blank strip of paper was used to cover up one of Aemilia's lines. Next to it, a note by Schröder written in dark ink was inserted: "12 Zeilen Plaz in den Rollen" [[Leave] 12 lines of space in the actors' parts]. This presumably referred to a planned (but not yet decided upon) change in the manuscripts to be handed out to the actors at a later point. These changes, or at least one of them, were then finally integrated into the prompt book. They were written on the second piece of paper glued into the book that now covered the whole page. The type of paper used in both cases was similar to the original; the new handwriting was, once again, Schröder's. The visual organisation of the glued-in page suggests that these changes were carried out somewhat hastily: the notes about the scene and its characters have been added right in the middle of Othello's lines in the preceding scene, while the names of the characters have been neither underlined in red nor spelled out entirely. However, the distinction between the two types of script has been retained, although it is now between German and Latin cursive. (Cf. figure 50.)

*Figure 50: O, 71v, glued over.*

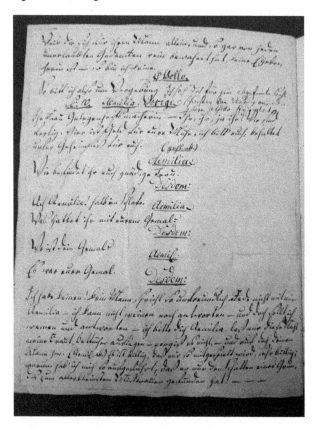

While the focus of Schröder's original version is Desdemona's self-reproach, in the new version, she urges Aemilia to fetch her husband of all people, the conniving Iago, and "diese Nacht meine Braut bettücher auflegen" [to put out my bridal sheets this night]. At this point, Schröder (or a collaborator) seems to have consulted an English Shakespeare edition available in print.[98] (Schröder could easily have asked someone to bring one back from London or could have come into possession some other way.) By faithfully following his template, Warburton's controversial 1740s *Works of Shakespeare*,[99] Wieland's translation had left out the lines "Prithee tonight / Lay on my bed my wedding sheets"[100] – with all their importance for the psychological minutiae, i.e., the subsequent sexualised strangulation. Accordingly, the lines had also been left out in both Schmid's and Steffens's Wieland adaptations. In order to consult Eschenburg's revision of Wieland, Schröder would have had to have waited some time until 1777, but he clearly chose a leaner version than Eschenburg's later "Diesen Abend lege doch die Bettücher von meiner Brautnacht auf mein Bette"[101] [This evening, why don't you lay the sheets of my bridal night on my bed].

The reintroduction of Shakespearean text by Schröder stresses the disruption to Desdemona's and Othello's relationship. The upcoming night is now built up as a crucial moment in the plot. Importantly, Aemilia is already involved in the events. At the end of the scene, she emphatically tells the audience about her concern regarding Desdemona's peculiar behaviour. A few scenes later, this concern will allow her to sense the danger hovering above her mistress, to get help, and to save her from being murdered. The corrections in Act IV, Scene 10, were made as a combined addition of text and paper because the changes could not have been inserted in any other way. Although the everyday practices of the theatre business almost certainly led to enrichments in the prompt book at some point, the visual organisation of most prompt books is not conducive to such change. Neither margins, nor line spacing, nor any other formatting allowed for any more extensive enrichments. Paste-ins therefore provided space to revise the content of the corrected section and thereby visually erased the original version. Because of this visual erasure of the replaced text, such "over-pasting" differs from the far more common corrective procedure of adding a changed text as close as possible to the passage to be replaced not only materially but also in terms of its "graphic dimension", i.e., in terms of the "conditions for perceiving the crossed-out expres-

---

98  Schröder's biographer claims that it was 1779 when Schröder started reading English editions of Shakespeare. Cf. Meyer 1819a, 290.

99  Cf. Warburton 1769. Despite the early English criticism of Warburton's opinionated edition (cf. Edwards 1970, from 1748) Wieland followed his mentor Bodmer's recommendation and chose Warburton as a template. Cf. Kofler 2008, 394.

100  Shakespeare 2016, 2141; cf. Warburton 1769, 262–265; cf. Wieland 2003, 749–751.

101  Eschenburg 1779, 165f.

sion"¹⁰². In most cases, the cancelled validity has been signalled by one of the most common forms of cancellation, where what has been cancelled has been marked but not erased – and thus remains legible as something that has been retracted.¹⁰³

Most corrections in *Theater-Bibliothek: 571* are of the latter type. With regard to the plot, they accelerate the action and intensify the tension, sometimes outdoing Shakespeare, Wieland, and his adapters. At the end of Act III, Scene 9, Othello no longer wants his wife's supposed lover out of the way "in den nächsten dreyen Tagen" [in the next three days] (as it says in the fair copy that follows Wieland, who is taken up by both Schmid and Steffens) but "in dieser Nacht" (O, 54v) [this night] in the revision, which intensifies the plot and at the same time emphasises the character's determination and willingness to use violence. On the other hand, Othello's desire to kill Desdemona has been somewhat downplayed. Schröder's Othello originally wanted "auf ein schnelles Mittel denken, den schönen Teufel aus der Welt zu schaffen" [to think of a quick means to rid the world of the beautiful devil] as in Wieland and all other sources. Now, after the revision, Othello first wants to be convinced of the legitimacy of his jealousy, i.e., "von der Schandtat mit dem Schnupftuche aus ihrem eignen Munde überzeugt werden" (O, 55r) [to hear of the infamy with the handkerchief from her own mouth]. (Cf. figure 51.)

*Figure 51: O, 54v and 55r.*

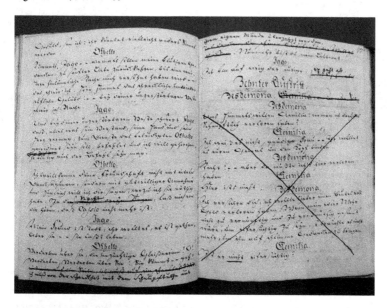

---

102 "graphischen Dimension", "Wahrnehmungsbedingungen des gestrichenen Ausdrucks", Wirth 2011, 26.
103 Cf. Grésillon 2010, 289f.

In order to relieve the now heightened tension, Schröder followed Steffens at the end of Act IV. The chamber maid Aemilia realises that Desdemona's life is in acute danger. At this point, an entire additional scene inspired by Steffens, for which there is no template in Wieland, Shakespeare, or Schmid, has been inserted on top of a page habitually left blank at the end of the act, i.e., text has been added without the addition of any extra paper. On the previous manuscript page, an indication that Act IV is going to end has been retracted, and a small manicule has been inserted to signal the addition: Aemilia remains alone on stage; in a soliloquy she expresses her concern for her mistress and ponders if there is a way out (cf. figure 52).

*Figure 52: O, 77v and 78r.*

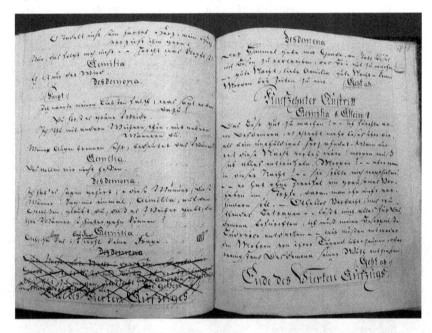

The template now being used was Steffens's. In his adaptation, Aemilia's vigilance paves the way for Desdemona's survival. Schröder not only shortened Steffens's scene but made it more pointed. In Steffens's version, Aemilia's meditations on what is about to happen had been mostly informative and explanatory:

> Mein Herz sagt es mir, es ist ein Unglück unterwegs. Wenn nur erst diese Nacht vorbey wäre. Morgen soll sich vieles ändern. [...] Seine Eifersucht ist reif und sie kann bald, bald in Wuth und Grausamkeit ausbrechen. Wer so weit gegangen ist, der besinnet sich auch nicht lange, weiter zu gehen. Warum soll ich weggeschickt werden? War es ihm doch sonst nicht zuwider, wenn ich ganze Nächte hindurch an der Seite seiner Schlafkammer bey ihr blieb. Er hat ohne Zweifel ein grausames

Vorhaben im Kopfe, daran ich ihn nicht verhindern soll. Gut, daß ich daran denke; ich muß Schildwache halten, und fleißig patrulliren. Die kleine Thür hinter der Tapete soll mir den Eingang eröfnen, wenn es nöthig seyn sollte. Vor allen Dingen aber muß ich mit unsern beyden Gästen Abrede nehmen.[104] [My heart tells me there is a disaster on the way. If only this night were over. Tomorrow, much will change. [...] His jealousy is ripe and could soon, soon break out in rage and cruelty. He who has gone so far does not have to think long about going further. Why should I be sent away? At other times, he had no problem with me staying with her all night long at the side of his bedchamber. He undoubtedly has a cruel plan in mind, which he does not want me to hinder. It is good that I realise this; I must keep watch and stay diligent on my patrol. The small door behind the wallpaper shall act as an entrance for me if necessary. Above all, however, I must make arrangements with our two guests.]

Schröder's version of the soliloquy dramatizes Aemilia's realisation into an inner back-and-forth, making it more pressing. She is now already planning to get help should the worst come to pass:

Das Böse gut zu machen! – – ich fürchte arme Desdemona, es schwebt mehr böses über dir, als dein unschuldiges Herz ahndet. Wenn nur erst diese Nacht vorbey wäre! morgen muß sich alles entwickeln. Morgen? – – aber wenn in dieser Nacht? – – sie sollte mich wegschicken! – – er hat ohne Zweifel ein grausames Vorhaben im Kopfe, daran man ihn nicht verhindern soll. – – Othellos Verdacht, und wüthendes Betragen – – läßt mich alles für Desdemona befürchten, ich muß meine Besorgniße Ludovico entdecken – – wir müßen entweder den Mohren von ihrer Tugend überzeugen, oder wenigstens Desdemona seiner Wuth entziehen. (O, 78r) [To make evil good! – – I fear, poor Desdemona, there is more evil hovering over you than your innocent heart suspects. If only this night were over! Tomorrow everything must unfold. Tomorrow? – – but if this night? – – she was to send me away! – – he has no doubt a cruel plan in mind, which he does not want to be prevented from carrying out. – – Othello's suspicions and angry behaviour – – make me fear all for Desdemona, I must reveal my concerns to Ludovico – – we must either convince the Moor of her virtue, or at least remove Desdemona from his rage.]

As mentioned before, we must reconstruct how exactly Desdemona was recused in *Othello* from contemporary accounts. There are no further revisions in *Theater-Bibliothek: 571* after a certain point in the fifth act. Nevertheless, this very point is precisely the one at which the decisive twist has been added. It is the simple, almost inconspicuous crossing-out of three words that, however, points to the

---

104 Steffens 1770, 86f.

greatest possible change in content. Towards the end of Act V, Scene 5, in the fair copy, Desdemona is murdered – as she is in Wieland and Schmid as well. Her pleas for Othello to desist from his terrible deed, or to at least to postpone it, go unheard. Accordingly, the prompt book contains the respective instruction as adapted from Schmid: "Er sticht sie" (O, 84v) [He stabs her]. Since Desdemona is now to survive, the instruction can no longer apply. Five small ink strokes have struck through the stage direction – and therefore the decisive moment of revision in the *Othello* prompt book. Due to the previous interventions inspired by Steffens, this kind of change is now dramaturgically plausible. They signify nothing less than the fact that the deed has been omitted: Othello does not stab her after all. The material performance and the stage performance, i.e., the inobtrusive material revisions and radical interventions into the course of the action in *Othello*, could not be any further apart at this moment (cf. figure 53).

*Figure 53: O, 84v.*

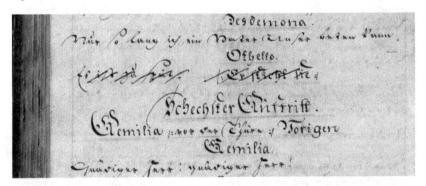

After this, the revisions stop. The stage direction "giebt ihr noch einige Stiche" (O, 85r) [gives her several more stabs][105] on the next folio has not been retracted. Getting the revised version to the actors seems to have taken priority at this point. As stated above, the prompter probably made do with loose sheets for the next performances. After that, the prompt book was no longer needed.

The revision practices used during the enrichment of *Theater-Bibliothek: 571* can be distinguished with respect to their form but were identical in their effect: they suspended certain parts of the dramatic text and, if necessary, substituted updated content. At the same time, they demonstrate how this dramatic text in the prompt book may have been the basis of the performance but was also an object of use in everyday theatre practice. It therefore had to be adapted to the circumstances, i.e., specific requirements. These requirements were not only artistic or

---

105 Schröder increases the intensity from Schmid's single "giebt ihr noch einen Stich" [stabs her once more] (Schmid 1772, 275).

technical but also social: in the case of *Othello*, it was first the intervention and then the absence of the paying audience that effected the transformation of the prompt book. Viewer expectations and habits, which are interwoven with poetic norms of representation, have thus been inscribed into the Hamburg *Othello* prompt book through very concrete material practices. But it was the choice of printed German Shakespeare translations, adaptations, and perhaps even an English edition of the "original" Shakespeare that these practices took up, collated, and transformed.

## V. Prompt Books on the Censor's Desk: Handwriting, Print, and Shakespeare

It was not only the paying audience that necessitated the handwritten revisions in the prompt books for the Hamburg Shakespeare performances. As explained in Chapter 4 with regard to *Die Sonnen-Jungfrau*, the company also had to take the authorities into account. Obscene or seditious language or actions were not permitted. Unlike in Vienna, the Hamburg prompt books of the time do not seem to have been submitted to a common approval procedure. There are no signs of acceptance or rejection in the written artefacts. There are no indications of visits from the authorities to control whether the text spoken on stage was the same as the one that had been permitted.[106] This by no means indicates that a more liberal attitude was being taken. Schröder's private company was in many respects in a much more precarious position than, for example, the Vienna court theatre. The ability to obtain performance permits depended on a whole range of factors. There was, for example, an entrenched tradition of hostility towards the theatre in the Hamburg clergy. It was near impossible to put on performances on weekends or during Lent.[107] Interventions such as Schröder's downplaying of the pregnancy in *Die Sonnen-Jungfrau* and his mitigation of Shakespeare's coarse language probably addressed demands being made by the paying audience and Hamburg authorities at the same time.

However, towards the end of Schröder's life, there was an official censorship office in place for three years, from 1811 to 1814. Schröder still owned the theatre (and the prompt books)[108] but, in 1798, he had retired from his position as principal and actor to a country estate at the gates of Hamburg. However, from 1811 to 1812, Schröder came out of retirement for more than a year. The aim was presumably to utilise his national and international prominence to improve the standing of the

---

106 Cf. Pieroth 2018, 19–22. For theatre censorship in general, cf. Wagner 2023.
107 Cf. Malchow 2022, 31–46.
108 Cf. Uhde 1879, 6f.

company in view of rising censorship pressures.[109] The revival of one of his Shakespeare productions from the late 1770s is perhaps the most prominent example of this, which we will discuss in detail below.

The French army had captured Hamburg in 1806. As the capital of the newly founded Bouches-de-l'Elbe department, the city formed part of the French Empire from late 1810 until the expulsion of the occupying forces in 1814. Napoleon decreed the reintroduction of censorship in France in 1810; the new laws were applied in the new territories in the course of 1811.[110] The central Direction de l'imprimerie et de la librairie [Department of Printing and Publishing] in Paris had a Hamburg-based agency that was closely aligned with the local police. Besides controlling printing and bookselling, the agency's resident censor was former Hamburg journalist Johann Philipp Nick (1777–1815),[111] who was responsible for newspapers and all published literature, as well as for the stage. Playbills, which advertised the venue, the date, and the name of the play, needed to be bilingual. An overall list of the plays to be performed had to be presented to Nick's supervisor, Louis-Philippe Brun d'Aubignosc, for approval. D'Aubignosc had the power to prohibit the performance of a play and to close down a theatre if his orders met with resistance. He could also intervene after the fact in the event that an approved play was deemed to have had an undesirable effect upon the public.[112]

As the local censor, Nick would note down pages in need of changes, suggest and insert amendments, and sign the final version with "vu et approuvé" [seen and approved] by "Nick censeur" [censor Nick] or simply "Nick". The 136 written artefacts that bear the censor's, i.e., Nick's, signature[113] account for nearly all the plays known to have been performed during his tenure from 1811 to 1814. The overwhelming bulk of them have been signed with the aforementioned "vu et approuvé" in black or brown ink. In various prompt books, page numbers have been listed on one of the final pages, referring to pages with objectionable content. They contain minor or major annotations as well as edits but – as in the case of *Die Sonnen-Jungfrau* – do not seem to have been made by Nick himself. Only in very few cases did prompt books include rejection notices: the most explicit one is on display in Gustav Hagemann's 1790 one-act-comedy *Leichtsinn und Edelmuth* [Frivolity and Magnanimi-

---

109  Cf. Meyer 1819b, 317–322.
110  Cf. Hellmich 2014, 123–124.
111  Cf. Schröder/Klose 1870, 519; cf. Hellmich 2014, 30f.
112  Cf. Hellmich 2014, 124–27.
113  Cf. Stoltz 2016 and according to the index of the Hamburg Staatsbibliothek "Handschriftenkatalog". Stoltz counts 135 because he does not yet include the *König Lear* prompt book analysed below. The written artefact clearly belongs to the Theater-Bibliothek but was found by one of the authors of this study in the general inventory of the Hamburg Staatsbibliothek in 2015 (based on references in Drews 1932 and Hoffmeier 1964). It has since been included in the special collection.

*ty*]. It had been performed on a regular basis until 1798 but was deemed by Nick to be too critical of the military. His rather genial commentary on the last page reads:

> In einem monarchischen Staate kann und darf der Soldatenstand als kein Unglück betrachtet werden. Der 15. Auft[ritt] wirft auf jeden Fall ein ungünstiges Licht auf ihn. Die anderen Scenen sind nicht gantz von diesem Vorwurfe frei. Sie werden es mir daher nicht übelnehmen hochzuverehrender Herr Director! wenn ich dieses Lustspiel nicht genehmigen kann.[114] [In a monarchy, the military cannot and must not be regarded as a misfortune. In any case, the 15th scene shows it in an unfavourable light. The other scenes are not entirely free of this reproach. You will therefore not hold it against me, Honourable Director! if I cannot approve this comedy.]

In general, plays needed to avoid statements that could be construed as being critical of France and all things French. Enemies like the English were best not mentioned – or at least not drawn in a favourable light. Words such as "homeland", "patriotism", "freedom", "tyranny", "oppression", etc. were to be avoided. As a matter of consequence, the agency tended to reject works by popular authors such as Friedrich Schiller wholesale.[115] However, Schröder and others found that many of the plays that reached Nick's desk were treated with a great deal of good will and attention to detail, while other plays hardly suffered any interventions at all.[116]

Whereas Nick signed off on the somewhat revised prompt books that had been in use for decades for *Die Sonnen-Jungfrau* and *Hamlet*, some other written artefacts that bear his signature look like they were newly produced copies instead of the existing prompt books of long-term productions. The previously used prompt books had possibly been worn out by their long-term use; the information stored in them might have been deemed too valuable to be messed around with by a (perhaps) temporary occupying power. An additional layer of writing by an outside hand was always at risk of rendering the prompt book as a whole illegible and thus unsuitable for practical use. When the theatre company feared a play might be problematic, Nick seems to have received freshly created written artefacts, i.e., prompt books that were produced from scratch and then – once they had Nick's signature of approval – further amended during what was sometimes decades of use.

In fifteen instances, the company did not create a new manuscript at all but used an existing print copy of the respective play as a basis. Usually, the print copy was not interleaved in order to prevent it from becoming too bulky to be handled in the prompt box. However, it was given a new cover and one or two extra sheets for blank

---

114 *Theater-Bibliothek*: 477, 34v; cf. Stoltz 2016.
115 Cf. Stoltz 2016. (Dominik Stoltz was part of the team that compiled the Theater-Bibliothek index but has only published this blogpost.)
116 Cf. *Allgemeine Zeitung* 1815, 1236.

pages in the front and back. The print was then enriched in handwriting that added technical information or changes to the content of the play. The print copy thus served as the primary layer of a hybrid printed and handwritten document. Revising a print copy was convenient (and common practice) whenever the stage adaptation of a play would not differ greatly from a published version of a text. Most of the fifteen "hybrid" prompt books signed off on by Nick were commercially successful (and politically non-threatening) comedies that had been part of the Hamburg repertory for a long period of time. Submitting a prompt book based on a print copy also conveyed the not-so-subtle point that a work allowed in print should also be allowed on stage.

Submitting a print-based prompt book also made sense in cases where the theatre company itself had published a particularly successful stage adaptation, as had been the case for some of the Hamburg Shakespeare productions back in the 1770s. Although the intellectual discourse and debate on Shakespeare had moved on since the 1790s, these adaptations were still the ones being performed in the 1810s. Out of the five Shakespearean plays performed under Nick's aegis, two were classified as comedies (the 1777 *Kaufmann von Venedig* [*Merchant of Venice*] and the 1792 *Viel Lärmen um Nichts* [*Much Ado About Nothing*]) and made use of the original revised handwritten artefacts (the inspection book *Theater-Bibliothek: 429a* for the *Merchant*, the prompter's version *Theater-Bibliothek: 948b* for *Much Ado*). With *Hamlet*, the company itself had switched to a print copy of Schröder's own version at some point, probably in the 1780s. As a family drama (and without the Fortinbras plot), there was little that could have unsettled the censor. Two other Shakespearean plays with potentially problematic content, however, were submitted to the censor as print copies with handwritten enrichments. Like *Hamlet*, Schröder's 1770s Hamburg adaptations of *Maaß für Maaß* [*Measure for Measure*] and *König Lear* had both privileged the family drama over the political dimension, but they still included tales of revolutionary struggle that could have been deemed problematic by the French authorities. Submitting them as print copies with handwritten enrichments thus meant less work for the scribes in the event of a possible rejection. If they were accepted, the company would now take the print copy as a starting point for the new prompt book. The resulting hybrid of print copy and multi-layered handwriting by multiple users made it easier to distinguish between the starting version (i.e., the play submitted to Nick), the additions made for the censor, and possible responses and counteractions. Additional technical information could then be seamlessly added at a later point in time.

## VI. A 1778 *König Lear* Print Copy and Its 1812 Context

The 1812 prompt book for *König Lear, Theater-Bibliothek: 2029*, is of special interest. This print copy with handwritten enrichments has been preserved at the Theater-Bibliothek, while former versions that may have been in use from the 1770s to the 1800s have not survived. Against the backdrop of French censorship, it seems at first rather curious that an adaptation of William Shakespeare's tragedy was performed at all – and frequently at that: five times in the course of 1812.[117] This play by a playwright from one of France's enemy nations is set in a mythical (or early medieval) England and portrays the disintegration of authority, various instances of brutal upheaval, and the invasion of a French army.[118] Many of the red flags that Nick's censorship office disapproved of can be found here. On the other hand, it had by this point been more than a decade since Shakespeare had been appropriated by the German Romantics. He was widely considered to be more at home in the German-speaking world than in the London theatre districts.[119] In the growing Romantic imagination, the England-based *Lear* plot had more the makings of a fairy tale than of an analogy of current political events. Above all, Schröder's own performance as the lead character had arguably been his greatest critical achievement as an actor from the 1770s to the 1790s.[120] Next to its success on a national level (aided by some guest performances in Mannheim and Vienna), it also received a three-page description in Mme de Staël's 1810 famous, quasi-ethnographic exploration of Germany for the French reading public, *De l'Allemagne [On Germany]*.[121] Despite the subsequent ban on de Staël's work, its stunning initial success would have contributed to whatever standing Schröder's Shakespeare-adaptations had with the French censorship office in Hamburg.

---

117 According to the playbills accessible on Jahn/Mühle/Eisenhardt/Malchow/Schneider (https://www.stadttheater.uni-hamburg.de), performances took place on 13, 20, 22, and 25 March as well as on 11 May and 28 October.

118 Cf. Shakespeare 2016, 2507–2513, 2540–2543, 2549f.

119 Cf. Habicht 1994a; cf. Paulin 2003, 211–296; cf. Blinn 1982.

120 Schröder's performance was generally considered to have set a new benchmark for a psychologically intricate, subtly nuanced, yet immediately comprehensible style of acting. For a comprehensive analysis of Schröder's König Lear, his acting style, and its contexts, cf. Hoffmeier 1964, 119–266; cf. Schäfer 2017. From 1778 to 1827, *König Lear* was performed fifty-four times in Hamburg based on Schröder's adaptation: nine in 1778; four in 1779; three in 1780; three in 1786; one each in 1787 and 1788; two in 1789; one in 1790; two in 1791, 1793, 1794 and 1795; one in 1796; two in 1798; three each in 1802 and 1806; five in 1812; two in 1816; one each in 1817 and 1818; two in 1819; and one each in 1822, 1823, and 1827. Schröder played Lear for the last time in 1798. Cf. Jahn/Mühle/Eisenhardt/Malchow/Schneider (https://www.stadttheater.uni-hamburg.de).

121 Cf. de Staël Holstein 1810, 293–96.

After the failure of his 1776 *Othello*, Schröder initially refrained from staging the other "great" tragedies. But he had not given up on the idea of establishing Shakespeare on the Hamburg stage, preferably with an at least similar ending to the ones known from the printed books. Schröder took time to prepare his audience. In 1777, the company staged two Shakespearean plays. Both were classified as comedies at the time and had their own finales. However, they both included a dark and tragic subplot for some of the characters, which Schröder accentuated. In *Der Kaufmann von Venedig* [*The Merchant of Venice*], Schröder shortened the love story and strengthened the parts of the plot in which Antonio's life is under threat. He kept the happy ending, of course, but toned down the serenity and reconciliatory mood that it had in the original and the print translations.[122] In *Maaß für Maaß*, which has been considered a model example of a hard-to-classify Shakespearean "problem play" since the twentieth century, Schröder got rid of the entire premise of his template: the near-tragic end to Angelo's rule was now no longer a test of his skill; Schröder's duke did not intervene by chance alone. Instead, the duke was now portrayed from the outset as an energetic figure who then learns about his regent's misdeeds. What had been a lucky interference in Shakespeare thus became a hero's intervention in Schröder.[123] While the content of the handwritten prompt book *Theater-Bibliothek: 514* had originally been classified as the "Lustspiel" [comedy] that it had been in Wieland's print translation, the first syllable was crossed out at some point and changed into a simple "Schauspiel" [play][124].

Overall, it seems as if Schröder made use of his audience's preference for comedies to get them used to the more serious aspects of Shakespeare. In July 1778, Schröder ventured into the "great" tragedies once more. It was not only his renowned acting skills that allowed not-yet-thirty-four-year-old Schröder to shine as the aging king – he also chose a different approach from that of *Othello*. The adapted Lear that he developed in collaboration with his brother-in-law Johann Christoph Unzer[125] was a less complex character than Shakespeare's had been. The first scenes in which the old absolute monarch gives away his kingdom to his two evil daughters while banishing the loving one to exile were turned into a messenger's report. The audience first encountered Lear as a frail man who had been mistreated at the hands of his children. As in *Hamlet*, the political dimension of the play faded into the background while the family conflict received greater attention. There was no trace left of the Shakespearean ambivalence. Schröder's Lear implored

---

122 Cf. Hoffmeier 1964, 120.
123 Cf. Hoffmeier 1964, 120f.
124 *Theater-Bibliothek: 514*, title page (recto of folio 1, but numbered differently in the written artefact itself).
125 Cf. Drews 1932, 27.

compassion; he died of exhaustion and old age rather than grief.[126] Having learned from the audience's reaction to Desdemona's death, Schröder also saved Lear's innocent and loving daughter Cordelia. Instead of having a mourning Lear carry her murdered corpse out onto the stage, Cordelia merely fainted and remained unconscious in Schröder's initial version. For the Hamburg audience, however, this was still too ambiguous, as several sources report. An actor playing a corpse could hardly be distinguished from an actor pretending to have blacked out. In response to the protests (even though they were milder than those regarding Desdemona's death), Schröder had Cordelia wake up at the end – only to lay eyes on her deceased father and dramatically faint once more.[127] Now, there was no doubt that she was still alive but had fainted as she glimpsed the horror, much like the female audience members were rumoured to have done in the case of *Othello*.[128]

Shortly after the play's initial success, Schröder had the version in which Cordelia's fainting had been further mitigated published as a printed book "nach Shakespear"[129] [after Shakespeare]. In 1781, it also became part of his *Hamburgisches Theater* series.[130] It was soon reenacted at other German theatres, but also received competition from another German *Lear* with an even happier ending. Schröder's former collaborator, Johann Christian Bock, produced a version of *König Lear* at the Leipzig court theatre in 1779 in which Lear survived and took the reins once more.[131] Bock's adaptation was soon also available in print.[132] Theatres sometimes performed hybrids of the two and published a bootlegged printed book that mixed the two templates.[133]

In Hamburg, Schröder's version was last performed in 1827, nearly fifty years after its premiere. But generally speaking, Schröder's and Bock's adaptations persisted on German stages until the 1840s.[134] In retrospect, this is surprising as the intellectual discourse about Shakespeare had shifted dramatically since the late 1790s. There was a new paradigm for the German Shakespeare in print! Starting in the mid-1790s, August Wilhelm Schlegel (in collaboration with his partner, Caroline Böhmer, and with theoretical input from his brother Friedrich) had taken a lead role in the early German Romantics' translations of Shakespeare according to aesthetic and poetic principles, i.e., in metric form instead of Wieland's and Eschenburg's prose. The Romantics no longer revered Shakespeare as "nature's child" but for the

---

126 Cf. Schäfer 2016, 528–533.
127 Cf. Schröder 1778c, 110; cf. Hoffmeier 1964, 142f.
128 Cf. Schäfer 2018, 49.
129 Cf. Schröder 1778c, 1.
130 Cf. Schröder 1781.
131 Cf. Schäfer 2016, 528–539.
132 Cf. Bock 1779.
133 Cf. Bock/Schröder 1779.
134 Cf. Drews 1932, 92f.; cf. Gazdar 1979, 227–231.

artistry of his language and plot construction. While the new translation captured previously overlooked dimensions of Shakespeare, it also adjusted the plays to reflect the new aesthetic trends. The more drastic aspects of Shakespeare were still softened but also sublated into a highly stylised language that closely resembled the one that the now older Goethe and Schiller were working on for the Weimar stage. In addition, the proto-naturalistic acting style that Schröder had championed in Hamburg was no longer considered avantgarde. In a lot of places, it had gone out of fashion in favour of emphatically artificial delivery, i.e., "declaiming" lines, which fitted in well with the aesthetics of the new print translations.[135]

However, such differences were not clear-cut oppositions. The Schlegel translation took time to become established among readers and more so on the stage. Schlegel himself temporarily stopped translating in 1804, after finishing a good half of the plays, and then came to a complete stop in 1810.[136] The circle surrounding Ludwig Tieck began by completing the Romantic translation in 1817, but did not finish until the 1830s, with their German *König Lear* only appearing in 1832.[137] Rival translations did not catch on. The Wieland approach to Shakespearean language often existed alongside the Romantic one, while Schröder's approach to theatre persisted alongside the one put into practice in Berlin and Weimar. At the height of the Weimar "Classicism" period, in 1806, Goethe commissioned Johann Heinrich Voß, son of the renowned translator of Homer, to translate *King Lear* in the Romantic mould. Voß delivered the translation (and then swiftly published it in print),[138] but Goethe then relied on Schröder's tested stage adaptation after all.[139] Vice versa, Schröder's 1777 prose version of the *Kaufmann von Venedig* [*Merchant of Venice*] was performed seven times during its first year and then twenty-five more times from 1781 to 1822. Six took place during the French censorship period. But at some point, the pasted-in pieces of paper that enriched prompt book *Theater-Bibliothek: 429b* started following the text of Schlegel's 1799 metric translation. This was probably for purely pragmatic reasons: the Schlegel edition was what the guest actor playing Shylock from 1816 onwards was used to.[140] With respect to the Hamburg *Hamlet*, the preserved playbills show that the Schlegel translation was performed twenty-six times between 1830 and 1850. (It has survived as prompt and inspection book *Theater-Bibliothek: 1982 (2) a&b*.) But until 1843, there were also six performances of the 1770s Schröder adaptation, with fifteen performances of Schlegel during the same period.[141]

---

135 Cf. Heeg 1999.
136 Cf. Paulin 2003, 315–330.
137 Cf. Paulin 2003, 344–348; cf. Baudissin 1832.
138 Cf. Voß 1806.
139 Cf. Ermann 1983, 224–226, 231.
140 Cf. Eickmeyer 2017, 102f.
141 Cf. Jahn/Mühle/Eisenhardt/Malchow/Schneider (https://www.stadttheater.uni-hamburg.de).

## Chapter 5. Prompt Book Practices in Context 175

Although no longer considered avantgarde in intellectual circles around the turn of the nineteenth century, the Hamburg theatre largely stuck to Schröder's aesthetics and continued to enjoy some success with the audience. However, theirs was no longer an educational mission. Accordingly, in-house adaptations no longer made it from the handwritten prompt book to the published printed book. One last attempt had been Schröder's *Maaß für Maaß* adaptation. Having been a steady part of the repertory from the end of 1777 to autumn 1778 (i.e., shortly after the premiere of their *König Lear*), the production was dropped until March 1789. After four performances that year, Schröder had his (rather liberal) adaptation published in 1790, a few years before the onset of the Romantic project. This time, "von Schröder" [by Schröder] was added to "nach Shakespeare" [after Shakespeare][142]. The prompt book *Theater-Bibliothek: 514* is the handwritten 1777 prompt book that was used originally and then slightly revised, probably for the 1789 reprisal. It then provided the content for the 1790 print version, which was part of a new publication series of plays as adapted by Stadt-Theater. After only one additional performance of *Maaß für Maaß* in 1791, two performances in early 1813 under French censorship were the last times that Schröder's adaptation, and Shakespeare's *Measure for Measure* altogether, were performed in Hamburg for decades. On these two occasions, a print copy of Schröder's adaptation provided the basis of the prompt book handed in to the censor and signed off by him, *Theater-Bibliothek: 948a*. What seems to be the inspection book, but may also have been used as a draft to try out the changes for the censor, was also based on a print copy, *Theater-Bibliothek: 948b*.[143] In 1813, hardly any changes seem to have been deemed necessary or required by the censor. It was only at the very end that Schröder's more heroic duke received four additional, probably explanatory handwritten lines. An initial draft has been erased before the final one is also written out in graphite pencil in the inspection book. It was probably then copied into the prompt book in ink. In contrast to Schröder's published adaptation, the duke no longer has the final word, which goes to the people, who applaud his rule – and thus affirm any authority, including that of the occupying French forces: "Es lebe unser Herzog!"[144] [Long live our duke!] – Such was the context in which, one year earlier, Schröder's *König Lear* had been staged. Schröder no longer played the lead but was at the helm of the theatre once more, on the brink of his final retirement.

---

142 Schröder 1790, 1.
143 While text and layout in both copies are identical, only *Theater-Bibliothek: 948b* has the date of publication, the publisher and the "nach Schröder" on its first page. *Theater-Bibliothek: 948a*, with only "Maaß für Maaß / Ein Schauspiel in fünf Aufzügen / nach Shakespear", could very well be a readily available bootlegged version.
144 *Theater-Bibliothek: 948a*, 125; *Theater-Bibliothek: 948b*, 125.

## VII. Appeasing the Censor: The Handwritten Revision of *Theater-Bibliothek: 2029* in 1812

It was against this political and aesthetic backdrop that Nick, the censor, received a revised print copy of the original, fabled, but now old-fashioned 1778 *König Lear*, *Theater-Bibliothek: 2029*. The company used a copy of the original 1778 print edition rather than one of the 1781 or 1785 editions.[145] Next to the printed "after Shakespeare", Schröder's own hand had added "von Schröder" [by Schröder] in black ink on the title page: the famous principal was not so much asking to stage a play by the English enemy as he was stressing the local aspect of the play (and his authority as a renowned artist). As a whole, *Theater-Bibliothek: 2029* consists of fifty-nine folios, fifty-five of which (4–58) are the printed pages. In addition, some empty sheets have been glued inside the front and back of a similar, sprinkled yellowish-brown cover to that of the *Othello* prompt book, i.e., a prompt book that Schröder considered part of his personal collection. In black ink, a faded sticker on the cover not only states the title "König Lear" and the numbers of an earlier index (47 29) but also clearly assigns the book to the "Soufleur" [prompter] in Schröder's own handwriting.

On both sides of the second folio, a set list and prop list have been written out in black ink. A different hand using a red pencil has added some other minor information.[146] On the recto of the third folio, more prop information has been inserted by different hands writing in black ink and in a faded grey pencil that has also cancelled out some of the black ink. Presumably, the same grey pencil was at work on the verso of the last folio and the inside of the back cover. A list of eight or nine single words might contain the performers' last names but is largely illegible. However, none of the last names on the existing Hamburg *König Lear* playbills from the 1770s to the 1820s are an obvious match. On the fifty-five printed folios, at least the same three writing tools have left their mark. But a graphite pencil has clearly been used by different hands at different points in time, while a hand that has added technical remarks made use of a pencil as well as some black ink. At least three different hands (including Nick's) used ink. One of them, which has made some textual additions, was clearly Schröder's himself. Altogether, eighty-two of the 110 printed pages in *Theater-Bibliothek: 2029* have been slightly or heavily redacted by sometimes more than one hand and often more than one writing tool or ink. The modes of written artefact enrichment range from the addition of technical information (entrance, exits, or sound cues) to textual changes. Inter-

---

145 For this reason, scholarship has considered the prompt book to be the one from the original production until now. Cf. Drews 1932, 42f.; cf. the figures and explanations 24–29 in the appendix of Hoffmeier 1964; cf. Schäfer 2016, 527.

146 Cf. added flyleaves before page 1 of the printed pages in L.

Chapter 5. Prompt Book Practices in Context    177

ventions that were either carried out by the censor himself or that addressed censorship demands feature prominently in the latter category. (Cf. figures 54 and 55.)

Figure 54: L, verso of second folio with prop list, and Figure 55: L, 1.

 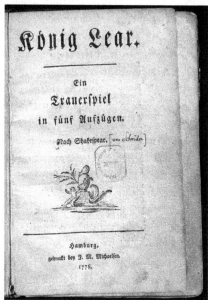

The more than 200-year-old enrichments made in graphite pencil (which are mostly technical and were probably added by an inspector or prompter at some point) are not only near-impossible to decipher but also difficult to distinguish by means of material analysis. A material analysis was carried out, however, on the different shades used, from black to brown ink (with some instances of red). But matters become complicated here as well. The different shades sometimes seem to indicate that the ink in the quill was running out; sometimes they seem to have been caused by the process of yellowing; sometimes they belong to three different types of red ink (ochre, realgar, and an unidentifiable substance that is probably organic) and two types of plant-based ink,[147] all used only occasionally. For the bulk of the enrichments, up to five different types of iron-gall ink might have been in play. However, the results for the latter are partly inconclusive. Other findings came back showing that up to three different inks were clearly being used for the same sentence or

---

147  Cf. the results of the ink analysis undertaken by Sebastian Bosch, in http://doi.org/10.25592/uhhfdm.13916 (Felser/Funke/Göing/Hussain/Schäfer/Weinstock/Bosch 2024, especially files: RD08[HandwrittenTheatre]2029_black_ink.xls.xlsm and RD08[HandwrittenTheatre]2029_red_final.xls.xlsm).

word in the same hand, which seems rather unlikely. At some points, that may have been due to the quill being re-dipped or an instruction being retraced later. Generally speaking, it seems that the prompt book's state of preservation means that it simply does not lend itself to the examination of miniscule details. However, there are two additional iron-gall inks which are more distinctive and were clearly used at other points in the prompt book, one of them by Nick, the censor.

To complicate matters further, Schröder's hand, which seems to have been responsible for many of the content revisions, clearly used different inks on different occasion. The same goes for another hand, which seems to have been in charge of making technical changes. While some changes were made to the technical setup in the prompt book and then retracted, very few of the content revisions seem to have been changed when *König Lear* was staged after the French left, between 1816 and 1823. Thus, the different inks seem to have been employed to make scattered and perhaps even occasional updates to *Theater-Bibliothek: 2029* with whatever ink was at hand.

Nevertheless, it is possible to draw some conclusions. The bottom of the last page of the printed text has been signed by Nick's hand in the aforementioned brown ink: "Vu et approuvé par ordre / de Mr le directeur général / de la haute police / Nick censeur"[148] [Seen and approved by the order / of the general director / of the state police / censor Nick]. On the next, empty end page, page numbers have been listed at the top, but in a different ink – the same one used for the prop list at the beginning, i.e., an ink that could have been used in the theatre and not by the censor. It seems that all the pages in the list were considered to be in need of amendment. Similar paratextual indices can be found in various written artefacts submitted to Nick. It is possible that page numbers like these were added when there was an expectation that a given version of a play was not going to be accepted or would be rejected wholesale. According to the ink analysis, it is unlikely that the numbers were added by the censor, meaning that there were probably other means by which to communicate with him. In this instance, each referenced page number has been separated from the next by a full stop: "S. 6. 7. 11. 13. 49. / 66. 67. 69. 74. 78. 85. 96 [or 97]. / 109." (L, 111) The second number after the 9 has been blotted out, but pages ninety-six and ninety-seven both have similar entries to the other ones. Another blot next to the 96 (or 97) looks like a mistake or a correction (cf. figure 56).

---

148 Similar marks of approval in other books include a date but often lack the reference to the "directeur general". Cf. Chapter 4 on *Theater-Bibliothek: 1460*.

*Figure 56: L, 110 and 111.*

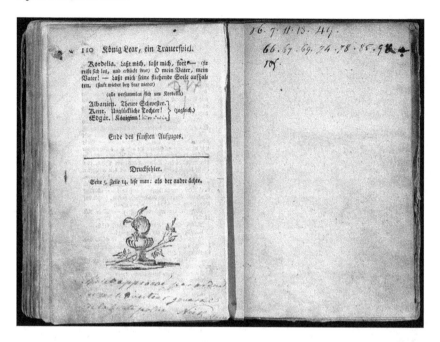

In the print copy, page ninety-seven contains the end of Act IV. The whole of the short Scene 9 has been cut by means of a square frame and three cursory slashes made in a plant-based ink. "Actus" [act] has been written in thick pencil above the scene and indicates that the curtain is to fall earlier. The hand writing in iron-gall ink that was responsible for most of enrichments has scrawled "Ende" [The End] in the right margin and has also added a diacritical sign (probably highlighting the cessation of the music) above it. While in Scene 8, Cordelia takes care of her recovering father, in Scene 9, she goes from being a loving daughter to a military commander. A knight informs her that "das Brittische Heer [...] das unsere angegriffen [hat]" [the British armies have attacked ours] (L, 97), a line that might have attracted protest-like applause in Hamburg at the time. Together with the mercurial rejoinder made by the Queen of France, the line has been unceremoniously cut – and thus a whole scene that a censor would certainly have found insidious.

Page ninety-six also reveals a correction made for the censor: most pages noted at the end include references to the names "England" and "France". In Shakespeare's play, Lear's daughter has been simultaneously promised to the Duke of Burgundy and the King of France – and after her banishment, she is married to the latter without a dowry. In his 1778 adaptation, Schröder had cut the part of Burgundy and only featured the King of France (to reduce the number of actors needed). Thirty-four years later, all respective references and salutations were changed into the Duke of Burgundy instead. Cordelia is consequently addressed as "Duchess" rather than "Queen" throughout the play. These changes amount to eight of the thirteen listed, deficient pages.

Figure 57: L, 4.

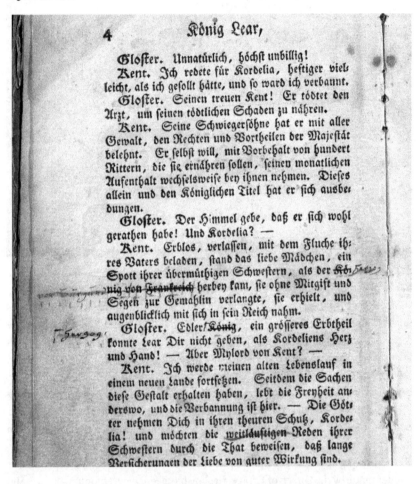

However, the reintroduction of a character taken from the original Shakespeare play was clearly not the censor's work but that of the theatre. While the respective strike-throughs could very well have been made in the same ink and hand as the final approval note, the corrections themselves have been written by a different hand, mostly Schröder's, and most of the time in a clearly different ink, i.e., one or more of the aforementioned three closely related types. Moreover, the changes do not start on page six, as suggested by the list, but right in the *dramatis personae* register on page two, where "France" has been changed to "Burgundy". The first time that the King of France is mentioned in the main text of the play is on page four. Here, a fascinating back-and-forth between different writing tools, and perhaps different hands as well, takes place. "König" [King] has been crossed out twice in black ink; "Duke of Burgundy" has been written in the blank space in the left margin in what is probably the same ink. A hand writing in thick red crayon has then retracted the correction; red dots beneath the strike-through nullify the previous cancellation. A graphite pencil seems to have had the last word: grey dots underneath the red strike-through cancel out the previous cancellation of the correction. Grey vertical lines through the strike-through and its retraction in the main text reinstate the primary retraction (cf. figure 57).

The comparatively clear differences between the editing stages make it much easier to identify the revision layers by the writing tools used in the written artefact as a whole. Nevertheless, it remains unclear when the back-and-forth took place. It could very well be that it bore witness to a discussion among the members of the theatre company before the prompt book was presented to the censor. After all, later mentions of France have all duly been crossed out and corrected. It is also likely that the interaction between the grey and red pencils took place when performances of Schröder's *Lear* version were being revived years after the occupation. Twelve additional performances between 1816 and 1823 have been identified. The red crayon revisions suggested changing "Burgundy" back to "France"; the hand working in graphite pencil disagreed and seems to have gained the upper hand – as it is then displayed throughout the rest of *Theater-Bibliothek: 2029*. Indeed, the preserved playbills demonstrate that Cordelia remained the Duchess of Burgundy for as long as Schröder's version was being staged in Hamburg.[149] Perhaps it was the enmity with post-war France that led to such a preference; perhaps it was a matter of convenience as the play was only taken up again every few years for one or two performances. This miniscule but time-consuming change to the prompt book would have had to be copied into all the actors' parts as well. Overall, surprisingly little seems to have been changed back after the occupation ended. The overall spirit of the censorship revisions seems to have fitted in neatly with the deference to authority prevalent in the post-Napoleonic era. Nevertheless, the initial change from "France" to "Burgundy" on pages two and four might have been an initial suggestion made by the theatre for the censor. The censor would have taken up the theatre's suggestion and then demanded that it be consistently implemented on some of the additional pages listed at the end of *Theater-Bibliothek: 2029*.

Apart from references to France and England, most of the other numbers refer to pages containing passages of a seditious nature. On page eleven, old Gloster's

---

149 As stated above Jahn/Mühle/Eisenhardt/Malchow/Schneider (https://www.stadttheater.uni-hamburg.de), list two performances in 1816, five in 1817, one in 1818, two in 1819, and one each in 1822 and 1823.

(the Germanised version of Shakespeare's Gloucester) long monologue about what he perceives to be the deterioration of politics and private morals has been largely cut by a slash made in the ink used by the theatre to mark most changes. In the midst of it all, Gloster states, "in Städten Empörung, in Provinzen Zwietracht, in Pallästen Verräthrrey" [in cities, mutinies; in countries, discord; in palaces, treason]. Traces of red varnish in the margins of the middle of the page, at the end of his monologue, indicate that a piece of paper had been glued over the last parts of the section. The addition was then removed at some later point, probably after the occupation had ended. Under the removed sheet, there is only one part that has been cut, with horizontal strike-throughs over three lines made in the ink that was also used to sign Nick's name. The fatalistic "Ränke, Treulosigkeit, Verrätherey und alle verderblichen Unordnungen verfolgen uns bis ans Grab" [Plots, disloyalty, treachery, and all pernicious disorders haunt us to our graves] (L, 11) seems to be the only part of the passage that had caught the censor's eye at first. Pasting over the rest of the passage meant playing it safe on Schröder's part. However, the strike-through underneath still stood after the additional sheet had been torn out; so, too, did the initial cancellation (cf. figure 58).

Similar changes pertaining to form and content were made using a similar writing tool throughout *Theater-Bibliothek: 2029* on the pages that were not singled out at the end. In his 1778 version, Schröder had already moved the section deemed most scandalous in the eighteenth century to the off, where the brutal blinding of old Gloster now took place.[150] The respective passages on pages seventy and seventy-one are now surrounded by a box that was also drawn in the same ink as the censor's signature. There is a strike-through from the top left to the bottom right indicating a complete retraction of the respective scene. Here, the treason in the palaces lamented earlier is in full swing: not only is the character of Gloster brutalised by a fellow nobleman in his own home, but the perpetrator, in turn, is also attacked by a defiant subordinate. Evidently, even the messenger's report was too seditious for the censor. Again, none of these cancellations were reversed after occupation, except for one minor sentence. On the contrary, the aforementioned hands working in red and grey pencils were also at work on these pages, using the latter to affirm and add retractions.

---

150  Cf. L, 70f.; cf. Wimsatt 1960, 98.

*Figure 58:* L, 11.

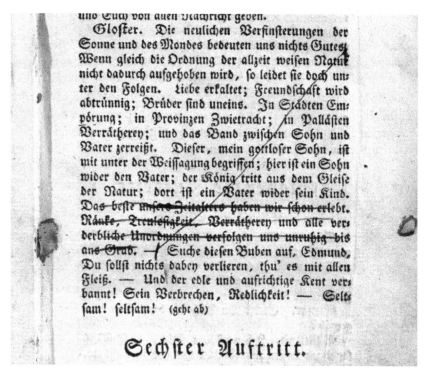

In the case of the Hamburg *König Lear*, restrictions on individual and artistic freedom seem to have started not with the reconstruction of the old European order after 1815 but with Napoleon's reintroduction of censorship. The various hands that interacted in *Theater-Bibliothek: 2029* in a multi-layered fashion were all working together towards the same goal: an even less brutal and inflammatory version than the tame one that the theatre had been staging in Hamburg since 1778. The ink that changed "France" into "Burgundy" was also behind an artistic choice that was in no way related to the necessities of censorship: the heavy reworking of the dialogues between Goneril, Lear's power-hungry daughter, and the Duke of Albany, her well-meaning husband. Goneril's part has been trimmed down by a thick graphite pencil. In turn, Schröder's own hand used ink to first cancel out Albany's lines and then to replace them altogether. Like Schröder's 1778 adaptation as a whole, the dialogue is based on Eschenburg's at the time freshly published prose translations, with a few throwbacks to Wieland whenever it seemed more apt. Schröder now replaced Albany's lines with parts from the new early nineteenth-century Romantic poetic translations and the aforementioned metric *König Lear* by the younger Voß, which was readily available in print.[151] In Schröder's 1812 update, however, the metric translation did not stand for an overall aesthetic principle but was intended to give additional contrast to the two characters. For example, Albany's line, "Vielleicht machst du dir zuviel Bedenklichkeit" [Perhaps you trouble yourself too much], uttered as he attempts to placate his wife's anger towards Lear, has been replaced by Voß's more rhythmic "Doch gehst du in der Furcht vielleicht zu weit" [But perhaps in fear you go too far].[152] Albany is presented as even more of a well-tempered nobleman. His wife's eight-line prose explanation has been cut down to one single line that remains faithful to Eschenburg; she is not only evil but brusque: "Besser, als zu viel Zutrauen haben" (L, 27) [Better than having too much trust]. As a contrasting rejoinder, Albany has been permitted some worldly metric wisdom in lines that the Shakespearean play had already compelled into an orderly rhyme. In Voß, Albany's "How far your eyes may pierce I cannot tell; / Striving to better, oft we mar what's well"[153] becomes "Wie weit ihr ins Verborgene dringt, ich weiß es nicht, doch raubt ein Streben nach dem Besseren uns oft das Gute" (L, 27). As a result, Shakespeare's complex, fully fledged characters, who Schröder's original version had at least partially captured, are presented more as clear-cut stereotypes of evil (woman) and good (man) in the revision of his own adaptation. The handwritten interjections taken from the print copy of a Romantic translation have been used to draw out this contrast rather than to render Shakespeare's aesthetic complexities in the style stipulated by the Schlegels. Always the pragmatist, Schröder would use whatever he could find – mostly in printed books – to create something he hoped would work on stage for the audience in question – be it the paying audience, the authorities, or both. On a material level, this led to *Theater-Bibliothek: 2029*'s hybrid form comprising the 1778 printed prose and the 1812 metric handwriting.

Of the five performances of the censored *König Lear* in 1812, three took place in late March, shortly before Schröder's ultimate retirement. Two took place later in the same year. The play was then taken up again nearly two years after the French left in January 1816.[154] (Schröder would pass away in September of the same year.) Some changes to the technical procedures such as lighting might date to this period. However, the handwritten simplification of Schröder's adaptation and its increased loyalty to the authorities presumably remained in place until *Thea-*

---

151 Cf. Voß 1806, 63; cf. http://doi.org/10.25592/uhhfdm.13916 (Felser/Funke/Göing/Hussain/Schäfer/Weinstock/Bosch 2024, especially file RFD08[HandwrittenTheatre]-Theater-Bibliothek2029-LEAR_Masterdatei.xls).
152 Voß 1806, 65.
153 Shakespeare 2016, 2513.
154 See above and cf. Jahn/Mühle/Eisenhardt/Malchow/ Schneider (https://www.stadttheater.uni-hamburg.de).

ter-*Bibliothek: 2029* was used one last time in 1827. But while the content of the *König Lear* adaptation had been simplified in the process of censorship and beyond, the process itself in *Theater-Bibliothek: 2029* reveals a complex scene involving multiple hands. They intervened into the print copy and also interacted with each other within it. The dynamics of the 1812 censorship procedure unintentionally turned the 1778 print copy into a unique hybrid comprising print and handwriting that simultaneously testifies to the negotiations of aesthetic standards taking place at the time as well as the demands being made by the audience and the censor. In the world of prompt book making and revision, the "author of authors", Shakespeare, was no different to any other, becoming a nodal point for diverse hands, tools, and writing and paper practices.

# Chapter 6. Doing Literature in Theatre: Schiller's Adaptation of Lessing's *Nathan der Weise* between Prompting and Stage Managing (1800s–1840s)

A dramatic text (or any other text, for that matter) which is adapted for a specific stage production is not an abstract entity. In addition to its immaterial presence in the minds and memories of the performers and all those responsible for seamless backstage operations, it also has material manifestations: in the written artefacts used to ensure that the same sequences of events can be repeated on stage and that the lines will be uttered in the same (or nearly the same) way in the next performance. The previous chapters have focussed on prompt books in the strict sense and mentioned other kinds of books only in passing. But in Hamburg in the late eighteenth and early nineteenth centuries, the prompter was not the only person making use of the written artefact containing the (valuable) complete adaptation of the respective play during a performance. Nor were prompt books the only written artefacts which were constantly being updated according to a specific area of responsibility. While the prompter was stuck in their box at the front of the stage, it was the inspector who oversaw the running of the performance backstage at the Stadt-Theater at Hamburg Gänsemarkt. According to Schröder's *Laws of the Hamburg Theatre*, the inspector also had general management responsibilities for the company's daily business such as overseeing the production of the costumes and the stage set. During the rehearsals as well as during the performances, they coordinated the various tasks of the dresser, the technical stage manager, the stagehands, the extras, and others.[1] In doing so, the inspector worked with a copy of the play, too, and that copy was also enriched with information relevant to the inspector's work (by the inspector themselves or by someone else). However, the division of labour was not that clear-cut. As we have sometimes indicated in previous chapters, the prompter also had a number of technical tasks to perform and needed to give signals for certain procedures or at least be in the know. For the technical cues, the inspector had to be aware of any technical updates that had been made as well. Adapting a play thus meant making it suit-

---

1 Cf. Schröder 1798, 41–46.

able for the stage on two levels at once: a textual one and a technical one. The focus of this chapter is on the written artefacts that were involved in this, the prompt book and the inspector's book, which sometimes interacted and sometimes existed independently of one another.[2]

In Hamburg at the turn of the nineteenth century, it was the prompter's responsibility (as a librarian) to ensure that all the written artefacts were brought in line and contained the same information. However, some deviations were to be expected. It is likely that actors often kept their booklets for as long as they did not relinquish their roles, and that the inspector's copy did not necessarily always make it back into the prompter's library. On a material level, it was these potentially divergent and often evolving written artefacts that comprised the stage adaptation of a play.

This chapter will take the example of the 1803 Hamburg production of Lessing's play *Nathan der Weise* [*Nathan the Wise*] to examine the correlation between the prompter's and inspector's books. The play that was published in print in 1779 was at that time referred to as a "dramatisches Gedicht" (Np, I) [dramatic poem] rather than a straightforward "play" or "drama". The text was immediately well received – but more as a closet drama made for reading than as a stage text. The lack of action in the wordy play seems to have made it unsuitable for the stage for nearly a quarter of a century.[3] This only changed with the advance of the aforementioned new theatre aesthetics introduced by Iffland in Berlin and then Goethe in Weimar. The more artificial style of acting was well suited to the declamatory mode of such a "dramatic poem". While this style was not on the agenda in Hamburg, the company at the Stadt-Theater swiftly followed suit after Iffland and Goethe both put on *Nathan der Weise* in 1801 and 1802. As we will discuss below, Hamburg's Stadt-Theater managed to win over Friedrich Schiller, who was, alongside Kotzebue, the most popular playwright of the day, to provide an adaptation for the stage, something he had already done for the Weimar production. Until the 1840s, the company at the Stadt-Theater then worked with their own updates of Schiller's adaptation. Both the prompt book and the inspector's book seem to have been continuously revised. However, they were both revised to varying degrees and in different ways. This chapter will place greater emphasis on the inspector's book than previous chapters and will shed more light on the inspector's use of the written artefacts. While examining some aspects of Schiller's adaptation of *Nathan der Weise*, it will look at the differences but also the similarities between the two types of written artefacts, where they overlap, and how their material performance took

---

2 The actors' booklets with their personal notes as well as all the written artefacts used in the respective production design sections (stage design, wardrobe, hairdresser) would also belong here but are not preserved at the Theater-Bibliothek.

3 Cf. Wessels 1979, 242f.

shape between prompting and stage management. The relationship between different media formats and their respective use will also play a role: the designated inspector's book, *Theater-Bibliothek: 1988a*, is an enriched manuscript, whereas the designated prompt book, *Theater-Bibliothek: 1988b*, is an enriched print copy.

## I. A Closet Drama, an Adapter's Work in Progress, and Two Related Written Artefacts

In 1798, Schröder resigned for the second time from the directorship of the Stadt-Theater at Gänsemarkt. As the owner, he leased its building and infrastructure, including the prompt book collection, to a group of, initially, five experienced members of the company, who ran the house until 1811.[4] Among them was Jakob Herzfeld, who had first joined the Hamburg theatre as an actor in 1791. He was not just closely connected to the two written artefacts that this chapter will focus on but also to the transition that took place in Hamburg to the post-Schröder era. When Schröder returned in 1811 for his last, two-year tenure and third "crisis" directorate during French occupation, Herzfeld was given an executive position. After Schröder's final departure in 1812, Herzfeld ran the theatre until his own death in 1826, spending the last eleven years as co-director.

Herzfeld's relationship to the two written artefacts in question began in 1801, when he sent a letter to Weimar, approaching one of the most well-known poets and playwrights of the time, Friedrich Schiller, on behalf of the Stadt-Theater's directorate. In his letter, Herzfeld expressed the directorate's wish to stage Schiller's latest and future plays, and asked if he would be prepared to sell manuscripts of the "Meisterstücke Ihrer dramatischen Muse"[5] [masterpieces of your dramatic muse] to the Stadt-Theater. Herzfeld's letter was the start of a productive collaboration.

---

4 One of them, actor Johann Karl Wilhelm Löhrs, died in 1802, while another, actor Karl Daniel Langerhans, resigned the same year. The other three men, actor and singer Gottfried Eule, actor, singer, and composer Carl David Stegmann, and actor Jakob Herzfeld remained in charge until 1811. Only a few years after they took office, however, a full-blown scandal broke out. Various media accused the directors of neglecting the theatre while unduly enriching themselves. Schröder was explicitly considered the benchmark for a level of quality that was no longer being achieved. This criticism was evidently being increasingly shared by some sections of the audience. In 1801, the directors were called on stage at the beginning of a performance of Kotzebue's *Menschenhass und Reue* [*The Stranger; or, Misanthropy and Repentance*] and confronted with a series of accusations concerning role assignments and engagements, as well as the state of the costumes and stage design. The increasingly heated situation was apparently only defused after Stegmann issued a public apology. The scandal has been extensively documented, contextualised, and analysed in M. Schneider 2017.

5 Schillers Werke. Nationalausgabe. 39.I, 71 (hereinafter cited as "NA").

Schiller not only sold manuscripts of stage adaptations of his own plays, filling his letters to Herzfeld with instructions and suggestions on how to stage them, but also offered manuscripts of stage adaptations he had made of other authors' plays, initially for Goethe's theatre in Weimar.[6] They included Gotthold Ephraim Lessing's *Nathan der Weise*, which had premiered in Weimar in 1801 in Schiller's adaptation.[7] Schiller's engagement with the play, as he wrote in one letter to Herzfeld, mainly consisted of making abridgements.[8] While this was a common procedure when adapting a play for the stage,[9] Schiller also smoothed out the ruptures he created while bridging them with some minor additions, interjections, and tweaks of his own. Schiller seems to have further fine-tuned his version of *Nathan der Weise* whenever he sold a new copy to another theatre. Until 1805, performances are known to have taken place in Berlin, Braunschweig, Breslau, Frankfurt, Stuttgart, and Mannheim.[10] The preserved written artefacts differ markedly from the enriched print edition that was presumably used in Weimar in 1801. (The Mannheim version published in the *Nationalausgabe* of Schiller's works was probably the last one he worked on.) Schiller created his Hamburg version in the midst of his involvement with the play; he seems to have sent a copy to Hamburg in September 1803, where *Nathan der Weise* was first staged in December. Even after taking Schiller's changes into account, a performance still lasted more than three hours – at least according to a note made in pencil on the last empty page of the print-based *Theater-Bibliothek: 1988b*, right below the information that no special lighting effects or paper props such as letters were required for the production.[11]

---

6 For an overview of his stage adaptations, see Rudloff-Hille 1969, 183–201; for more detail, see Müller 2004.

7 Cf. Albrecht 1979; cf. Müller 2004, 171–193; cf. Niefanger 2021, 123–143; for the early stage history of the play, cf. Wessels 1979, 242–280.

8 Cf. NA 31, 122.

9 However, these revisions slightly mitigated some of the topics, as they made criticisms of Christianity and the important role of money less explicit. Moreover, they accentuated some of the characters somewhat differently. Scholars have evaluated these changes in various ways. While Barner, for example, disqualifies Schiller's adaptation as a "nachgerade verstümmelnde Version" [almost mutilating version] (2000, 182), Borcherdt praises Schiller as a "Meister theatralischer Kunst" [master of theatrical art], who "vom Hören zum Sehen, vom Lesen zum Spiel umzuformen sucht" [seeks to transform from hearing to seeing, from reading to playing] and who achieves a "Steigerung und Stilisierung" [enhancement and stylisation] of the characters in the play (NA 13, 318). Albrecht 1979 emphasises the great importance of the adaptation for Schiller's own engagement with Lessing and for the play's stage career. He is more nuanced in his presentation, analysis, and valuation, as is Müller 2004, 171–193. They both either stress the purposeful, shared character of the changes or explain and contextualise them, citing political and poetological or aesthetic reasons.

10 Cf. Müller 2004, 182.

11 Cf. Np, 239.

A few days after the first two performances, a happy Herzfeld informed Schiller of the production's great success as well as the audience feedback, which had exceeded his expectations.[12] *Nathan der Weise* was off to a very successful start in Hamburg, with seven performances alone in the first month of its staging. After that, it remained a steady part of the repertory for many years. It was performed forty-seven times before 1847 and explicitly announced as an adaptation by Schiller until 1846.[13]

Two written artefacts that contain a copy of Lessing's play can be found at the Theater-Bibliothek. They both relate to Schiller's adaptation, albeit to varying degrees and in different ways. Nonetheless, the history of their use as well as their material biographies are strongly intertwined. *Theater-Bibliothek: 1988a* contains a handwritten version of Schiller's adaptation that was probably copied from the one he had sent to Hamburg. It was written out by a single scribe using a dark ink on two clearly distinguishable types of paper. The scribe switched from lighter to darker paper that was a little rougher from the sixth of thirteen quires onwards, starting with the end of the last scene of Act II. This base layer was revised by at least three other hands. One of them added technical information in graphite pencil. The others cancelled, added, and replaced content using dark ink as well as graphite pencil and red crayon.

*Theater-Bibliothek: 1988b* was initially based on a print version of Lessing's play. It is a copy of the third edition of *Nathan der Weise*, published in 1791 by the Vossische Buchhandlung in Berlin. In order to align the original copy of the print version with the template of Schiller's adaptation, the printed book was heavily revised. Dark ink and red and grey pencil were used as well as blue ink and blue pencil. However, it is not possible to say exactly how many hands were involved. Many passages were revised more than once. Sometimes several writing tools performed the same operation; at others, the various layers modified each other or cancelled each other out again. Either way, the order of their use does not remain the same throughout the book. A substantial part of the revisions consists of extensive cancellations of text, most of which served the same purpose: shortening Lessing's play in accordance with Schiller's adaptation.

At first glance, one might assume that the print-based *Theater-Bibliothek: 1988b* had served as a trial copy before being used for performances. Instead of faithfully

---

12 In his letter from December 6th Herzfeld writes: "Es ist bereits 2 mahl, von einem zahlreichen Publicum, mit einer ausgezeichneten Aufmerksamkeit gehört und gesehen, und von *allen* Theilen desselben mit einem Beifall aufgenommen worden, der all' meine Erwartung übertraf" (NA, 40.I, 155f.) [It has already been heard and seen twice by a large audience paying excellent attention, and received by *all* parts of the same with applause that exceeded all my expectations].

13 Probably due to its pacifist content, no performances were put on during the censorship era. There is thus no signature from the censor and there are no respective revisions.

transcribing Schiller's template, the director or someone close to him might have used the template as a proposal rather than a prescription. The back-and-forth between the multiple hands might have been a discussion of which cancellations to accept, which to reject, or how to forge a new path. Schiller might have also reworked his submission, meaning that the print version had to be revised again. But even though the content of the print version and the manuscript largely match, neither the first drafts nor the final revisions of *Theater-Bibliothek: 1988a* and *Theater-Bibliothek: 1988b* are fully identical. (Cf. figure 59.)

*Figure 59: covers of Nm and Np.*

It is fair to assume that the manuscript was not a transcription of the updated print version and that the two written artefacts were created independently of one another. However, both written artefacts seem to have been repeatedly put to use between 1803 and 1847, sometimes simultaneously, but sometimes probably not. It would make sense for them to have been used simultaneously as *Theater-Bibliothek: 1988a* was designated as an inspector's copy and *Theater-Bibliothek: 1988b* as a prompter's copy. This kind of allocation can also be found in other plays by Schiller at the Theater-Bibliothek for which both handwritten and print copies were used.[14] It was easier for a prompter in their dimly lit box to work with a print copy during a performance as print was more legible than handwriting – at least as long as it did not contain a myriad of updates.[15] Below we will discuss how the scope and types of revisions in *Theater-Bibliothek: 1988a* seem to have impaired its legibility – and thus the most crucial quality of a prompt book.

It is immediately striking how the material performances of the two written artefacts sometimes fundamentally differ – and not just due to their materiality and respective visual organisation or layout as a manuscript and a printed book. Rather, they also differ in the ways in which they were revised and updated, for example, when the same operation was carried out in a different style or using different writing tools. On the other hand, because certain amendments can only be found in one of the two books, there are modifications in *Theater-Bibliothek: 1988a* with no corresponding changes in *Theater-Bibliothek: 1988b* and vice versa. This might suggest a period or periods when the two books were being used independently of one other. It also raises the question of whether the designations on their front covers (one for the prompter in their box, one for the inspector backstage) were always adhered to or whether the two written artefacts were put to different uses at various points in time.[16]

Many of the differences in content relate to Schiller's adaptation of Lessing's play. *Theater-Bibliothek: 1988b*, the enriched print version, contains extensive abridgements, made to establish a Schillerian version of the text. But in the manuscript version *Theater-Bibliothek: 1988a*, some parts of Lessing's text that Schiller had left out have been reinserted. These and other modifications, which were the

---

14 See the written artefacts that contain *Dom Karlos, Die Braut von Messina, Maria Stuart*, and *Die Jungfrau von Orleans: Theater-Bibliothek: 1989a* and *b*, *Theater-Bibliothek: 1991a* and *b*, and *Theater-Bibliothek: 2022 a* and *b*, *Theater-Bibliothek: 2023a* and *b*. In these cases, the "a" shelf mark designates a handwritten inspector's copy, while the "b" shelf mark designates a printed prompter's copy.

15 For the preference of print, cf. Düringer/Barthels 1841, 1006. However, Blum/Herloßsohn/Marggraff 1846a, 36f., propose a manuscript that leaves an empty page (for notes) next to each written one.

16 In his discussion of Schiller's *Nathan der Weise* adaptation and the corresponding prompt books used at the Stuttgart court theatre, Niefanger also assumes there were "mehrfunktionale Nutzungen" [multi-functional uses] of the written artefacts (Niefanger 2021, 125).

result of technical requirements rather than aesthetic considerations of the integrity of Lessing's play, not only led to differences in both prompt books but also created two versions of the play for its Hamburg stagings. Both differ in several aspects from the third print edition of Lessing's text published in 1791, but also from what scholarship has come to refer to as Schiller's ultimate adaptation of *Nathan* – and they differ from each other as well.

The following considerations will provide a close analysis of the two prompt books with regard to the interrelations that have shaped the material dynamics of both written artefacts. The adaptation of Lessing's drama for the stage would not only come to bridge the gap between print and handwriting but also between prompting and stage management. The rest of this chapter will thus examine the characteristics and practices of, as well as the reasons behind, identical, similar, and distinct revisions, and the patterns and dynamics of the prompt books' use.

## II. The Author as Adapter: Schiller's Template in *Theater-Bibliothek: 1988a* and *Theater-Bibliothek: 1988b*

The practical use of at least one of the two written artefacts was at some point discontinued or at least called into question. Another look at the cover of *Theater-Bibliothek: 1988a*, the manuscript designated for the inspector, shows a note that labels the book as "nicht brauchbar" [unusable]. This is remarkable because the book was clearly being used over a long period of time, whereas the same cannot be said for certain about the print version. Several indications in the written artefact attest to this: right inside the cover, an extra sheet of paper has been pasted in. It contains a cast list which refers to the performances of the year 1846 (cf. figure 60).

However, the list does not include the guest star of the 1846 performance, actor Eduard Jerrmann from the K. K. Hofburg-Theater in Vienna, who portrayed the main character, Nathan. He is only mentioned on the respective playbills[17] and in the book itself, namely in a note on folio 65r (cf. figure 61).

---

17  Cf. Jahn/Mühle/Eisenhardt/Malchow/M. Schneider (https://www.stadttheater.uni-hamburg.de).

*Figure 60: Nm, cast list.*

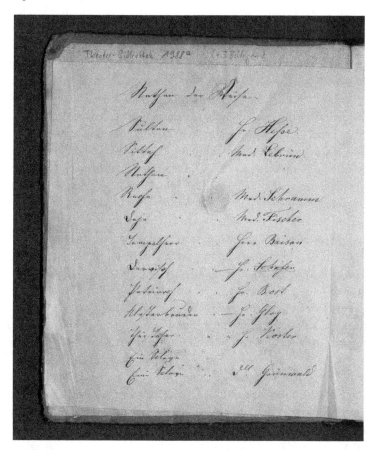

*Figure 61: Nm, 65r.*

While it seems fairly certain that *Theater-Bibliothek: 1988a* was in use up until the mid-1840s, other modifications and content features allow us to narrow down when it was first used and thus when the written artefact was created. Some of the hands who updated the book can be identified, namely Herzfeld and Barlow, the prompter at the time.[18] Based on their involvement, the first possible use of the book could have been as early as 1803 or as late as 1816, as the latter was the last time the play was staged while both men were still alive.[19] Many traces clearly point to the earlier date and are linked to the person responsible for the model of *Theater-Bibliothek: 1988a*. While Schiller sent copies of his adaptation to theatres in Hamburg and other cities, he still continued to work on it himself. What has been deemed the final edition of his *Nathan*, the version staged in Mannheim in 1806 and written down shortly before Schiller's death in 1805,[20] is included in the *Nationalausgabe* – the comprehensive and authoritative German edition of Schiller's works. However, this version is not identical with the content of *Theater-Bibliothek: 1988a* or *Theater-Bibliothek: 1988b*. In fact, there are several instances in which the primary layer of the Hamburg prompt book differs, presumably because it was based on an earlier version of Schiller's adaptation, i.e., the one he sent to Herzfeld in 1803.[21] Most of these differences relate to only minor details.[22] A typical example is folio 97v, where Saladin's second speech starts with: "Komm, liebes Mädchen, / Komm! Nimm's mit ihm nicht so genau" [Come, dear girl, come! Don't take him so seriously]. In Lessing's version, the reply is a little longer, and several verses precede it.[23] They are left out in Schiller's adaptation and accordingly in *Theater-Bibliothek: 1988a*. However, Schiller evidently revised the passage again after completing his work for the Stadt-Theater, adding a few words and extending the first of the two verses. Unlike in *Theater-Bibliothek: 1988a*, the respective verses in the final published edition read: "Komm, liebes Mädchen, höre nicht auf ihn! / Komm! Nimm's mit ihm nicht so genau"[24] [Come, dear girl, don't listen to him! Come! Don't take him so seriously].

Another addition not only supports the theory that *Theater-Bibliothek: 1988a* was put to use in 1803 but also suggests that Schiller either communicated some

---

18  Cf. Chapter 2, sections two and three.
19  There was also a performance of *Nathan der Weise* in 1820, the year Barlow died, but only after his death.
20  Cf. Müller 2004, 182.
21  And this one was probably not identical to the version that had premiered in Weimar a year and a half earlier, cf. Albrecht 1979, 41f.
22  Cf. Felser/Funke/Göing/Hussain/Schäfer/Weinstock/Bosch 2024 (http://doi.org/10.25592/uhhfdm.13916).
23  Cf. Lessing 1993, 622.
24  NA 13/1, 281.

later revisions after the fact or that the theatre had access to an updated version at some point. While Schiller in most cases added just a few words of his own to the text, as in the first example, he rewrote an entire speech in Act I, Scene 3. The revision mainly concerns the lines spoken by dervish Al-Hafi, who explains his decision to act as treasurer for the sultan. In Schiller's last version, Al-Hafi does not accept Saladin's offer out of vanity but rather, and much more clearly than in Lessing's original, emphasises his idealistic motivation to use the office to do good.[25] At some point, this new text became part of *Theater-Bibliothek: 1988a*, the manuscript. It was added on two sheets of paper in Act I, Scene 3, and was written out by the same scribe who had written the fair copy and pasted over the lower part of folio 12v and the upper part of folio 13r (cf. figures 62 and 63).

*Figure 62: Nm, 12v.*

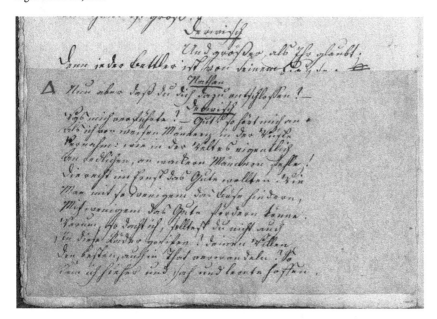

---

25 In this scene, Schiller's new text does not fundamentally change the character of Al-Hafi. Rather, it emphasises a trait already inherent in the figure and makes it explicit. There is another part in the play where Schiller rewrote the text, namely at the beginning of Act III, Scene 4. In contrast to the revision in Act I, Scene 3, it was part of the content of *Theater-Bibliothek: 1988a* from the outset (cf. Nm, 47r). This addition, too, does not so much change the character as it expands on a trait already implied by Lessing, making it more dramatically explicit. Schiller thereby turns Sittah into a schemer who urges her brother Saladin to set a trap for Nathan in order to get his money. On the Hamburg stage, however, it was obviously not intended to be portrayed in this way. The passage was cancelled in *Theater-Bibliothek: 1988a* and not even included in *Theater-Bibliothek 1988b* (cf. Np, 110f).

*Figure 63: Nm, 13r.*

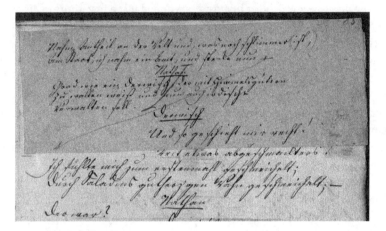

These revisions did not replace Lessing's version of the scene, but they intervened into an earlier phase of Schiller's adaptation. When turning back the pinned-in sheets containing Schiller's text, we find a shorter version of the original passage.[26] It appears that it was not rewritten until *Theater-Bibliothek: 1988a* had already been created and the theatre in Hamburg had gotten hold of the updated version – perhaps provided by Schiller himself (cf. figures 64 and 65).

*Figure 64: Nm, 12v, primary layer.*

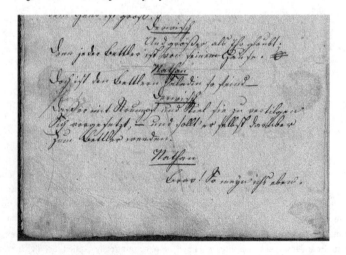

---

26 Folios 12v and 13r were restored at the Staats- und Universitätsbibliothek Hamburg Carl von Ossietzky in such a way that the two sheets can now be folded in towards the inner margin of the book.

*Figure 65: Nm, 13r, primary layer.*

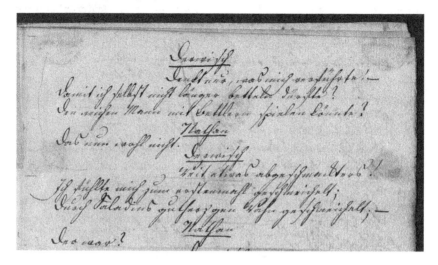

This example also shows that, alongside theatrical requirements, audience expectations, and political pressure, an author or someone in an authorlike position could be responsible for making amendments to a play and contributing to the material performance of a prompt book. From the second half of the eighteenth century onwards, an increasing amount of authority was being attributed to the figure of the author.[27] However, in the theatre, the products of such singular authorship were dealt with pragmatically, as the traces of use in the prompt books analysed here show. More important than the supposed completeness of an author's dramatic work was its functional integration into the changing dynamics of a theatre production. Nevertheless, despite all interventions, the dramatic text was still attributed to its original author.[28] In the case of *Nathan der Weise*, the performances were explicitly advertised with reference to two famous (authors') names – Lessing and Schiller. And as the exchange between Schiller and Herzfeld exemplarily shows, new ideas from and changes made by the author were certainly included in the theatrical processes – but the author did not have ultimate, unquestionable authority.

Director Herzfeld and playwright Schiller negotiated this type of influence in their correspondence. Herzfeld, for instance, asked Schiller for a toned-down version of *Maria Stuart*[29] and justified reducing the role of the chorus in the Hamburg

---

27 As discussed in Chapter 5.
28 Cf. Weinstock 2022.
29 Cf. NA 39.I, 71.

staging of *Die Braut von Messina* [*The Bride of Messina*].[30] On the other hand, Schiller accompanied his manuscripts of *Die Jungfrau von Orleans* [*The Maid of Orleans*] and *Wilhelm Tell* [*William Tell*] with suggestions about how to stage them.[31] The simultaneous negotiation and recognition of authority and authorship is even more evident when it comes to the plays Schiller adapted. Even though he was not their author, Herzfeld attributed something akin to authorship to Schiller and therefore involved him in any planned changes. When Schiller made suggestions about his own translation and adaptation of Louis-Benoît Picard's comedy *Der Neffe als Onkel* [*The Nephew as Uncle*] (based on the play's Weimar staging[32]), Herzfeld did not respond but explicitly asked for Schiller's "Erlaubnis" [permission][33] to make changes of his own. Herzfeld described these changes as minor, although he did in fact modify the entire last scene of the play.[34] A similar dynamic can be identified in Schiller's adaptation of Carlo Gozzi's *Turandot*: Schiller sent later updates and changes to Hamburg after making initial suggestions and receiving counter-requests from Herzfeld.[35]

Against this backdrop, the addition of Schiller's own text to Act I, Scene 3, in *Theater-Bibliothek: 1988a* seems to demonstrate the influence of an authorial figure on the theatrical treatment of a play and the corresponding prompt book. It becomes apparent, however, that both forms of engagement with the dramatic text, i.e., the author's literary activity and the pragmatic use of his work in a theatre, coincided with respect to their inherent open-endedness. Potentially, they would never be finished. The materiality of the written artefact is the place where this incompleteness manifests itself. Schiller, here, continuously updated the text of his adaptation in a manner similar to all the other updates that were continuously made to prompt books during their use. Nevertheless, this chapter aims to demonstrate how such reference and reverence to a notion of authorship also shaped the material performance of the prompt book – regardless of any actual contact and exchange between the theatre and the playwright. Both the manuscript *Theater-Bibliothek: 1988a* and the print-based *Theater-Bibliothek: 1988b* put such a material performance on display.

Including Schiller's text in our analysis helps us to date the beginning of the use of *Theater-Bibliothek: 1988a*. It seems to have been included relatively soon after the creation of the prompt book around 1803, while Schiller was working on further versions of his adaptations – but before he finished what Schiller schol-

---

30 Cf. NA 40.I, 68.
31 Cf. NA 39.I, 101 and NA 32, 117.
32 Cf. NA 32, 56.
33 NA 40.I, 178.
34 Cf. NA 40.I, 178.
35 Cf. NA 31, 122; cf. NA 39.I, 244.

arship considers to be the final version.³⁶ The cast list, Jermann's name, and the respective playbills all indicate that the prompt book was being used well into the 1840s – for more than four decades altogether.

Similar dating of the use of the print-based *Theater-Bibliothek: 1988b* is not possible. Unlike in the case of *Theater-Bibliothek: 1988a*, there are no clear indications of a specific year or period of time. But it is fair to assume that it was created equally early, as, after all, a copy for the prompter was an indispensable part of a production. Furthermore, it seems that *Theater-Bibliothek: 1988b* was in use for quite some time as well. Several layers of revisions, their cancellations, and sometimes even the cancellations of those cancellations have contributed to a complex material performance that is unlikely to have evolved quickly. We will examine this in more detail below.

## III. The Work of the Inspector in *Theater-Bibliothek: 1988a*

The supposedly "unusable" manuscript *Theater-Bibliothek: 1988a* not only contains references to the period of its use but also to its designated purpose as a copy for the "inspector". As a relative of today's stage manager, the inspector's tasks included aspects of supervision and organisation. On the one hand, the inspector liaised between the staff and the directorate. It was their duty to communicate the former's complaints to the latter but also to meticulously record and report to the latter all sorts of mistakes, instances of negligence, and misconduct on the part of staff that occurred during rehearsals and performances. On the other hand, the inspector was involved in these processes themselves. As can be gleaned from Schröder's *Laws of the Hamburg Theatre*, they attended rehearsals and performances and helped to ensure they ran smoothly. The inspector had to make sure that procedures regarding costumes and props worked well, i.e., that everybody received what they needed, and that everything was available and in its proper place. To this end, they coordinated closely with the people in charge of the respective divisions. An inspector also had to know what kinds of sounds or sound effects were to take place at what point during a performance and set the respective cues. The same applied to directions for actors' entries and exits, stage left or stage right. In all matters, it was the inspector's duty to make sure that the arrangements set out in the book were respected. Furthermore, the inspector was in charge of the extras, giving them instructions, checking their costumes, and keeping an eye on their behaviour.³⁷

---

36 Cf. Müller 2004, 182.
37 The duties and responsibilities of an inspector were set out in the theatre regulations of the time. See Schröder (1798, 41–46) and Düringer/Barthels (1841, 1174–75), who follow Schröder, but further differentiate between the inspector's responsibilities for rehearsal and performance processes. However, Schröder's regulations were directly linked to Hamburg and shaped con-

However, the inspector not only contributed to the successful execution of theatrical processes but also made sure that those processes could be repeated in the next performance. Structurally, most of their tasks during the performance were identical to those of the prompter, but they took place backstage. The means to perform their task were also the same: both aspects, execution and repetition, depended on a "script", which in this case was a written artefact used and updated by the inspector. The inspector wrote down information concerning their tasks and duties for each production (or had it written down), usually in a copy of the respective play. This could include lists of names, props, or even the stage design, written down in varying degrees of detail on the inner covers, on vacat pages, or blank folios, probably often copied from the main lists provided by the prompter-librarian.[38] The information also included technical and organisational annotations made right next to the sections they concerned, added to the book in the same way that a prompter's copy would be updated. Nevertheless, some of the amendments and updates differed. The information that was relevant to the inspector tended to turn the written artefact they used into more of an organisational and technical score for the performance. However, there were also changes that were important to and/or characteristic of both books. Aside from the same operations performed to update the text (that were typical of the use of written artefacts employed in the context of a theatre production), some of the updates themselves were identical as well. Extensive changes to dialogue or retractions of passages, entire scenes, or characters concerned not only the prompter but potentially also the inspector. This was also the case for stage directions that were either not important for the use of the book in question or not taken into account in a production. Crossing out didascalia like stage directions might have supported not only the prompter's but also the inspector's tasks in that it distinguished between information that was relevant for their tasks and information that was not.

Many of these features can be found in the manuscript *Theater-Bibliothek: 1988a*. The fact that they were added systematically strongly indicates that it was indeed a copy used by an inspector at a certain point. Folios 14r and 15v contain the transition from the fourth to the fifth scene of the first act, which includes a change of characters and scene (cf. figures 66 and 67).

---

crete theatre practice there. In contrast, the 1840s dictionary formulates more of an ideal, typical conception that is as much descriptive as it is prescriptive. It is striking, however, that in the first version of Schröder's regulations, which appeared in the *Annalen des Theaters* in 1792, there is not yet a section with regulations pertaining to the inspector alone. They only become part of a later version printed in 1798.

38 By the middle of the nineteenth century, the written artefact ideally used by the inspector was a "Scenarium" [scene book], which visually connected the different types of technical information and cues with the respective sections of the play in different columns, almost like a table (cf. Düringer/Barthels 1841, 958–964).

*Figure 66: Nm, 14v.*

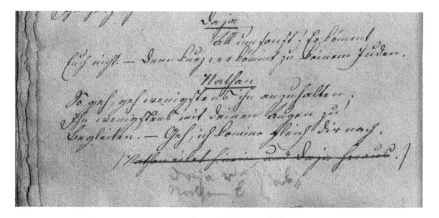

*Figure 67: Nm, 15r.*

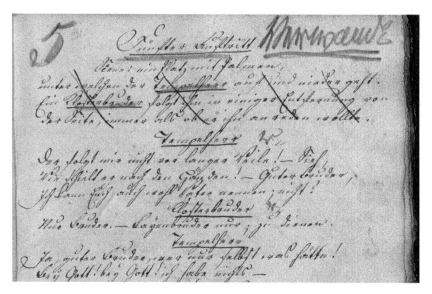

At the end of Act I, Scene 4, Nathan instructs Daja, his adopted daughter Recha's companion, to go and approach the young Templar, Recha's saviour, who is walking up and down a palm-fringed square nearby. Nathan himself intends to follow her shortly afterwards. However, a stage instruction that refers to their exits – "Nathan eilet hinein und Daja heraus" [Nathan hurries in and Daja out] – has been crossed out in dark ink at the bottom of folio 14v. The writing tool used here indicates that this strike-through was part of more extensive amendments to didascalia that would be of great consequence. This operation was performed throughout *Theater-Bibliothek: 1988a* in this kind of ink, which can also be seen at the beginning of the fifth scene on folio 15r. If needed, information about technical stage procedures was added, generally in pencil. Here, an addition of this type indicates that Daja and Nathan were to exit the stage in opposite directions. It says "Daja r | Nathan l ab" which means that Daja exits stage right ("r" for "rechts"), Nathan stage left ("l" for "links").[39] Accordingly, additions on folio 15r specify from which side the characters enter the stage in Act I, Scene 5. The "r" right next to his first mention means that the Templar enters stage right, as does the Friar who follows him, which is indicated in the same way. These additions replace the crossed-out stage directions. We read: "Szene: Ein Platz mit Palmen, unter welchen der Tempelherr auf und nieder geht. Ein Klosterbruder folgt ihm in einiger Entfernung von der Seite, immer als ob er ihn anreden wollte" [Scene: A square with palm trees, under which the Templar is walking up and down. A Friar follows him at some distance from the side, as if he might address him at any minute]. Here, the stage directions apparently provide information that is relevant for the technical process of performing the text on stage. They describe the actions of the characters – one following the other – but also the changes that have been made to the stage set on which they are now to take place. While the sentence itself has been crossed out, the corresponding technical information for the inspector has been condensed and added in pencil. The word "Verwandlung" [transformation], written prominently right next to the scene title at the top of folio 15r, immediately signals that the stage set needs to be changed between the two scenes. This was a common way of indicating such changes in prompt books.

A related, but less frequently appearing instruction can be found at the transition from Act II, Scene 4, to Act II, Scene 5, on folio 31r (cf. figure 68). On the upper right-hand side, the word "abräumen" [clear away] has been added. It is an instruction that refers to the props and decorations that were to be taken off stage. At this point, the stage had to be transformed from a chamber in the sultan Saladin's palace into a square near Nathan's house. We can only speculate as to whether the instruction "abräumen" in addition to "Verwandlung" underscored that the scene change would be particularly complex and detailed (as it probably included the scattered elements of a chess set that Saladin had wiped off a table two scenes earlier). However, the addition was clearly directed at an inspector rather than the prompter in their box. It is a type of information that translates the fictional processes and settings of the dramatic (secondary) text into concrete instructions for their technical realisation on stage.

---

39  Our translation is imprecise. In the German-speaking countries, stage right and stage left are defined from the perspective of the audience, which also happens to be the perspective of the prompter in their box. It is the other way round in English-speaking countries where stage left is to the left of the actor facing the audience. While there could not be any confusion for the German prompter as to where to direct the actors, this was an entirely different matter for the German inspector backstage.

*Figure 68: Nm, 31r.*

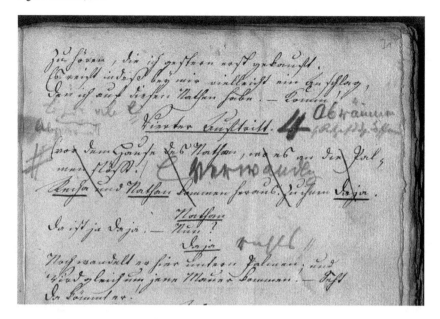

These pieces of information have not only been added next to or near the content they refer to but are also summarised at the end of the book in two lists, one on the verso side of the last vacat page, one on the inner back cover. Such lists are also typical of an inspector's copy (cf. figures 69 and 70).

In *Theater-Bibliothek: 1988a*, these lists give a brief overview of the technical process involved in the staging, or more precisely, of certain elements of that process, with the list on the vacat page providing the most detail. It enumerates keyword information for each act that would have been relevant to the inspector. This includes procedures such as the aforementioned scene changes or the clearing of the stage as well as references to the setting, decorations, props, and the characters they related to.

*Figure 69: Nm, verso side of the last vacat page, and Figure 70: Nm, inner back cover.*

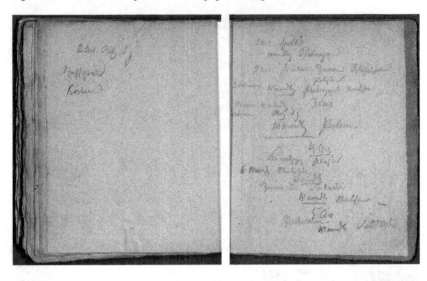

Not included in this kind of list or summary are references to extras and silent roles.⁴⁰ Some notes regarding them have been added on 102r and the otherwise empty folio 102v, but somewhat more illegibly than the more organised form of a list (cf. figure 71).

*Figure 71: Nm, 102v.*

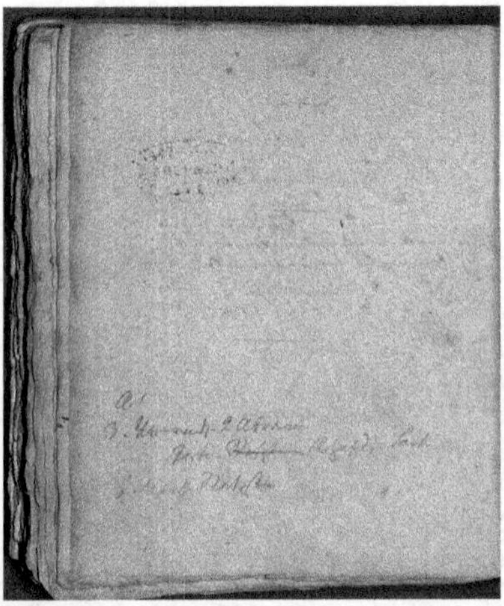

---

40  Such silent roles were also played by regular members of a company, but apparently not always with the necessary degree of professionalism. Schröder's theatre regulations explicitly urged the inspector to report any negligence to the directorate if their instructions were not followed (cf. Schröder 1798, 4f.).

However, extras and silent roles were not only mentioned in summaries towards the end of *Theater-Bibliothek: 1988a* but also appear in the scenes they were part of. This is the case at the beginning of Act II on folio 23v. This scene is set in a room in Saladin's palace, where the sultan and his sister Sittah are playing chess. An addition made in pencil at the top of the folio concerns the associated chess set, which seems to be a particularly important prop. Two other additions in pencil now refer to someone who was presumably an extra. In the beginning, there is also another person on stage: a male slave stands in the open door of the room ("Ein Sclave steht in der offenen Thür" [A slave stands in the open door]) and exits shortly afterwards ("Sclave ab" [Slave exits]) on the order of his master Saladin. This character was not part of the dramatic text or the initial content of the written artefact and was added when the play was performed in Hamburg. The corresponding references were added to *Theater-Bibliothek: 1988a* at some point while the book was being used for a production (cf. figure 72).[41]

*Figure 72: Nm, 23v.*

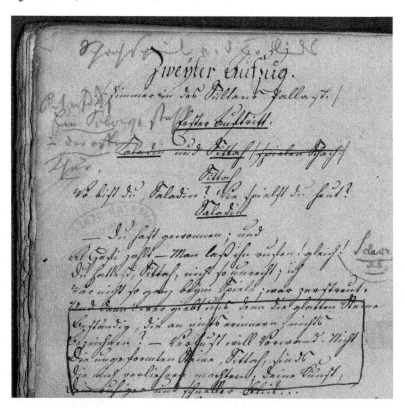

---

41   *Theater-Bibliothek: 1988b* also has an addition refering to the slave. Cf. Np, 50.

The character is also included in the cast list at the beginning of the written artefact. The fact that there is no actor's name accompanying it supports the theory that he was played by an extra. However, two additional characters who had similarly minor roles in the scene were probably played by people more closely connected with or even part of the theatre company. The cast list mentions their names: "Eine Sclavin" [a female slave] was played by one Fräulein Grünwald in the 1846 staging, the "Thürsteher" [doorman] by a Herr Koster.[42] In their scenes, additions refer to these names instead of the characters' names, which indicates that they played extras on a permanent basis (cf. figures 73 and 74).

Figure 73: Nm, 43r.

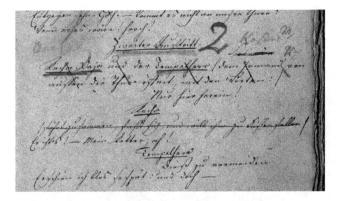

Figure 74: Nm, 95v.

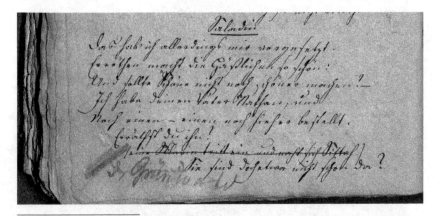

---

42 This might have had to do with the fact that these two characters are, unlike the male slave, also part of the dramatic text. The doorman, however, was not a designated character. The secondary text only mentions "jemand" [someone] who opens the door of Nathan's house and shows the arriving Templar in, saying something like, "Nur hier herein" [Here this way] (cf. Lessing 1993, 544).

Additions like these were made because the inspector was responsible for extras, silent roles, and other similar parts. The reference to guest star Eduard Jerrmann on folio 65r has a comparable purpose. It indicated when the actor (who was not present on stage for a few scenes) could change his costume.[43]

These various examples demonstrate that *Theater-Bibliothek: 1988a* was clearly put to use by an inspector. Information that was necessary for managing certain processes during a performance – i.e., organising scene changes, decorations, props, extras, and silent roles – was added systematically throughout the book and transformed the written artefact into a technical score for the performance.

## IV. Transforming a Print Copy into a Prompt Book: Technical Requirements for Creation and Use in *Theater-Bibliothek: 1988b*

The use of the enriched, print-based *Theater-Bibliothek: 1988b* is largely characterised by dynamics different to those of *Theater-Bibliothek: 1988a*. Despite any similarities and correspondences, the revisions made to the designated prompter's copy differ significantly. There were often other intentions behind the operations, and the operations themselves were often either different or were carried out in a different way. This was due to the book's main purpose: because it was used by a prompter, it always had to contain the latest version of the dramatic text, which was the main objective of its updates. It also had to do with the written artefact's mediality: *Theater-Bibliothek: 1988b* was based on a print copy with a different layout and different content that varied from the outset. Accordingly, it had to be modified in a different way to *Theater-Bibliothek: 1988a*. Furthermore, traces of various writing tools and multiple layers of updates throughout the book indicate that a number of people were involved in the process. All of this has contributed to a particularly complex material performance that might appear illegible to an outside eye. It is not always possible to identify the final layer, i.e., the latest version of the content, or to reconstruct the interplay between the various layers. Many of the modifications are not immediately comprehensible and raise questions about the book's practical usefulness. *Theater-Bibliothek: 1988b* is an example of how continuously updating a prompt book could increasingly impede one of its main purposes: to be used during a performance as a prompting tool, with the prompter providing the latest version of the dramatic point of reference for the performance with only the poor lighting of a candle to read by – but immediately and clearly.

Apart from its enriched content, *Theater-Bibliothek: 1988b* contains another register of additions directly related to the performance. Like some of the additions

---

43 The addition says "Umzug Jerrmann" (Nm, 65r) [change Jerrmann].

to the manuscript of *Theater-Bibliothek: 1988a*, this information pertains to technical stage requirements. One might think that the attributions made on the covers might not always have been correct, i.e., that neither the manuscript *Theater-Bibliothek: 1988a* nor the print-based *Theater-Bibliothek: 1988b* was used by the inspector or prompter alone.[44] However, the technical additions can also be explained in another way: besides feeding the actors lines, the prompter also had to carry out coordination tasks during a performance and was thus also involved in technical processes. Some of these included areas of responsibility that were also relevant to the inspector. It was the prompter's task to give cues from their box at the right time so that the inspector could then supervise changes made to the stage, but also so that the curtain could be lowered. It was common in nineteenth-century theatre for two cues to be given for each. In the event of changes, the prompter first gave a signal to clear the stage, then another to set up the new scene. When the curtain was about to fall, they gave a first signal to the technician in charge to get ready and then a second signal to carry out the process. Timing was crucial for both processes. The cues were not to be given too early or too late in order to ensure that the end of the scene would not be disturbed and that transitions take place smoothly.[45]

*Figure 75: Np, 146 and 147.*

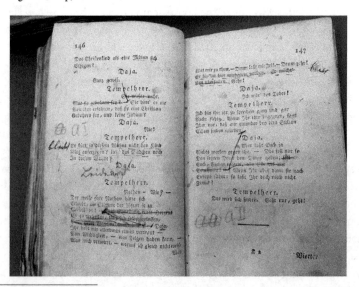

---

44  And it would not be entirely unusual either. Such a change in function has obviously also taken place in the case of *Theater-Bibliothek: 1987a* and *Theater-Bibliothek: 2022b*. The former is a manuscript of *Die Räuber* [*The Robbers*] that was initially used as a prompter's copy and then as an inspector's copy; the latter is a print copy of *Maria Stuart* that was used for both functions.

45  Cf. Düringer/Barthels 1841, 1137f.

There are additions to *Theater-Bibliothek: 1988b* that can be attributed to both processes. The lowering of the curtain at the end of an act was indicated by the letter "a" for "actus", which appears twice in the last scene of every act (cf. figure 75).

Like the cues for scene changes, the first sign, "a I", was added towards the end of the scene, but while it was still running. This should have given the stagehands in charge enough time to prepare everything required for the curtain to then be lowered after the last reply. The cue for this was indicated by the second sign, "a II".

Related processes seem to have taken place in a slightly different fashion: scene changes are indicated using the letters "v" or "w" for "Verwandlung" or "Wandlung" [both meaning "transformation"], with "w" used in the most recent layers (cf. figures 76 and 77).

*Figure 76: Np, 130.*  *Figure 77: Np, 131.*

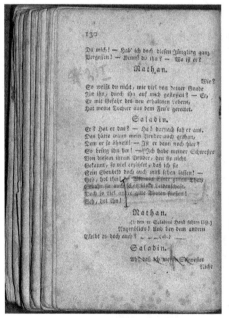 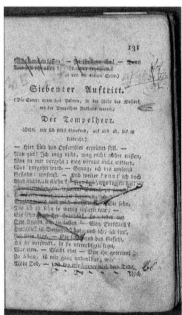

Figure 77 shows that the second of the two signs, "W II", was added at the end of the scene, where the two actors exit the stage. The first sign, "W I", however, was added at a point in the book where the scene was actually still running. It is debatable whether the stage would have been cleared when, as in the present example, Nathan and Saladin were still engrossed in their dialogue. However, in order to avoid interruptions between two scenes within one act, it was not uncommon to move the last part of a scene to the front of the stage and to lower the drop curtain, behind which the scene could then be changed.[46] It seems probable that this was also the case in the Hamburg performances of *Nathan der Weise*.[47] (The temporary reduction in stage space would have also fitted in with the content: at the end of the dialogue, Nathan and Saladin come to talk about the young Templar and the closeness they both feel with him.)

Only a few changes in *Theater-Bibliothek: 1988b*, the print-based prompt book, were technical additions. It was inevitable that the book would undergo extensive modifications; the decision to use a print copy of Lessing's published version of the play as the basis for a prompter's copy of the Schiller adaptation called for alignment. The Lessing content needed to be revised and, accordingly, the underlying printed text in *Theater-Bibliothek: 1988b* had to be enriched in handwriting.

The revisions concerned details as well as the overall structure of the play. Since Schiller's *Nathan der Weise* was considerably shorter, the revisions initially consisted of cancellations that ranged from single verses to entire speeches and complete scenes. Several writing tools and paper practices were involved in this process. One example of a rather minor alignment can be found in one of Saladin's speeches on pages 115 and 116: two of his lines have been crossed out in accordance with Schiller's adaptation. Evidently, this operation was carried out repeatedly. A dark ink, a grey pencil, and a red pencil were used successively to do the same: to cross out the two lines (cf. figures 78 and 79).

*Figure 78: Np, 115.*

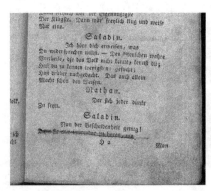

*Figure 79: Np, 116.*

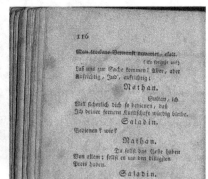

---

46 Cf. Borcherdt in NA 13, 294f.

47 Borcherdt mentions this practice in Leipzig and Dresden stagings of Schiller's *Fiesco* and *Don Carlos* (cf. NA 13, 295). It was more usual for the drop curtain to be lowered only after a scene had ended in order to change the rear part of the stage, while the next scene was played in front of the drop curtain (cf. Birkner 2007; cf. Malchow 2022, 322–333 and 371–378). However, Malchow also mentions the possibility of lowering the drop curtain within a scene in connection with Schröder's staging of *Der Kaufmann von Venedig* [*The Merchant of Venice*], cf. Malchow 2022, 378.

Characteristically of the material performance of *Theater-Bibliothek: 1988b*, passages were often revised more than once. These three writing tools were used in many cases, though not always at once or in the same order. The way they interacted, however, stayed the same: they took up previous revisions which they either repeated and emphasised or modified. The modifications in particular indicate that the approximation of Schiller's version was a process and the outcome of multiple layers of updates. This can be seen, for example, on page seven. The cancellations in the lower part of the page add up to a version that corresponds to Schiller's. Both pencils and the dark ink were involved (cf. figure 80).

*Figure 80: Np, 7.*

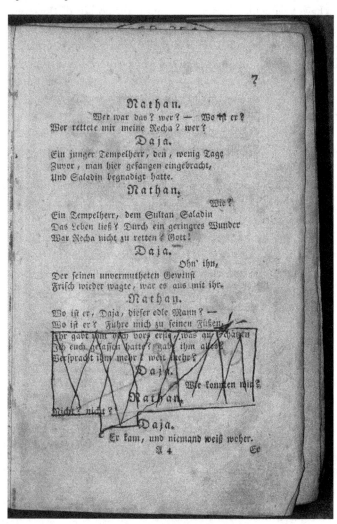

At first, the grey pencil has struck through one part of Nathan's third speech and Daja's reaction, thus connecting Nathan's third and his fourth speeches. The red pencil has then modified this retraction, extending it to cover larger parts of the third and fourth speeches. A hand working in dark ink has emphasised this, initially with just a diagonal line, before ultimately framing and emphatically crossing out the entire section.

Often, these retractions also extend to the next page or even pages. On some occasions, they are accompanied by additional signs or notes that did not concern the dramatic text itself but had a pragmatic purpose. They were not updates but instructions directed at the reader of the book, tips that helped them to use it. Below the printed text at the bottom of page 107, for example, the subsequent two speeches have been added in dark ink, minimally abridged. However, the next page, where these speeches form part of the printed text, has been cancelled out completely by a diagonal line that has been drawn in what is presumably the same dark ink. This cancellation extends to the top of the following page. Now, at the bottom of page 107, next to the two speeches, there is another addition: the letters "vi=". The equals sign indicates that a word has been divided; the missing part of the word can be found at the top of page 109. Right next to the end of the cancellation "=de" has been added. The use of the divided Latin word "vide" was common in prompt books and other written artefacts employed in theatre productions.[48] It was a tool used to signal a more extensive cancellation, to draw the user's attention to the beginning and the end of an invalidated passage, and to remind said user to carefully look at what was taking place in the written artefact. This may well have been necessary, as matters are not always clear in *Theater-Bibliothek: 1988b*.

On page twenty-five, at the beginning of a cancellation that is similarly extensive but more complex, as all the aforementioned writing tools were involved, the same kind of addition is accompanied by an indication of how far the retraction of the printed text extends. In this way, the user of the book knew immediately which page to turn to. Interestingly, this highly practical type of information was not added systematically to the book, even though other abridgements were equally extensive and complex (cf. figure 81).[49]

---

48 Düringer and Barthels, for example, mention it in their list of usual abbreviations from theatre manuscript culture (cf. Düringer/Barthels 1841, 9–12).

49 See, for example, the respective sections in Act II, Scene 3, and Act II, Scene 4, or the at some point entirely cancelled scenes Act IV, Scene 5, and Act IV, Scene 6.

*Figure 81: Np, 25.*

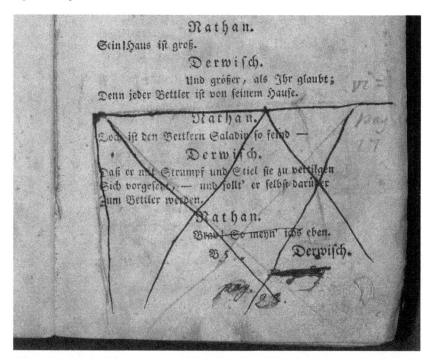

This complexity was not the result of any kind of ambiguity about the purpose of the operations. Rather, it was due to their materiality: the multitudes of layers and their various realisations tended to cause a certain amount of confusion and repeatedly required increased attention. Sometimes, the extensive abridgements have been changed again and parts of the cancelled-out texts have been reintegrated. Other parts have been revised so intensively that they are no longer immediately comprehensible.

The end of Act III, Scene 1, provides one example of the former. It seems that, at some point, the retraction of the printed text began at the bottom of page ninety-nine and extended to page 101, but not quite to the end of the scene. The last two verses were not included in these retractions as they provided for a transition to the next scene. But in what was presumably a later revision, the cancellations on page 100 were partially cancelled out once more. The red and grey pencil were apparently erased, the ends of Recha's and then Daja's lines in the middle of the page were thus rendered valid again, and only then the dark ink – apart from slightly modifying Recha's lines – repeated and emphasised the further course of the cancellation as a final layer (cf. figures 82 and 83).

*Figure 82: Np, 100.*     *Figure 83: Np, 101.*

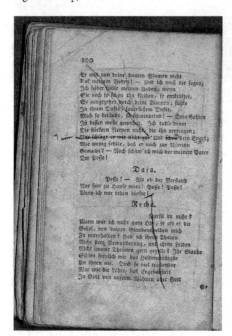
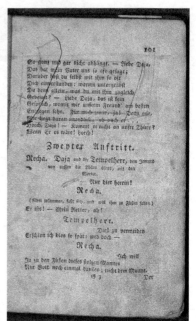

A passage from Act IV, Scene 4, illustrates the latter. Here, a part of the dialogue between the Templar and Saladin seems to have been revised over and over again. In this part, Saladin defends Nathan against the Templar's accusation that Nathan actually believes his own religion to be superior and explicitly praises him for not making that mistake ("Nathans Loos / ist diese Schwachheit nicht" [This weakness is not Nathan's lot]). At least, this was what he did before the revisions and what, according to the logic of the character, he should have still been doing afterwards. It does not seem entirely clear, however, whether the praise really emanates from him at the end of the enriched version; the excessive material performance makes it unclear which version of the text was ultimately valid (cf. figure 84).

Due to the materiality of the enrichment, there is uncertainty about whether the Templar's reply above the framed section ("Der Aberglauben schlimmster ist, den seinen / Für den erträglichern zu halten" [Considering one's own superstition to be the more tolerable one is the worst superstition]) has been cancelled out or not. The red pencil and ink lines beneath it seem to reinstate its validity because the same lines were also drawn in red pencil below the lines of praise, which the different versions all have ended up with. Also contributing to this impression is the word "bleibt" [remains] written in dark ink in the outer margin next to the Templar's lines.

*Figure 84: Np, 170.*

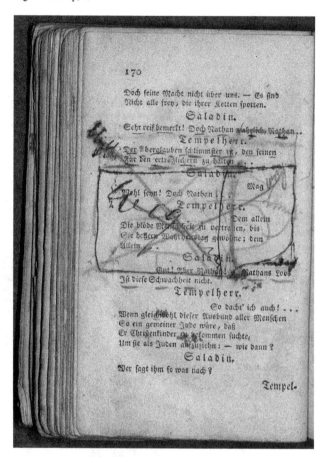

On the other hand, the reply might have been cancelled out yet again by the diagonal stroke made in red pencil. Then there is also the slightly bent vertical line drawn in dark ink on the right-hand side. Once we realise that this vertical line is a bit shorter and coextensive with the frame, it is the Templar's underlined speech that the praise of Nathan is connected to. Otherwise, it would have to be connected to Saladin's prior response, which is also underlined. The facts speak for the latter. It simply would not make any sense at this point if the Templar were praising Nathan for not succumbing to self-righteous religious delusion when that is precisely what he has just accused him of. The multiple layers of revisions and the back-and-forth between cancellations and their cancellations create material ambiguity, even where there is great clarity with regard to the content.

However, the complicated and sometimes confusing material performance of *Theater-Bibliothek: 1988b* has not only been shaped by the different writing tools and their interplay; rather, other paper practices were in use too, sometimes to implement more extensive changes. In his adaptation, Schiller left out the first two scenes of the fifth act. Accordingly, they were not included in *Theater-Bibliothek: 1988a* from the outset. In *Theater-Bibliothek: 1988b*, however, they were part of the initial content and needed to be cancelled out. Two practices were combined to do so: pages 193 to 198 were folded at the lower outer edge so that pages 194 to 197, which contain most of Act V, Scene 1, could be skipped when the reader turned the page. The beginning of Act V, Scene 1, on page 193 as well as Act V, Scene 2, on pages 198 and 199 have been thoroughly crossed out using a red pencil. These cancellations frame the pages invalidated by the folding (cf. figure 85).

*Figure 85: Np, 193.*

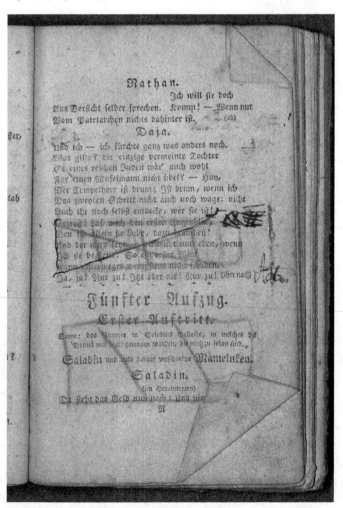

However, these revisions could have been easily reversed, at least in part: if required, the pages could have simply been unfolded again. Radically irrevocable, on the other hand, were the revisions to Act II, Scene 2. In Lessing's version, the beginning of the scene is dominated by the chess game between Saladin and Sittah, in which the rather absent-minded sultan shows minimal interest in winning before their conversation turns to the unstable political situation and the impending conflict with the Templars. Schiller shortened large parts of this scene, in particular most of the chess game. This was also done in *Theater-Bibliothek: 1988b*, but not by crossing out parts of the text or by folding over the respective pages. Instead, six pages were physically cut out – and rather unceremoniously at that, it would seem (cf. figure 86).

*Figure 86: Np, 51, margin of cut pages.*

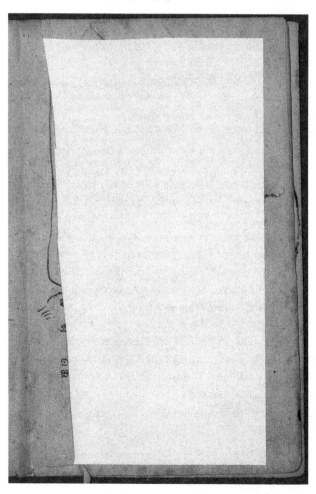

It would be fair to assume that this irreversible modification was motivated by the content of the scene. The materiality of the written artefact may have factored in as well. The sequence with Saladin and Sittah playing chess and commenting on each other's moves might be interesting for readers, but not so much for viewers, which is why this part of Lessing's text is not really appealing as a potential part of a performance. Accordingly, it was very unlikely that the scene would ever be reintegrated, no matter how true the staging of the play remained to Schiller's version over the years or to what degree it differed. Moreover, the fact that *Theater-Bibliothek: 1988b* is based on a print copy of the play might have made the decision easier. If necessary, a new book could have been obtained more quickly and with less effort than in the case of a manuscript. The easy availability of the printed book at least allowed for a different pattern of use: it did not fundamentally change the operations used to update the book, but it did affect the potential consequences of some of those operations.

Because the pages have been cut out, the scene now continues on page fifty-seven in the middle of a lengthy speech by Saladin, which has itself been shortened using the three writing tools mentioned above. In order to make a coherent connection here, the beginning of the scene also had to be changed. This modified beginning was added to the book on an extra sheet pasted in on page fifty, right under the stage instructions (cf. figure 87).

It is not the operation itself that is of significance here but what it adds to the book. The content on this extra sheet differs both from Schiller's later final version[50] and from the manuscript *Theater-Bibliothek: 1988a*.[51] Although the beginning of Act II, Scene 1, in *Theater-Bibliothek: 1988a* is not identical with Schiller's 1805 version either, these differences are only minor and derive from the different work stages to which both versions correspond.[52] The revision in the print-based *Theater-Bibliothek: 1988b* seems to have been developed more specifically within the Hamburg theatre context: the scene is still somewhat shorter than Schiller's. The newly added text corresponds neither to Lessing's 1791 print nor to Schiller's 1805 version. On a technical level, however, it was created in a similar way: it omits parts of Lessing's text, recombines others, and adds a minimal amount of new text, although the newly added text has been taken from the textual material of the Lessing template. In this context, the omission of Saladin's now futile dream of marrying his siblings off to those of the Christian King Richard is particularly striking. Thus, the possibility, albeit brief and purely imaginary, of lasting inter-

---

50 Cf. NA 13, 191.

51 Cf. Nm, 23v–24r.

52 Saladin's first reply in *Theater-Bibliothek: 1988a*, for example, begins with "Du hast gewonnen" [You have won] (Nm, 23v), which Schiller extended in his final edition to "Gleichviel! Du hast das Spiel gewonnen" [All the same! You have won the game] (NA 13, 191).

religious and intercultural peace has been deleted from the play without compensation. We will discuss a number of other changes in this vein below.

Figure 87: Np, 50.

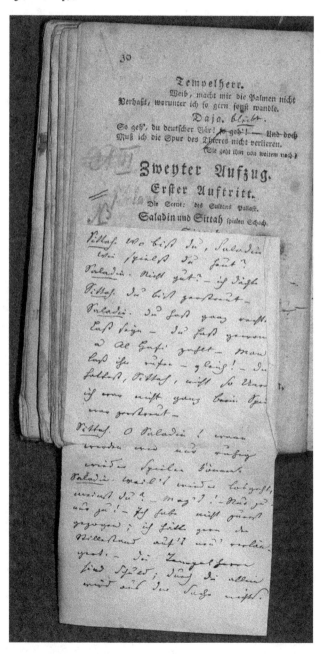

## V. The Evolution of an Adaptation I: Simultaneous or Non-Simultaneous Use

The beginning of Act II, Scene 2, exemplarily reveals the relationship between the two written artefacts to each other (and also to Schiller's later 1805 version). It is a case in point for the variations and differences that developed during the use of the two books. The reason for some differences may have been the different purposes served by the written artefacts. In other instances, the significant differences indicate that the manuscript *Theater-Bibliothek: 1988a* and the print-based *Theater-Bibliothek: 1988b* were not used simultaneously by a pairing of inspector and prompter at all times – or that they were, but that it did not really matter on a pragmatic level if a book was not up to date. It seems that, for both books, the revisions that followed from their use were generally guided not by the authority of a dramatic author (Lessing's or Schiller's template) but by pragmatic considerations.

### Correlations and Disparities

There are revisions that were only made in one of the two written artefacts. Often, they are not complex on a material level, nor do they change the content in a similar way to the revisions in Act II, Scene 2. But they have various effects that go beyond shortening overlong speeches. Take, for example, the Templar's lines at the top of page 171 in *Theater-Bibliothek: 1988b*, the designated prompt book. Disappointed and angered by Nathan's behaviour, which the Templar views as a rejection of his courtship, the Templar reveals Recha's Christian origins to Saladin in Act IV, Scene 4. Some of his lines were crossed out over time: at first, half a line was struck through in red pencil, followed by the preceding two and a half lines in the now faded grey pencil, an action that was then repeated once more in dark ink and thereby reinforced. These cancellations ensured greater focus on the main information provided in the reply – the revelation that Recha is only Nathan's adopted daughter. In *Theater-Bibliothek: 1988a*, however, the reply has not been revised at all. Backstage, the inspector might not have been in need of the latest version of the text – as long as the change did not interfere with their overall technical responsibilities (cf. figures 88 and 89).

*Figure 88: Np, 171.*

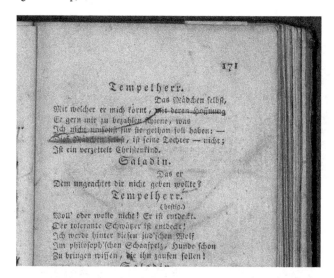

*Figure 89: Nm, 75r.*

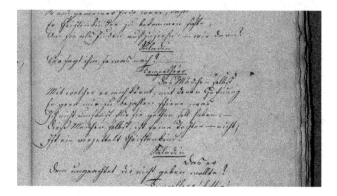

There are, on the other hand, revisions that were made in both written artefacts, but whose execution differs fundamentally on a material level. On folio 28r in *Theater-Bibliothek: 1988a*, one of Sittah's speeches and the beginning of Saladin's response have been cancelled out. As a consequence, two of Saladin's speeches have become one. To highlight this connection and to indicate where the new speech continues after the cancellation, a vertical sinuous line has been drawn (cf. figure 90).

*Figure 90: Nm, 28r.*

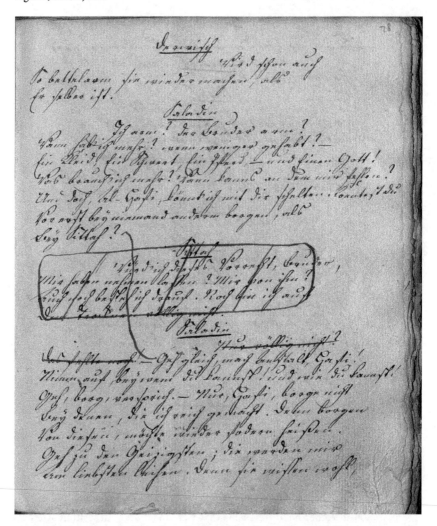

Of course, in *Theater-Bibliothek: 1988b*, the print-based prompt book, much greater effort was required to create the same dialogue. The content of one and a half pages has been cancelled out and partly replaced with the help of a piece of paper pasted over the upper half of page sixty-six. Its content is thus to follow the lines at the top of page sixty-five. The valid text continues right below the piece of paper. The result is an identical dialogue in both books – a dialogue that differs from both Lessing's version and presumably the one sent in by Schiller in 1803 (and definitely from Schiller's ultimate 1805 version). It gives an example of how the template Schiller had submitted in Hamburg in 1803 was the starting point for a work in progress (cf. figures 91 and 92).

*Figure 91: Np, 65.*  *Figure 92: Np, 66.*

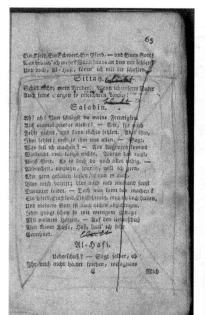
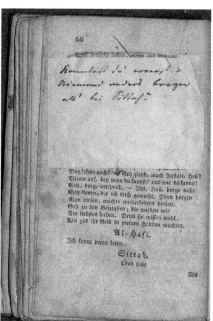

However, it took several layers of revisions for the print-based *Theater-Bibliothek: 1988b* to arrive at the same result. Extensive cancellations on page sixty-five in red crayon and graphite pencil were taken back at some point. But this disavowal of the retraction was in turn retracted once more. The word "bleibt" has been added several times and then crossed out again in dark ink – thus reinforcing the original cancellation anew.

There are repeated modifications of the same passages in both books. After initial parallel revisions, these modifications sometimes diverged again at a later date. This was the case in scenes like Act V, Scene 5: at the bottom of folio 89v in *Theater-Bibliothek: 1988a* (the manuscript), parts of the Templar's lines have been crossed out in dark ink up to the top of folio 90r. The same hand presumably also retracted his last reply on the same folio (cf. figures 93 and 94).

226   Martin Jörg Schäfer and Alexander Weinstock: Theatre in Handwriting

*Figure 93: Nm, 89v.*

*Figure 94: Nm, 90r.*

In *Theater-Bibliothek: 1988b*, the print-based written artefact, the same lines were crossed out, in grey and red pencil on page 210 and in faded red pencil on page 211. Both sections were then revised further. The strike-through of the Templar's lines on page 211 has been withdrawn, as the underlining and "bleibt" show, but only in *Theater-Bibliothek: 1988b* (cf. figures 95 and 96).

*Figure 95: Np, 210.*

*Figure 96: Np, 211.*

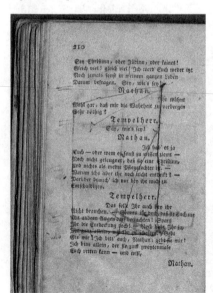
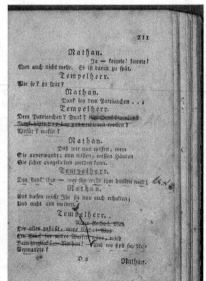

The Templar's other speech became the subject of further revisions and more extensive cancellations in both books. But these cancellations are not entirely identical. In fact, they each allow for different accentuations. In the print-based *Theater-Bibliothek: 1988b*, the passage has been modified by several layers, some of which have faded. The latest version has been established in the dark ink. The cancellation made using this ink begins at the top of the page, right after the Templar's first speech, and ends in the same place on the page as the initial cancellation. The result is a contracted speech by the Templar that already starts on page 209. The new ending attached to it by the abridgement further intensifies the urgency of the Templar's courtship of Recha, which is under threat from the Patriarch: "Sey, wie's sey! Gebt / Sie mir! Ich bitt' euch!, Nathan; gebt sie mir! / Ich bins allein, der sie zum zweitenmale / Euch retten kann – und will" (Np, 210) [Be that as it may! Give / her to me! I implore you, Nathan; give her to me! / I am the only one who can save her for you for the second time – and wants to do so].

In the manuscript *Theater-Bibliothek: 1988a*, on the other hand, the section has been revised less intensely. In fact, there is just one more layer. Two pencil strokes on folios 89r and 90v have established the latest version. It resembles *Theater-Bibliothek: 1988b* but is not identical: the cancellation starts a little later and extends a little further, or so it seems. This has led, firstly, to the inclusion of more lines by Nathan, in which he addresses the Templar's insinuations. Secondly, it appears to eliminate the Templar's explicit, urgent request for Recha. The cancellation goes so far that the Templar now merely emphasises that he alone can still save her without explicitly responding to Nathan's question: "Nathan: Ihr wähnt / Wohl gar, daß mir die Wahrheit zu verbergen sehr nöthig? / Tempelherr: Ich bins allein, der sie zum zweitenmale Euch retten kann – und will" (Nm, 89v–90r) [Nathan: It seems you believe that I very much need to conceal the truth? Templar: I am the only one who can save her for you for the second time – and wants to]. This potentially contributes to the Templar taking a somewhat more distanced attitude towards Nathan – something that is quite inherent in the character's distrustful, almost suspicious side.

This passage from Act V, Scene 5, illustrates how close the traces of parallel and apparently independent use are to each other in the entangled material performance of the manuscript *Theater-Bibliothek: 1988a* and the print-based *Theater-Bibliothek: 1988b*.[53] Identical, similar, and different revisions resulting from varying layers, which are generally more numerous in *Theater-Bibliothek: 1988b*, characterise the relationship between the two written artefacts. The material effort required to carry out the revisions was sometimes disproportionate to the content

---

53 What also contributes to the impression of independent use is the modification of the Templar's second speech in the middle of page 211 in *Theater-Bibliothek: 1988b*. Parts of it have been cancelled out here but not in *Theater-Bibliothek: 1988a*; cf. Nm, 90r.

of the changes. This was due to the different versions of the play with which the books started out (Schiller's adaption in the manuscript, Lessing's third edition in the print-based prompt book) as much as it was due to the different media comprising their primary layer: a manuscript and a printed book.

## Reintroducing Segments from the Canonised Print Version

Two more features need to be mentioned with regard to the dynamics of the prompt book and the inspector's book: the growing importance of Lessing's print template for the manuscript *Theater-Bibliothek: 1988a* and the extra time the ending takes in both written artefacts – apparently created at the theatre, independently of Lessing and Schiller. Both concern the entanglement between the dramatic text and its theatrical staging as well as the authority of the author in relation to the practices of the stage.

It has already been pointed out that Schiller's adaptation was the model for many of the enrichments in *Theater-Bibliothek: 1988b*, the print copy of Lessing's play. What is striking is that there are traces of an opposing dynamic in the manuscript *Theater-Bibliothek: 1988a*: modifications reinsert passages of Lessing's text that had been left out in Schiller's revision. Such reinsertions can be found several times in the written artefact. In Act III, Scene 2, in the Templar's first speech on folio 44v, for instance, there is a small triangle and a small # symbol. The same symbols were also drawn on an extra piece of paper pasted onto the folio like a subsequent sheet (cf. figures 97 and 98).

*Figure 97: Nm, 44v with symbols indicating insertion.*

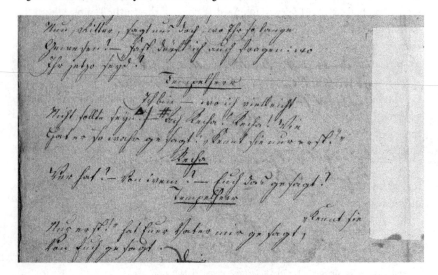

*Figure 98: Nm, extra sheet glued to 44v.*

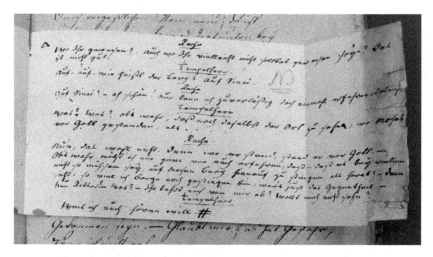

The content of this extra sheet was supposed to be added between the triangle and the # symbol on folio 44v, right in the middle of a verse that Schiller had created out of two different speeches from Lessing's text. The sheet contains lines from Lessing's original version of the play that once again extend the abbreviated scene – more specifically, part of the dialogue between the Templar and Recha, in which she asks him in a somewhat naïve and innocent manner about his experience ascending and descending from Mount Sinai. The reinserted lines from Lessing provide stronger motivation for the subsequent expression of the Templar's blossoming affection.[54]

Although the scribe of *Theater-Bibliothek: 1988a* has not yet been identified, we do know who was responsible for the writing on the extra sheet: the writing is by Herzfeld, the person who had not only ordered a copy of Schiller's adaptation to begin with but who, at some point, also seems to have been the driving force behind the partial realignment of the book with Lessing's original template. This is also evident in other scenes. Three loose sheets have been preserved with the book, each of which can be precisely assigned to specific folios. They all contain parts of Lessing's published print edition of the play. Herzfeld was the one responsible for the writing on two of the sheets (cf. figure 99).

---

54 Some of the respective section in the print version was cancelled at some point, but this cancellation was repealed again in a later revision (cf. Np, 104).

*Figure 99: three sheets with additional content.*

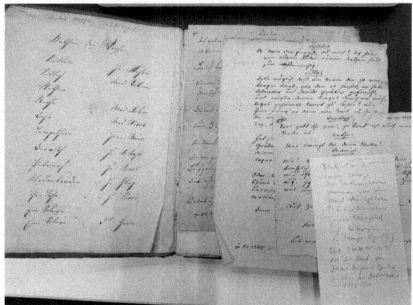

The content of the first sheet belongs to folio 12v, one part of Act I, Scene 3. Two diacritical signs[55] – a circle crossed out twice and a triangle – indicate where on the folio it was supposed to be added: right before the previously mentioned revision of the passage using Schiller's own text. These signs also provide a crucial clue about the order of the revisions. The triangle was added to the pasted-in sheet, which was accordingly added first.[56] In other words, while the prompt book had been initially further updated in the sense of Schiller's adaptation, it was then later readapted to the version of Lessing's play available in print.

In Act I, Scene 3, Herzfeld's addition brings a topic back into the play that Schiller had largely omitted: the great importance of money, which is closely associated with economic power and dependence.[57] Nathan is not only wise but also rich; he talks about tolerance but also about money and business. Saladin, too, is

---

55 They were also used in *Theater-Bibliothek: 728* and are described in Chapter 4.
56 Cf. Nm, 12v.
57 Scholars have given various reasons for this against different aesthetic and poetological backdrops. In his NA comment, Borcherdt talks about a "bewußtem Idealisierungsprinzip" [conscious idealisation principle] according to which "die Motivwelt [...] ihrer materiellen Bedingtheit entkleidet werden soll" [the imagery is to be stripped of its material conditions] (NA 13, 318). Müller (2004) also argues that the repeated discussion of the sultan's financial needs is inappropriate with regard to the *Ständeklausel* [estates clause] in theatre (cf. Müller 2004, 183). On the role of economics in the play, see, for example, Weidmann 1994 and Schönert 2008.

driven by financial worries in the face of a renewed conflict with the Templars. Both levels are by no means mutually exclusive in Lessing's version. The addition in Herzfeld's hand reincludes this aspect of the play.[58]

This is also the case with regard to the other major addition made in his hand. The content of the second loose sheet belongs to Act II, Scene 3. A triangle and a letter "Q" on folio 30v indicate that it was also supposed to be added in the middle of a verse that Schiller had created out of two separate speeches (cf. figure 100).

*Figure 100: Nm, 30v.*

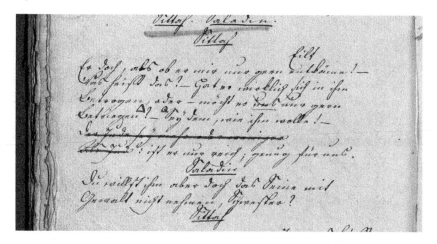

The reinserted passage extends the dialogue between Saladin and Sittah. They now explicitly discuss Nathan's wealth, which they both attribute to his successful trading activities. Moreover, the part of the conversation in which the rumours about the mysterious origins of his fortune are mentioned has also been integrated back into the version of the play found in *Theater-Bibliothek: 1988a*.

Apart from these sheets, Herzfeld also added other short passages from Lessing's text. They set the same accents in the content. At the beginning of Act V, Scene 6, Saladin, who has just rid himself of his financial worries, emphasises the importance of money for merchants. The respective lines have been squeezed in using dark ink on folio 96r, right next to the lines that Schiller had left them out of (cf. figure 101).

---

58 However, the resulting version does not seem entirely smooth. The transition from Lessing's reinserted text on the loose sheet to Schiller's text on the pasted-in sheet reads: "Nathan: Auch Zins vom Zins der Zinsen? / – Derwisch: Freilich! – Nathan: Bis / Mein Kapital zu lauter Zinsen wird. Nun, aber, daß du dich dazu entschlossen? – Derwisch: Was mich verführte? Gut! so! hört mich an!" [Nathan: Also interest from the interest of interest? / – Dervish: Of course! – Nathan: Until / My capital becomes pure interest. But now, that you have resolved to do this? – Dervish: What tempted me? Good! so! hear me!].

*Figure 101: Nm, 96r.*

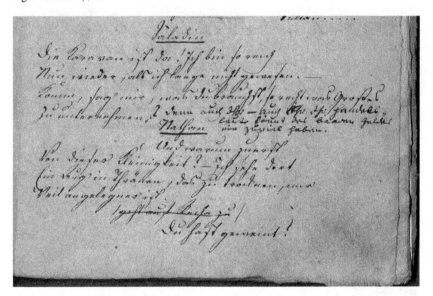

In a similar fashion, some of Recha's lines have been revised in Act V, Scene 4. A few of them have been cancelled out and some new content added in the limited free space right next to them (cf. figure 102).

*Figure 102: Nm, 93v.*

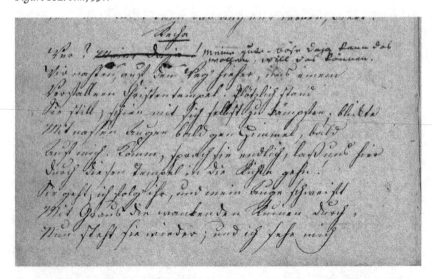

This addition does not really make any significant changes to the content, but it does highlight one of the character's traits. Recha now answers Sittah's question about who would want to force another father on her in the same way that she does in Lessing's original print publication, i.e., in an almost childlike manner.[59] This character trait is emphasised in another revision at the beginning of the same scene: a crossed-out circle and a triangle on folio 92v indicate that content was supposed to be added after Sittah's second speech (cf. figure 103).

*Figure 103: Nm, 92v.*

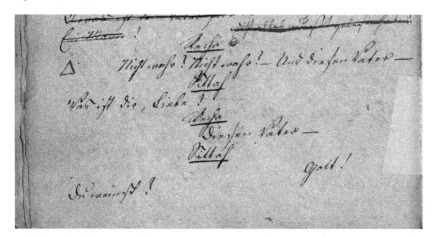

The content in question was written on the third loose sheet. This time, though, not by Herzfeld but by Barlow, the prompter. The addition of content to the folio itself has also been made in his hand, as has at least the retraction to the left of it. These crossed-out lines have not been cancelled out but moved to the end of the loose sheet; the same connection has thus been retained but relocated. In the extended, Lessing-based version of this section, Recha confesses that she can hardly read due to her father's aversion to scholarship based on dead signs. But now, in response, Sittah exclaims admiringly, "O was ist dein Vater für ein Mann!"[60] [Oh, what a man your father is!]. This revision now strengthens the accentuation of Recha's obedience and inexperience as a daughter who is dependent on her father.

---

59 Instead of, "Wer? Meine Daja!" [Who? My Daja!], she now says again, "Wer? Meine gute-böse Daja kann das wollen, will das können" [Who? Why my good-evil Daja can want that, wants to be able to do that] (Nm, 93v).

60 This is indeed a little irritating, because the part of the dialogue where Recha explains that her father himself educated her remains left out instead. It would have provided a more convincing motivation for the admiration felt by Sittah, who evidently agrees with Nathan that book-based education only leads to affectation and self-alienation (cf. Lessing 1993, 614f).

This is one of the two shifts that take place with the reintegration of Lessing's text into a written artefact based on Schiller's adaptation: the childlike, innocent, almost naïve side of Recha is now emphasised – which once again brings her closer to the daughter character that figured prominently in the bourgeois theatre of the time. She is an unaffected and virtuous young woman with the closest possible affective ties to her father and who is also confused by her feelings for a young man who is drawn to her. The other shift relates to the economic dimension of the play, i.e., the significance and value of money. Wealthy merchant Nathan's financial power makes him interesting to Saladin – the sultan himself knows that this is an indispensable prerequisite for maintaining political and military power. The renewed emphasis on this theme ensures that the dramatic diegesis, which is otherwise shaped by abstract ideals, becomes more tangible and specific. The reintroduced theme also refers to the social fields and structures for which ideals like tolerance and wisdom are presented as more than necessary.[61]

## Ending Extemporaneously

Among the revisions that directly relate to the Hamburg theatre context, one change stands out. It has its model in neither Lessing nor Schiller and instead seems to be related to the dynamics specific to the Hamburg performances. At some point, the already conciliatory ending of the play was amplified, apparently for greater stage effect. A few lines were added below the original reference to "the end" of the play. This extended ending was written in ink in the print-based prompt book *Theater-Bibliothek: 1988b* and in pencil in the inspector's manuscript book, *Theater-Bibliothek: 1988a*. On the one hand, the (very similar) additions encompass lines to be spoken while on the other hand pointing to the improvisational character of the extended finale. In addition to the dialogue, "p. p." ("perge perge", meaning "continue") has also been added in the print-based prompt book. However, it seems that this extended version did not become a permanent fixture in the play and was taken back again. In the modified ending, Saladin explicitly invites Nathan to join the reciprocal embraces indicated in the final stage directions. He refers to the central ring parable of the play and amicably affirms Nathan's moral authority as he exclaims, "Komm in meine Arme! – Nathan – deine Hand! Wie wars mit deinem Ring? – bist du mit mir zufrieden?" [Come into my arms! – Nathan – your hand! What was it about your ring? – are you satisfied with me?] (Np, 238) (cf. figures 104 and 105).

---

61 Interestingly, almost all of these sections look different in *Theater-Bibliothek: 1988b*. Not only is the degree of revision often very different, but the versions resulting from these revisions are usually only similar and not identical with *Theater-Bibliothek: 1988a* either.

*Figure 104: Nm, 102r.*  *Figure 105: Np, 238.*

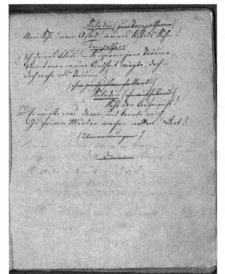 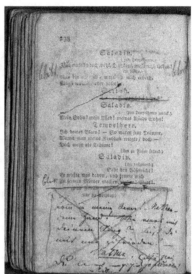

The untidy incompleteness of the addition is striking in both written artefacts. In the manuscript *Theater-Bibliothek: 1988a*, Nathan's final reaction has not been written out at all and is merely hinted at instead. In the print-based *Theater-Bibliothek: 1988b*, it has been written down so sloppily that some parts are scarcely legible. Other parts simply consist of a continuous line ending in "p. p.": the extended ending seems to have been largely improvised.

In the manuscript, Saladin's additional lines are somewhat illegible. Not only have they been written very carelessly, but the pencil has faded – or an attempt has been made to erase it. This corresponds to the crossing-out of the new handwritten ending in the print-based *Theater-Bibliothek: 1988b*. Apparently the extemporaneous finale was not a permanent change to the play. After a hiatus, a new generation of actors (and a new artistic director) might have preferred to stick with the lines of a text that, by that time, had become canonised and was being widely read in print.

## VI. The Evolution of an Adaptation II: Negotiating Christianity in Public

There is another type of revision that can be found to varying degrees in both written artefacts. It is likely that these changes were also directly related to the context of the Hamburg performances. On a material level, they do not differ from the other revisions; the same operations were employed to carry them out. However, they seem to have been neither aesthetically nor technically motivated. Instead, it is reasonable to suspect that they had something to do with the changing tastes of the public and the changing morals of the time. (They might have also been another attempt to preemptively avoid a brush with the authorities.) They concern a topic that is central to the play but that was potentially quite explosive and also seem to indicate changes in the way that this topic was dealt with over the course of two written artefacts' use. It is now well-established that, in *Nathan der Weise*, the theme of tolerance gains particular traction in connection to interfaith relations and the religions' respective claims to power. This is necessarily linked to an overarching critique of religion as such, especially Christianity. The play presents prejudices and delusions, but also their overcoming. In the process, it explores ways of thinking about and realising community and belonging – independently of, or at least not primarily through, religion.

A number of revisions found in both written artefacts suggest that it was not possible to bring this topic on stage without further ado. The changes affected, on the one hand, the emphasis on religious identities and, on the other, the strong criticism of Christianity, which is particularly pronounced in the version of Lessing's play that was available in print.[62] There were evidently periods of revision in which both aspects were toned down. However, this does not apply equally to both books. In fact, the manuscript *Theater-Bibliothek: 1988a* proves to have undergone much more revision in this respect.

Both aspects pertain to certain characters in the play: the first one primarily concerns the Templar and Recha, the second one the Patriarch. There are several sections throughout the play in which the Templar is either referred to or refers to himself as a Christian and as a Templar at the same time. In several instances, however, references to his religious identity have been crossed out in *Theater-Bibliotek: 1988a*,[63] while in *Theater-Bibliothek: 1988b* this is only sporadically the case.[64]

Similarly, the emphasis on Recha's religious identity is somewhat downplayed. In *Theater-Bibliothek: 1988a*, the Templar no longer stresses to the Patriarch that Recha is baptised. And even when he speaks to Nathan, he no longer explicitly refers to her possible religious affiliation.[65] One reason for these changes may

---

62 This constellation was in any case not without its problems. After all, a performance of the play brought to the theatre stage a fundamental critique of an institution that itself had a history of pronounced and forceful hostility towards the theatre. See, for example, Wild 2003, 167–356; Krebs 2005; Kolesch 2012.

63 Cf. Nm, 34v, 63r.

64 Cf. Np, 83.

65 Cf. Nm, 68v, 89v. In *Theater-Bibliothek: 1988b*, the respective lines were also cancelled out at one point. However, the revisions have faded so much that they are hardly visible anymore. This makes it at least questionable whether they were valid until the end of the book's use (cf. Np, 155 and, in particular, 210).

be the interfaith love between the two characters, which the play ultimately resolves through the "revelation" that both are Christians. Up until that point, however, interfaith love is continuously brought up as a problem. It seems to have been too provocative for the stage in times that were less tolerant than the age the play anticipated. Another reason for the revisions, which has more to do with the changes affecting the Templar, is the negative portrayal of Christianity and the Church – after all, the Templar can barely hold back his pejorative opinion. The retractions now offer a slight mitigation in that the criticism is not explicitly voiced by a Christian but "only" by a Templar. The focus shifts minimally from his denomination to his profession.

In this sense, too, the Muslim Sittah's sharp criticism of Christian intolerance is cancelled out in single strokes of dark ink at the beginning of the second act in *Theater-Bibliothek: 1988a* – as are parts of Saladin's subsequent reaction. Although he urges that a distinction be made between Christians in general and the Christian Templars, he still mentions both together, whereas the strike-through now reinforces their separation. The threatening outbreak of a new conflict is thus attributed to military and political efforts alone – while any explicit religious component is distinctly excluded.[66]

In the extensive revision to this scene in *Theater-Bibliothek: 1988b*, the print-based prompt book, these passages were cancelled at the start. The new beginning of the scene, which has been integrated into the prompt book on the pasted-in sheet, has been modified by means of abridgments and by recombining the text material in such a way that it no longer contains any explicit criticism of religion.[67]

Both written artefacts build on a strategy that had already defined Schiller's adaption, as Marion Müller has shown. She points out that Duke Karl August himself demanded retractions on two pages in Act II, Scene 1, before the play was staged in Weimar. Müller demonstrates that these pages included the part of the dialogue that contained detailed and explicit criticisms of Christianity.[68] The respective verses were consequently omitted by Schiller. They therefore did not form part of his Hamburg adaptation, as they had not been part of the version in *Theater-Bibliothek: 1988a* either, the manuscript copied from Schiller's template. Lessing's explicit and unsparing critique of Christian intolerance and self-righteousness as expressed in the scene with Sittah[69] was presumably radically shortened for political reasons. However, the far-reaching revisions of the dialogue in the two written artefacts used in the Hamburg theatre context demonstrate that, even decades later, remarks about Christianity had lost none of their political explosiveness.

---

66 Cf. Nm, 24r and v.
67 Cf. Np, 30.
68 Cf. Müller 2004, 178–180.
69 Cf. Lessing 1993, 517.

Having said that, not all negative portrayals of Christianity were so permanently erased. This applies above all to the treatment of the figure of the Patriarch, who was drawn by Lessing as an autocratic fanatic in an all-round pejorative manner. Looking at the revisions in both written artefacts, we see that, in the course of their use, attitudes changed regarding how negatively this supreme Church representative could now actually keep being depicted on the Hamburg stage. Almost all of the relevant passages in both books were the subject of two layers of revision. In the process, the second layer took back the first layer while retaining the primary layer. Apparently, concerns about portraying the Patriarch too negatively on stage played only a temporary role while *Theater-Bibliothek: 1988a* and *Theater-Bibliothek: 1988b* were in use.[70]

Take for example the beginning of Act IV, Scene 2: this is the first scene in which the Patriarch appears in person. He enters the stage not as a humble, pious man but in a stately, pompous manner. The part of the dialogue that demonstrates that this is inappropriate and rather questionable was retracted in the manuscript *Theater-Bibliothek: 1988a*, meaning that the character does not immediately appear in a bad light upon his first appearance. The corresponding lines have been framed in dark ink and crossed out with a single stroke. However, this retraction was taken back again. A "bleibt" was added in dark ink next to the framed section. This second layer cancelled out the validity of the first, restoring the initial negative impression (cf. figure 106).

*Figure 106: Nm, 67r.*

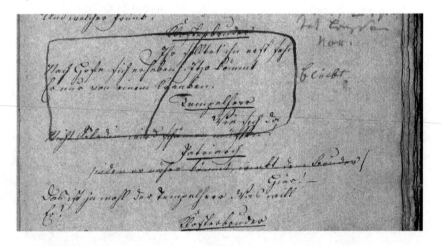

---

[70] This may indicate a somewhat more liberal climate in Hamburg. In Munich, for example, the play was only allowed to be staged at all after the character of the Patriarch was removed altogether, cf. NA 13, 419.

In *Theater-Bibliothek: 1988b*, the print-based prompt book, there is a related retraction at the beginning of the scene. It is somewhat less extensive and includes only one of the two speeches that were retracted in *Theater-Bibliothek: 1988a*. An initial diagonal pencil stroke has been repeated once more in dark ink. Unlike in the manuscript, there is no doubt about the inappropriateness of the Patriarch's conduct, even after a first layer of revision. Nevertheless, in a second layer, the already minimised critique has been fully withdrawn once more: a "bl" for "remains" has been added in pencil right next to the crossed-out lines. Even though the revision phases differ in both books, the scene was identical at the end of both processes (cf. figure 107).

Figure 107: Np, 152.

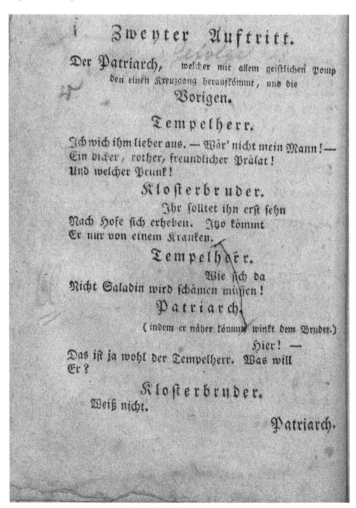

A comparable material dynamic is at play where the scheming, nefarious actions of the Patriarch, who has been identified as an intriguer and adversary of interfaith tolerance all along, are named outright. The Templar in particular makes sure of this. He repeatedly refers to the Patriarch as a "Schurke" [villain] and to his actions as "Schurkerey" [villainy]. The respective passages were cancelled in a first layer of revisions in both written artefacts. Their content may have been somewhat delicate, declaring on stage that the highest church official in Jerusalem was morally deficient – thereby explicitly making him the play's antagonist. Although the Patriarch appears in a dubious light from the outset, it is solely through the Templar in Act V, Scene 3, that he is so harshly evaluated in the play. The words of this character, although they merely express what the audience might have felt already, nevertheless overtly direct the viewers' perception (cf. figures 108 and 109).

*Figure 108: Nm, 87v.*

*Figure 109: Np, 205.*

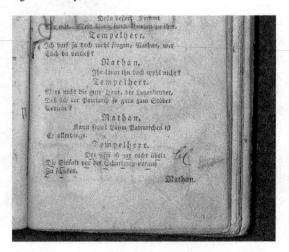

Whatever the reasons for these changes, they do not seem to have been compelling enough. The respective retractions were themselves retracted in both written artefacts. And yet, it is not possible to say whether this happened after a short period of time or after years of use. In the print-based *Theater-Bibliothek: 1988b*, the cancellation of the retraction has been indicated in ink strokes below the verses, in addition to the "bl" also used as "bleibt" in the manuscript *Theater-Bibliothek: 1988a*. Again, there are differences in the material performance of the two books. While the retractions in both passages have been taken back in *Theater-Bibliothek: 1988b*, this is only true of one retraction in *Theater-Bibliothek: 1988a*. Instead, the retraction of the still somewhat explicit criticism of the Patriarch on folio 89r has actually been reinforced by yet another layer of revisions. It is possible that the repetition of the Templar's plain words in one scene was thought to be too drastic. In this way, the negative portrayal of the character remained part of the performance, but much less emphatically (cf. figures 110 and 111).

*Figure 110: Nm, 89r.*              *Figure 111: Np, 209.*

 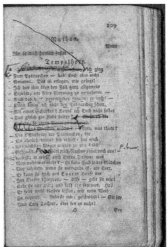

In view of this divergence, it is a matter of debate whether the revisions concerning the sensitive topic of religion originated from the simultaneous use of both written artefacts. It is possible that this was at least partly the case. With regard to the figure of the Patriarch, both books were only initially updated in parallel – or rather, from a certain point, updates made to the actors' parts were negligently only made in one of the books. On the other hand, it is also possible that the same requirements, the same need for changes, and the same basis for decision-making affected theatre operations during phases in which the books were being used independently of each other – without this having to result in completely identical revisions. Rather, it is precisely the characteristic mixture of parallel, merely similar, and completely divergent changes that makes both scenarios seem plausible. What is certain in any case is that the portrayal of Christianity and Church representatives was more problematic from a theatrical point of view than from a literary one, and that, even decades after the second "Hamburger Theaterstreit" [Hamburg Theatre Controversy], the company apparently felt compelled, or at least thought it advisable, to cut potentially explosive passages about Christianity. The version of Lessing's play available in print and Schiller's stage adaptation in manuscript form were able to go further. But when the content of those written artefacts became an element of theatrical processes, such openness was no longer possible without further ado. This is evident in the material performances of both books as well as in their relationship to Lessing's and Schiller's versions – in strike-throughs, cuts, and omissions. However, the extra-theatrical pressure seems to have softened over time (or the production had been a little too cautious from the outset). In many cases, the retractions that affected the portrayal of the Patriarch as an antagonist were ultimately taken back.

## VII. Entangled Purposes, Complementary Materialities

The example of *Theater-Bibliothek: 1988a* and *Theater-Bibliothek: 1988b* has vividly shown how the authority of literary authors (whether they were creators of "original" works or adapters of others' works with a literary reputation of their own) and their literary texts played a role in shaping the use of the Theater-Bibliothek prompt books and how that authority became interwoven with the other forces that manifest themselves in the material performances of these written artefacts. The intertwining of *Theater-Bibliothek: 1988a* and *Theater-Bibliothek: 1988b* also points to the entanglement of various prompt book practices. In addition to the interdependencies between handwriting and print, which we have already discussed in previous chapters, the relationship between prompting and stage management has come into view in this chapter. We have shown that these prompt book practices (in the general sense pertaining to both the prompter's as well as the inspector's written artefacts) provided the framework for "doing literature in theatre".

Lessing's *Nathan der Weise* is a prime example of a (relatively) "stable" literary text that has been continuously reproduced in printed book copies since 1779. Its stage adaptation was just as much an evolving entity as the prompt books that served as its physical carriers. Through the prompt book and the inspection book, the adapted text of Lessing's play became entangled with the technical conditions and procedures of the Hamburg stage. As soon as we start viewing the adaptation as nothing but the text that Schiller wrote down (with the 1805 version as his ultimate goal), the adaptation loses the very context that made it the theatrical adaptation of a rather untheatrical play (a "dramatic poem") in the first place. Schiller's final adaptation is not the version presented in the *Nationalausgabe* (although it certainly was his last version of *Nathan der Weise*). Rather, Schiller's ever-evolving Lessing adaptation is the sum of all the different versions it metamorphosed into as it took on a life of its own: in its negotiations with its general context that became visible with respect to shifting attitudes towards religion, but also in the independent lives that the prompt book and the inspection book seem to have taken on – whether because they were not always being used simultaneously or because their upkeep became sloppy. Examining how literature was done in theatre at certain points in time means retracing the heterogenous layers that manifest themselves in the material performance of prompt (and inspection) books. For their part, the two written artefacts *Theater-Bibliothek: 1988a* and *Theater-Bibliothek: 1988b* bear witness to the theatre's intensive, long-lasting engagement with *Nathan der Weise* but also to the play's decades-long success in Hamburg – a success that endured far beyond the Schröder era.

As we have shown in previous chapters, the back-and-forth, i.e., the multiple revisions carried out with the help of different writing tools and paper practices, were fairly typical of the prompt books in use at the time. The practices of this theatre manuscript culture can be clearly identified in both written artefacts. These practices were carried out over time by several hands, some of which are no longer identifiable, and, as the enriched print-based book *Theater-Bibliothek: 1988b* demonstrates, they ran the risk of impairing the usability and functionality of the written artefact at a certain point – at least for any person other than a user involved in the revision process. Even though the practices are identifiable, the different layers can be "decluttered" to a certain extent, and much of the context can be reconstructed, it is no longer possible to fully decipher the actual history of the use of the two written artefacts – as is the case with most prompt books at the Theater-Bibliothek.

# Chapter 7. Outlook

In twenty-first-century European theatre, prompting[1] is often done electronically. At some "grand houses", actors receive their prompts via earbuds while prompters communicate via headsets. Sometimes, there is no prompter, and actors are expected to help each other out if they forget their lines. In German theatre, however, some of the bigger houses still employ more than one prompter,[2] and in the late twentieth- and early twenty-first-century tradition of "postdramatic theatre", appearances by the prompter have sometimes been incorporated into the performance as a self-referential device.[3] The Hamburg theatre audience of the late eighteenth and early nineteenth century was made aware of the box-like elevation at the front of the stage on a regular basis – of a peculiar disembodied voice that did not seem to belong to any of the actors. On the contrary, whoever was standing on stage was clearly not the one speaking in those moments and seemed eager to avoid revealing how carefully they were listening to the words, which only at first glance appeared to lack a specific location. In fact, the words were coming directly from the prompt box, which may not have been particularly eye-catching. They were spoken by a voice that was sometimes clear, sometimes less so, but always audible precisely when the dialogue being spoken on stage seemed to falter, an actor fell strangely silent, or the action on stage was in danger of coming apart at the seams. It is not without irony that the prompter ensured the progress of the performance while their – necessary – interventions completely suspended one of the principles deemed absolutely essential in the new theatre-aesthetic discourse of the time: the demand for scenic illusionism, i.e., a stage performance that would make the audience forget as much as possible that they were attending a theatre performance. This requirement was an integral part of the concept of theatre that redefined prompting and the profile of the prompter, regardless of the degree to which those aesthetic considerations were applied. After all, in theatre based on

---

1 Culturally, prompting as a concept has made its comeback in the work of "prompt engineers" who programme artificial intelligence prompts. Cf. Harwell 2023.
2 Cf. Oltmann 2023.
3 Cf., for the case of René Pollesch, Matzke 2012b, 127–129.

plays, i.e., dramatic texts created in line with literary standards, the prompter was not only entrusted with the task of feeding the actors lines. Rather, during the Hamburg era shaped by Schröder, they were also required to keep the respective text up to date with the latest content and technical revisions and, because the master copy in the prompt book was the foundation of the performance, to guard it like a treasure. It was therefore not just during the performance – where they were ever-present, even when they were not needed and remained silent in their box – that the prompter carried out their tasks. They did so throughout the process of preparing the play for performance,[4] while it remained in the repertory, and when it was taken up again after a hiatus.

There are a great number of aspects to consider here, such as the performances in the theatre and their preparation as well as the associated tasks and processes. But we also need to examine the demands that were made of the prompter, some of which had to do with the technical requirements of the stage, some with the overall cultural standing of the theatre. This relates to the aesthetic, cultural, and political expectations and stipulations that shaped the theatre as well as those which the theatre, vice versa, tried to shape for its part, in line with its new forms and aspirations. The intersections and interdependencies between these aspects can be examined by looking over the prompter's shoulder, as it were, and observing their most important tool: the prompt book. Through its use, this written artefact has become the scene of an entanglement between theatrical work, traditional as well as context-specific writing practices, and the norms and expectations that affected the theatre of the time. Accordingly, we have to focus our view over the prompter's shoulder to detect the corresponding relationships and connections. To put it in more general terms: the analysis of theatrical written artefacts requires us to take a special perspective that our study has attempted to develop.

In order to characterise the particularities of these prompt books and to situate them within their specific contexts by going beyond the respective written artefacts, the perspective we take has to be an interdisciplinary one, for which the specific, tangible written artefacts are the starting point. In this volume, we have applied a manuscript studies approach initially developed for objects preceding the European "age of print" and "age of books" to manuscripts that were often bound in a modern book format and sometimes formed hybrids with print copies. This approach has focussed on the specific materiality of the prompt books as well as the practices and techniques that shaped their daily use. Questions and perspectives at the intersection of literary and theatre studies are negotiating the causes, parameters, and effects of their use both in the practical terms of day-to-day operations and in the dramaturgical terms of performing a literary text in an

---

4 In the period examined here, significant parts of this process began to take the shape of rehearsals, cf. Matzke 2012a.

environment that was constantly changing. Sometimes these changes were considerable, as with the arrival of the French censor in Hamburg, sometimes ever so slight, as with respect to varying tastes and fashions. As we have elucidated over the course of this study, using a prompt book like this usually became a continuous process of revision that could never actually be said to come to an end.

We hope that our interdisciplinary analysis has not only grasped the specific features of prompt books and the practices associated with them but will also help to define and shift research questions and approaches in neighbouring disciplines. Our analyses have aimed to exemplify an understanding of written artefacts that not only encompasses how they were created, the materials they used, how they were made up, and the external shape they took but also the wider cultural contexts of their use. At the same time, we hope that our analyses have provided an example of what an examination of the mutually illuminating interplay between materiality, (writing) practices, and cultural contexts could look like.[5]

Conversely, prompt books have long been analysed in theatre studies with respect to their context rather than as material artefacts. From this perspective, prompt books have broadened our knowledge of historical performance practices. They have provided information about the shifting validity of agreements regarding stage procedures and their textual basis over a production's performance history as well as about the ways in which stage equipment and machinery were used. At what points was the stage set rearranged or changed, and how? At which point was which lighting mood to be used? Which scene sequences had to be changed and reworked for which dramaturgical or technical reasons? Which information from which parts of the text had to be redistributed or completely rewritten due to which kinds of updates concerning characters or dramatic scenes? Prompt book dynamics thus make tangible in equal measure what happened on stage, what was supposed to happen on stage, and what no longer had to happen there.

To a large extent, this is exactly how we have made use of the prompt books at the Hamburg Theater-Bibliothek. However, the preceding chapters have also drawn attention to how the prompt books that theatre practice depended upon were themselves reshaped by their practical use. Because it was always conceivable that further changes would be made, the process essentially always remained unfinished. It was limited only by the edges of the paper, which, at some point, were filled up, only for the content to continue further on sheets that were pasted in, pinned in, or attached in other ways. This process, however, exposes the specific materiality of the prompt books as something performative. Informed by media and cultural studies, our analysis of prompt books as performative mate-

---

5 For another example of an interdisciplinary approach to analysis, cf. Piquette/Whitehouse 2013. The volume brings together perspectives from archaeology and philology with a focus on the materiality of writing processes.

rial objects has thus built and expanded on the understanding and use of an essential theatre studies concept: materiality as performance. The use of the written artefacts led to the creation of multiple layers of revision; the written artefacts thus became the secret centre of the performances of literature-based theatre as it increasingly took shape in the course of the eighteenth century. Therefore, the materiality of prompt books was accompanied by a performative dimension from the outset, which not only emerged when prompters used their books to feed actors lines.[6] These kinds of material performances allowed for, informed, and determined the ways in which dramatic texts were adapted to the demands of the stage or, depending on one's point of view, the ways in which theatre as a cultural institution made literature performable. Either way, prompt books were objects of utility in the everyday business context of a theatre. Their specific materiality not only provided the infrastructure[7] for all artistic aspects of day-to-day operations but was in turn reshaped and transformed by them.

This materiality allows us to expand upon concepts and notions important for the study of literature as well. After all, prompt books were a central element of a theatre that, at least in the vision of some critics at the time, was to replace improvisation and loose scene sketches with dramatic texts containing firmly defined characters, elaborate psychologies, and distinct plots. However, the treatment of these texts within the cultural context of theatre conceived of them as the ever-adaptable foundations of what was to take place on the stage. The adaptation of literature in theatre practice thus undermined any understanding of literary texts as closed, untouchable entities. When they were performed on stage, dramatic texts were no longer finished works of art but one of many functional elements. This also had consequences for the status of the "authors" to whom these texts were attributed. Our analysis of selected prompt books has shown that there was often more than one person behind a performance once a dramatic text was in the process of being prepared for the stage. After all, the circumstances of the theatre – technical conditions, norms, expectations, and reactions – sometimes made it necessary to rewrite the dramatic text radically, sometimes at very short notice. At times, this had an impact on the progression of scenes, gave rise to new additions to the text, or even affected the plot of the play itself. The process of creating and updating a prompt book tended to involve several people, usually

---

6 In the sense of the somewhat earlier terminology coined by Paul Zumthor, they exhibit a special "degree of performance" ("Performanzgrad") in relation to other written artefacts (Zumthor 1988, 706). This stems not only from the many different ways that they were used during a specific theatrical performance but also and in a special way from the process of materially revising and updating them. This process points beyond the individual performance, but at the same time refers decidedly to the function of the prompt book over the course of the performance as a specific context.

7 For "infrastructuralism" as a perspective, cf. Peters 2015, 30–33; cf. Etzold 2023.

distinct from the person credited as the author of the dramatic text presented on stage (and even canonised) later in literary historiography. Under the name of the author printed on the playbills of the time, adaptations and revisions were made by prompters and principals within the scope of their everyday work.[8] This reveals a particular tension in the way that authorship took effect and lasting shape in the period around 1800 as a singular, often ingenious, individual achievement. However, the material performance of the prompt book, which the operation of literature-based theatre – which also took effect and shape in this era – ultimately depended on, points to how the work done on the dramatic text within the institution of theatre was always pluralistic from the outset. Consequently, analysing prompt books helps us to deepen our understanding of authorship in literary and cultural studies. In recent years, scholarship has been increasingly devoting itself to forms and constellations of non-individual authorship.[9] It is precisely because each prompt book remained tied to a particular author that examining them can contribute to research on the nature of authorship as well as to the scholarship of the particular authors analysed here. Prompt book research brings to light new text versions, contributes to their philological indexing, and in some cases allows us to catch a glimpse of the working methods of the people who created and worked on them. At the same time, it stimulates the productive scrutinization of the corresponding concept of the artistic or literary work (*Werk*), precisely because of the special way in which these texts were handled in the theatre.

Many of these cross-disciplinary impulses and lines of questioning have arisen from our specific, interdisciplinary focus on the actual practices of prompt book use. The previous six chapters have covered the writing and paper practices of prompt book production and revision, the adaptation of literary texts, and the theatrical and cultural practices that have manifested themselves in their materiality.[10] The emphasis we have placed on these practices has often been at odds with the concepts of and discourses on theatre, literature, and related written media that

---

8 Christof Hoffmann suggests a distinction between "writers" ("Schreiber") and "composers" ("Verfasser") for "writing positions" ("Schreibpositionen") outside of authorship, which, according to him, is based primarily on attribution. In the case of prompt books, "writers" are those who carry out the necessary updates – usually the prompters – while "composers" are also responsible for making those updates. Composers were usually the theatre directors (Hoffmann 2017, 166). In a related sense, Tobias Fuchs speaks of authorship as an "offer of roles" ("Rollenangebot") (Fuchs 2020, 11).

9 Such forms and constellations can be identified in many ways in the period around 1800. For an overview of forms of plural authorship, cf. Barner/Schürmann/Yacavone 2022. For concrete constellations around 1800, cf., for instance, Spoerhase/Thomalla 2020 or Ehrmann 2022.

10 Andreas Reckwitz has stressed the importance of artefacts for the analysis of social practices, as such practices are sometimes dependent on artefacts or can only take place at all by using them, cf. Reckwitz 2003, 282–301, in particular 290f.

emerged in the eighteenth century. There is often a glaring discrepancy between the purely functional adaptations of dramatic texts to the technical conditions of the Hamburg stage and the efforts made to elevate them in their integrity to cornerstones of literature-based theatre; between the open-ended material revisions of dramatic texts in prompt books and claims that the final versions of these texts are the ones that can be found in commercially available print copies; between the multiple agents involved in these revisions to varying degrees and the individual authors' names to which these literary texts are still attributed (e.g., on the front covers of print copies, on playbills, and on the title pages of prompt books).

What took place on the level of practices sometimes clearly differed from what simultaneously emerged on a discursive level and was then applied to, and sometimes superimposed upon, those practices. It would be wrong, however, to conclude that these two levels diverged and remained independent of each other. On the contrary: the material performance of a prompt book certainly takes place in something that, following Andreas Reckwitz, can be identified as a "practice/discourse formation".[11] In our case, the practice/discourse formation of prompt book practices means an area of contact rather than the separate identities of both levels. Prompt book practices and the discourses that permeated theatre as a cultural institution touched upon each other within the materiality of the prompt book: literary and theatrical, cultural and habitual, but also political norms, claims, and values circulated and took shape on a discursive level. All of them had an impact on the performance of the play that went beyond spatial, technical, or personnel factors. Accordingly, they determined how prompt books were created and revised, which left behind material traces in the processes of their use. The operations carried out for this purpose hardly differed in each case. It did not matter if there was a lack of actors, a problem with the length of the play, or a break in decorum: the contents of prompt books were retracted, added to, pasted over, etc. The practices involved in these revisions were generally the same from prompt book to prompt book. Knowledge of the discursive environment of prompt books and the norms and requirements that governed that environment make it (more often than not) possible to declutter, decipher, distinguish, and reconstruct how the layers of use came about and how, together, they have contributed to a unique material biography for each prompt book.

It is in these layers that the theatrical adaptations of literary texts performatively materialise. On a discursive level, claims were being made about literary texts forming the foundations of a theatre that was in the process of becoming socially acceptable, in part because it was increasingly passing as "high art". The use of prompt books in practice, however, shows that they were one functional element in processes of adaptation and revision which had to meet a great varie-

---

11 "Praxis-/Diskursformation"; cf., for example, Reckwitz 2016, 49–66.

ty of pragmatic, technical, and discursive requirements. Our study has retraced these connections, dynamics, and influences in selected individual prompt books and their respective material performances. In other words, it has attempted to shed some light in the dimness of that box at the front of the stage. It was only when something on that stage came to a standstill or got out of hand, and a disembodied whisper had to intervene, that the quiet voice caught the spectators' attention, and they heard the person reading from the prompt book. Without the prompt books that came into play from the box in those moments, the stage would have remained truly silent or would have become mired in utter chaos. The performance, the play, and the theatre itself depended on these written artefacts that were completely pragmatic at the time but that are equally enigmatic and fascinating today.

# List of Figures

Figure 1: textual and material enrichments in a prompt book for Lessing's *Nathan der Weise* (Nm, 44v and 45r) / figure 2: a handwritten 1777 and a printed 1812 prompt book for Shakespeare's *Maaß für Maaß* [*Measure for Measure*] (*Theater-Bibliothek 514*, 122 and 123, and *Theater-Bibliothek 948b*, 32 and 33) / figure 3: the front cover of an 1815 prompt book for Shakespeare's *Othello* (*Theater-Bibliothek: 586a*) / figure 4: the complete cover of *Theater-Bibliothek: 586a* / figure 5: *Theater-Bibliothek: 641*, 13v and 14r. Joseph Marius von Babo's heroic tragedy *Die Römer in Teutschland* (created presumably shortly before 1780) was a contribution to a writing contest / figure 6: *Theater-Bibliothek 1989b*, 54 / figure 7: Nm, 9v and 10r / figure 8: *Theater-Bibliothek: 1379a*, 86v and 87r / figure 9: *Theater-Bibliothek: 215a*, 118 and 119 / figure 10: *Theater-Bibliothek: 586a*, 100 / figure 11: *Theater-Bibliothek: 1379b*, 56 and 57 / figure 12: *Theater-Bibliothek: 1989b*, 291 / figure 13: *Theater-Bibliothek: 1982 (1)*, 36 / figure 14: Nm, 45r / figure 15: Np, 50 and 57 / figure 16: L, 50 / figure 17: L, 54 / figure 18: L, 55 / figure 19: Nm, 15v / figure 20: S2, 98r / figure 21: S1 and S2 in front of sheet music for *Die Sonnen-Jungfrau* / figure 22: S1, 31v / figure 23: S1, 77 / figure 24: S1, 118 / figure 25: S1, 150 / figure 26: S1, transversal view / figure 27: S1, 87 / figure 28: S1, 21v / figure 29: S1, 17v and 18a r / figure 30: S1, 26v / figure 31: S1, 29v / figure 32: S1, 19v / figure 33: S1, 20r / figure 34: S1, 22v / figure 35: S1, 30r / figure 36: S1, 21v and 22r / figure 37: S2, 68v and 69r / figure 38: S2, 95r / figure 39: S2, 28r / figure 40: S2, 55r / figure 41: S2, 27r / figure 42: S2, 70r and inlay / figure 43: S2, 92v / figure 44: S2, 11v and 12r / figure 45: playbill 22 August 1813 / figure 46: S2, 94v / figure 47: *Theater-Bibliothek: 1428b*, 235 / figure 48: O, 83v and 84r / figure 49: O, 71v, primary layer / figure 50: O, 71v, glued over sheet / figure 51: O, 54v and 55r / figure 52: O, 77v and 78r / figure 53: O, 84v / figure 54: L, verso of second folio with prop list / figure 55: L, 1 / figure 56: L, 110 and 111 / figure 57: L, 4 / figure 58: L, 11 / figure 59: covers of Nm and Np / figure 60: Nm, cast list / figure 61: Nm, 65r / figure 62: Nm, 12v / figure 63: Nm, 13r / figure 64: Nm, 12v, primary layer / figure 65: Nm, 13r, primary layer / figure 66: Nm, 14v / figure 67: Nm, 15r / figure 68: Nm, 31r / figure 69: Nm, verso side of the last vacat page / figure 70: Nm, inner back cover / figure 71: Nm, 102v / figure 72: Nm, 23v / figure 73: Nm, 43r / figure 74: Nm, 95v / figure 75: Np, 146 and 147 / figure 76: Np, 130 / figure 77: Np, 131 / figure 78: Np, 115 / figure 79: Np, 116 / figure 80: Np, 7 / figure 81:

Np, 25 / figure 82: Np, 100 / figure 83: Np, 101 / figure 84: Np, 170 / figure 85: Np, 193 / figure 86: Np, 51, margin of cut pages / figure 87: Np, 50 / figure 88: Np, 171 / figure 89: Nm, 75r / figure 90: Nm, 28r / figure 91: Np, 65 / figure 92: Np, 66 / figure 93: Nm, 89v / figure 94: Nm, 90r / figure 95: Np, 210 / figure 96: Np, 211 / figure 97: Nm, 44v with symbols indicating insertion / figure 98: Nm, extra sheet glued to 44v / figure 99: three sheets with additional content / figure 100: Nm, 30v / figure 101: Nm, 96r / figure 102: Nm, 93v / figure 103: Nm, 92v / figure 104: Nm, 102r / figure 105: Np, 238 / figure 106: Nm, 67r / figure 107: Np, 152 / figure 108: Nm, 87v / figure 109: Np, 205 / figure 110: Nm, 89r / figure 111: Np, 209.

# Bibliography

## I. List of Written Artefacts from the Theater-Bibliothek

Staats- und Universitätsbibliothek Hamburg Carl von Ossietzky, LA: Schröder, Friedrich Ulrich Ludwig: 49–50. Brief an August von Kotzebue (Hamburg, 11.10.1793).

Staats- und Universitätsbibliothek Hamburg Carl von Ossietzky, LA: Schröder, Friedrich Ulrich Ludwig: 49–50. Brief an August von Kotzebue (Hamburg, 28.11.1793).

Staats- und Universitätsbibliothek Hamburg Carl von Ossietzky, Theater-Bibliothek: 215a. *Frauenstand! Schauspiel in 4 Aufzügen von Iffland*. Earlier title: *Frauenstand! Schauspiel in fünf Aufzügen von Iffland*.

Staats- und Universitätsbibliothek Hamburg Carl von Ossietzky, Theater-Bibliothek: 374b. *Die Heimkehr. Trauerspiel in einem Aufzuge*.

Staats- und Universitätsbibliothek Hamburg Carl von Ossietzky, Theater-Bibliothek: 429a. *Der Kaufmann von Venedig. Ein Lustspiel in vier Aufzügen*.

Staats- und Universitätsbibliothek Hamburg Carl von Ossietzky, Theater-Bibliothek: 429b. *Der Kaufmann von Venedig. Ein Lustspiel in vier Aufzügen*. Earlier title: *Der Kaufmann von Venedig. Ein Lustspiel in fünf Aufzügen*.

Staats- und Universitätsbibliothek Hamburg Carl von Ossietzky, Theater-Bibliothek: 477. *Leichtsinn und Edelmuth. Lustspiel in einem Aufzuge*.

Staats- und Universitätsbibliothek Hamburg Carl von Ossietzky, Theater-Bibliothek: 492a. *Die Matrone von Ephesus. Lustspiel in einem Acte*.

Staats- und Universitätsbibliothek Hamburg Carl von Ossietzky, Theater-Bibliothek: 492b. *Die Matrone von Ephesus. Lustspiel in einem Aufzuge*.

Staats- und Universitätsbibliothek Hamburg Carl von Ossietzky, Theater-Bibliothek: 492c (1). *Die Matrone von Ephesus. Lustspiel in einem Aufzuge*. [Rollenbuch des Telamon].

Staats- und Universitätsbibliothek Hamburg Carl von Ossietzky, Theater-Bibliothek: 492c (2). *Die Matrone von Ephesus. Lustspiel in einem Aufzuge*. [Rollenbuch des Dromo].

Staats- und Universitätsbibliothek Hamburg Carl von Ossietzky, Theater-Bibliothek: 492c (3). *Die Matrone von Ephesus. Lustspiel in einem Aufzuge.* [Rollenbuch des Philokrates].

Staats- und Universitätsbibliothek Hamburg Carl von Ossietzky, Theater-Bibliothek: 492c (4). *Die Matrone von Ephesus. Lustspiel in einem Aufzuge.* [Rollenbuch der Mysis].

Staats- und Universitätsbibliothek Hamburg Carl von Ossietzky, Theater-Bibliothek: 492c (5). *Die Matrone von Ephesus. Lustspiel in einem Aufzuge.* [Rollenbuch der Antiphila].

Staats- und Universitätsbibliothek Hamburg Carl von Ossietzky, Theater-Bibliothek: 514. *Maaß für Maaß, ein Schauspiel in fünf Aufzügen nach Shakespeare.* Earlier title: *Maaß für Maaß, oder, Wie einer mißt wird ihm wieder gemeßen, ein Lustspiel in fünf Aufzügen nach Shakespeare.*

Staats- und Universitätsbibliothek Hamburg Carl von Ossietzky, Theater-Bibliothek: 571. *Othello, oder Der Mohr von Venedig ein Trauerspiel in 5 Aufzügen von Shakespear.*

Staats- und Universitätsbibliothek Hamburg Carl von Ossietzky, Theater-Bibliothek: 586a. *Othello, Der Mohr von Venedig. Trauerspiel in fünf Aufzügen, von Shakespeare. Neu für die Bühne bearbeitet.*

Staats- und Universitätsbibliothek Hamburg Carl von Ossietzky, Theater-Bibliothek: 641. *Die Römer in Teutschland, ein heroisches Trauerspiel in fünf Akten.*

Staats- und Universitätsbibliothek Hamburg Carl von Ossietzky, Theater-Bibliothek: 728. *Die Sonnen Jungfrau. Schauspiel in fünf Aufzügen.*

Staats- und Universitätsbibliothek Hamburg Carl von Ossietzky, Theater-Bibliothek: 948a. *Maaß für Maaß. Ein Schauspiel in fünf Aufzügen. Nach Shakespear von Schröder.* Schwerin und Weimar, in der Bödnerschen Buchhandlung. 1790.

Staats- und Universitätsbibliothek Hamburg Carl von Ossietzky, Theater-Bibliothek: 948b. *Maaß für Maaß. Schauspiel in fünf Aufzügen. Nach Shakespear.*

Staats- und Universitätsbibliothek Hamburg Carl von Ossietzky, Theater-Bibliothek: 1379a. *Viel Lärmen um Nichts, ein Schauspiel in 5 Aufzügen, nach Shakespeare.*

Staats- und Universitätsbibliothek Hamburg Carl von Ossietzky, Theater-Bibliothek: 1379b. *Viel Lärmen um Nichts, ein Schauspiel in 5 Aufzügen, nach Shakespear.*

Staats- und Universitätsbibliothek Hamburg Carl von Ossietzky, Theater-Bibliothek: 1403a. *Tarare. Eine Oper in vier Aufzügen.*

Staats- und Universitätsbibliothek Hamburg Carl von Ossietzky, Theater-Bibliothek: 1403b. *König Axur. Eine Oper in vier Aufzügen.*

Staats- und Universitätsbibliothek Hamburg Carl von Ossietzky, Theater-Bibliothek: 1403c. *Axur König von Ormus. Oper in fünf Akten.*

Staats- und Universitätsbibliothek Hamburg Carl von Ossietzky, Theater-Bibliothek: 1428b. *Die Kreuzfahrer. Schauspiel in 5 A.*

Staats- und Universitätsbibliothek Hamburg Carl von Ossietzky, Theater-Bibliothek: 1460. *Die Sonnen-Jungfrau. Schauspiel in fünf Aufzügen.*

Staats- und Universitätsbibliothek Hamburg Carl von Ossietzky, Theater-Bibliothek: 1982 (1). *Hamlet, Prinz von Dännemark. Trauerspiel in fünf Aufzügen. Nach Shakespear.*

Staats- und Universitätsbibliothek Hamburg Carl von Ossietzky, Theater-Bibliothek: 1982 (2)a. *Hamlet, Prinz von Dänemark. Trauerspiel in 5 Aufzügen von Shakespeare: übersetzt von A.W. Schlegel.* Earlier title: *Hamlet, Prinz von Dänemark.*

Staats- und Universitätsbibliothek Hamburg Carl von Ossietzky, Theater-Bibliothek: 1982 (2)b. *Hamlet, Prinz von Dänemark. Trauerspiel in 6 Aufzügen.*

Staats- und Universitätsbibliothek Hamburg Carl von Ossietzky, Theater-Bibliothek: 1987a. *Die Räuber. Trauerspiel in fünf Aufzügen.*

Staats- und Universitätsbibliothek Hamburg Carl von Ossietzky, Theater-Bibliothek: 1987b. *Die Räuber, ein Trauerspiel.* Mannheim, bei C. F. Schwan und G. C. Götz. 1802.

Staats- und Universitätsbibliothek Hamburg Carl von Ossietzky, Theater-Bibliothek: 1988a. *Nathan der Weise, ein Schauspiel in fünf Aufzügen von Lessing für die Bühne gekürzt v. Schiller.* Earlier title: *Nathan der Weise, ein dramatisches Gedicht in fünf Aufzügen von Lessing für die Bühne gekürzt v. Schiller.*

Staats- und Universitätsbibliothek Hamburg Carl von Ossietzky, Theater-Bibliothek 1988b. *Nathan der Weise. Ein Dramatisches Gedicht, in fünf Aufzügen.* Von Gotthold Ephraim Lessing. Dritte Auflage. Berlin, in der Vossischen Buchhandlung. 1791.

Staats- und Universitätsbibliothek Hamburg Carl von Ossietzky, Theater-Bibliothek: 1989a. *Dom Karlos, Infant von Spanien, ein Trauerspiel in fünf Aufzügen.*

Staats- und Universitätsbibliothek Hamburg Carl von Ossietzky, Theater-Bibliothek: 1989b (1). *Dom Karlos, Infant von Spanien von Friedrich Schiller.* Leipzig, bei Georg Joachim Göschen. 1787.

Staats- und Universitätsbibliothek Hamburg Carl von Ossietzky, Theater-Bibliothek: 1989b (2). *Dom Karlos, Infant von Spanien von Friedrich Schiller.* Leipzig, bei Georg Joachim Göschen. 1787.

Staats- und Universitätsbibliothek Hamburg Carl von Ossietzky, Theater-Bibliothek: 1991a. *Die Braut von Messina oder die feindlichen Brüder. Trauerspiel in vier A.*

Staats- und Universitätsbibliothek Hamburg Carl von Ossietzky, Theater-Bibliothek: 1991b. *Die Braut von Messina oder die feindlichen Brüder, ein Trauerspiel mit Chören in fünf Akten.* Tübingen, in der J. G. Cotta'schen Buchhandlung. 1803. Earlier title: *Die Braut von Messina oder die feindlichen Brüder, ein Trauerspiel mit Chören.*

Staats- und Universitätsbibliothek Hamburg Carl von Ossietzky, Theater-Bibliothek: 2022a. *Maria Stuart. Trauerspiel in fünf Aufzügen.*

Staats- und Universitätsbibliothek Hamburg Carl von Ossietzky, Theater-Bibliothek: 2022b. *Maria Stuart. Ein Trauerspiel*. Tübingen, in der J. G. Cotta'schen Buchhandlung. 1810.

Staats- und Universitätsbibliothek Hamburg Carl von Ossietzky, Theater-Bibliothek: 2023a. *Die Jungfrau von Orleans*.

Staats- und Universitätsbibliothek Hamburg Carl von Ossietzky, Theater-Bibliothek: 2023b. *Die Jungfrau von Orleans. Eine romantische Tragödie*. Tübingen, in der J. G. Cotta'schen Buchhandlung. 1816.

Staats- und Universitätsbibliothek Hamburg Carl von Ossietzky, Theater-Bibliothek: 2029. *König Lear. Ein Trauerspiel in fünf Aufzügen. Nach Shakespear [von Schröder]*. Hamburg, gedruckt bei J. M. Michaelsen. 1778. Earlier title: *König Lear. Ein Trauerspiel in fünf Aufzügen. Nach Shakespear*.

## II. List of Databases and Datasets

Deutsche Nationalbibliothek/Gemeinsame Normdatei: Entry for Christian Friedrich Zimmermann, Souffleur. https://d-nb.info/gnd/1243915552 (last accessed on December 23, 2023).

Felser, Anna Sophie/Funke, Tobias/Göing, Hannah/Hussain, Sophia/Schäfer, Martin Jörg/Weinstock, Alexander/Bosch, Sebastian (2024): Theatre in Handwriting. Hamburg Prompt Book Practices, 1770s-1820s [Data set]. http://doi.org/10.25592/uhhfdm.13916.

Hamburger Kulturgut Digital: https://digitalisate.sub.uni-hamburg.de/ (last accessed on December 23, 2023).

Jahn, Bernhard/Mühle, Friederike/Eisenhardt, Petra/Malchow, Jacqueline/Schneider, Martin: Digitaler Spielplan des Hamburger Stadttheaters 1770–1850. https://www.stadttheater.uni-hamburg.de (last accessed on December 23, 2023).

## III. List of Other Sources

[no author] (1845a): Allgemeine Theater-Chronik. Organ für das Gesamtinteresse der deutschen Bühnen und ihrer Mitglieder. Vierzehnter Jahrgang. Nr. 62. Leipzig: Sturm & Koppe.

[no author] (1845b): Allgemeine Theater-Chronik. Organ für das Gesamtinteresse der deutschen Bühnen und ihrer Mitglieder. Vierzehnter Jahrgang. Nr. 76. Leipzig: Sturm & Koppe.

[no author] (1845c): Allgemeine Theater-Chronik. Organ für das Gesamtinteresse der deutschen Bühnen und ihrer Mitglieder. Vierzehnter Jahrgang. Nr. 115. Leipzig: Sturm & Koppe.

[no author] (1846): Allgemeine Theater-Chronik. Organ für das Gesamtinteresse der deutschen Bühnen und ihrer Mitglieder. Fünfzehnter Jahrgang. Nr. 116. Leipzig: Sturm & Koppe.

[no author] (1815): Allgemeine Zeitung. Nro. 307, Friday 3, November 1815. Stuttgart: Cotta'sche Verlagsbuchhandlung.

Albrecht, Wolfgang (1979): Schillers Bühnenbearbeitung von "Nathan der Weise". In: Günter Hartung (ed.): Beiträge zur Lessing-Konferenz 1979. Halle (Saale): Martin-Luther-Universität Halle-Wittenberg, 32–60.

Andrist, Patrick/Canard, Paul/Maniaci, Marilena (2013): La syntaxe du codex. Essai de codicologie structural. Turnhout: Brepols.

Aristotle (2013): Poetics. Oxford: Oxford University Press.

Barner, Ines/Schürmann, Anja/Yacavone, Kathrin (eds.) (2022): Artistic Collaborations: The Practice and Aesthetics of Working Together/Künstlerische Kollaborationen: Zu Praxis und Ästhetik der Zusammenarbeit. Journal of Literary Theory (16/1).

Barner, Wilfried (2000): Goethe und Lessing. In: Nachrichten der Akademie der Wissenschaften in Göttingen. I. Philologisch-Historische Klasse (4), 163–190.

Bartelmus, Martin/Mohagheghi, Yashar/Rickenbacher, Sergej (eds.) (2023): Ressource "Schriftträger". Materielle Praktiken der Literatur zwischen Verschwendung und Nachhaltigkeit. Bielefeld: transcript.

Bate, Jonathan (1986): Shakespeare and the English Romantic Imagination. Oxford: Clarendon Press.

[Baudissin, Wolf Graf v. (tr.)] (1832): König Lear. In: Shakespeare's dramatische Werke. Übersetzt von August Wilhelm von Schlegel, ergänzt und erläutert von Ludwig Tieck. Achter Theil. Berlin: G. Reimer, 281–385.

Beal, Peter (2008): A Dictionary of English Manuscript Terminology. 1450–2000. Oxford: Oxford University Press.

Beit-Arié, Malachi (1993): Hebrew Manuscripts of East and West. Towards a Comparative Codicology. London: The British Library.

Benne, Christian (2015): Die Erfindung des Manuskripts. Zur Theorie und Geschichte literarischer Gegenständlichkeit. Berlin: Suhrkamp.

Birgfeld, Johannes/Bohnengel, Julia/Košenina, Alexander (eds.) (2011): Kotzebues Dramen. Ein Lexikon. Hannover: Wehrhahn.

Birkner, Nina (2007): *Hamlet* auf der deutschen Bühne. Friedrich Ludwig Schröders Theatertext, Dramentheorie und Aufführungspraxis. In: Das achtzehnte Jahrhundert (1), 13–30.

Bishop, Tom/Henke, Robert (2017): Institutional Frameworks for Theatre, 1400–1650: Mapping Theatrical Ressources. In: Robert Henke (ed.): A Cultural History of Theatre. Volume 3: In the Early Modern Age. London/New York: Bloomsbury, 15–33.

Blinn, Hansjürgen (1982): Einführung. In: Hansjürgen Blinn (ed.): Shakespeare-Rezeption. Die Diskussion um Shakespeare in Deutschland. I. Ausgewählte Texte von 1741 bis 1788. Berlin: Schmidt, 9–38.

Blum, Robert/Herloßsohn, Karl/Marggraff, Hermann (1846a): Allgemeines Theater-Lexikon oder Encyklopädie alles Wissenswerthen für Bühnenkünstler, Dilettanten und Theaterfreunde. Neue Ausgabe. Band 2: Boulanger–Devise. Altenburg/Leipzig: Pierer und Heymann.

Blum, Robert/Herloßsohn, Karl/Marggraff, Hermann (1846b): Allgemeines Theater-Lexikon oder Encyklopädie alles Wissenswerthen für Bühnenkünstler, Dilettanten und Theaterfreunde. Neue Ausgabe. Band 7: Situation–Zwischenspiel. Altenburg/Leipzig: Pierer und Heymann.

[Bock, Johann Christian] (1779): König Lear. Ein Trauerspiel in fünf Aufzügen. Nach Shakespear, von J. C. Bock. Leipzig: Christian Gottlob Hilcher.

[Bock, Johann Christian/Schröder, Friedrich Ludwig] (1779): König Lear. Ein Trauerspiel in fünf Aufzügen. Nach Shakespear, von J. C. Bock. Aufgeführt auf dem Churfürstlichen Theater zu München. Leipzig: Holle.

Bosse, Heinrich (2014): Autorschaft ist Werkherrschaft. Über die Entstehung des Urheberrechts aus dem Geist der Goethezeit. Neue, mit einem Nachwort von Wulf D. v. Lucius versehene Auflage. Paderborn: Fink.

Brandes, Johann Christian (1799): Meine Lebensgeschichte. Band 1. Berlin: Maurer.

Brandt, George W. (ed.) (1992): Theatre in Europe. A Documentary History. German and Dutch Theatre 1600–1848. Compiled by George W. Brandt and Wiebe Hogendoorn. Cambridge: Cambridge University Press.

Brauneck, Manfred/Müller, Christine/Müller-Wesemann, Barbara (1989): Theaterstadt Hamburg. Schauspiel, Oper, Tanz. Geschichte und Gegenwart. Reinbek: Rowohlt.

Brauneck, Manfred (2012): Europas Theater. 2500 Jahre Geschichte – eine Einführung. Reinbek: Rowohlt.

Brockett, Oscar G. (1999): History of the Theatre. Boston: Allyn and Bacon.

Bülow, Eduard von (1831): Friedrich Ludwig Schröders dramatische Werke. Mit einer Einleitung von Ludwig Tieck. Berlin: Reimer.

Burdett, Eric (1975): The Craft of Bookbinding. A Practical Handbook. Vancouver, BC: David & Charles Limited.

Campe, Rüdiger (2021): Writing Scenes and the Scene of Writing. A Postscript. In: MLN (136/5), 1114–1133.

Clair, Colin (1976): A History of European Printing. London et al.: Academic Press.

Colins, Franklin (1991): Shakespeare Domesticated. The 18th Century Editions. Aldershot: Scolar Press.

Dennerlein, Katrin (2021): Materialien und Medien der Komödiengeschichte. Zur Praxeologie der Werkzirkulation zwischen Hamburg und Wien von 1678–1806. Berlin: De Gruyter.

Derrida, Jacques (1978): Writing and Difference. Chicago: University of Chicago Press.
Derrida, Jacques (1984): Off Grammatology. Baltimore: Hopkins University Press.
Devrient, Eduard (1848): Geschichte der deutschen Schauspielkunst. Dritter Band: Das Nationaltheater. Leipzig: J. J. Weber.
Dewenter, Bastian/Jakob, Hans-Joachim (eds.) (2018): Theatergeschichte als Disziplinierungsgeschichte? Zur Theorie und Geschichte der Theatergesetze des 18. und 19. Jahrhunderts. Heidelberg: Winter.
Dickmann, Jens-Arne/Elias, Friederike/Focken, Friedrich-Emanuel (2015): Praxeologie. In: Thomas Meier/Michael R. Ott/Rebecca Sauer (eds.): Materiale Textkulturen. Konzepte – Materialien – Praktiken. Berlin/München/Boston: De Gruyter, 135–146.
Diderot, Denis (1936): Diderot's Writing on the Theatre. Cambridge: Cambridge University Press.
Dobson, Michael (1992): Making the National Poet. Shakespeare, Adaptation, and Authorship. Oxford: Clarendon Press.
Drews, Wolfgang (1932): König Lear auf der deutschen Bühne bis zur Gegenwart. Berlin: Dr. Emil Ebering.
Dupont, Florence (2007): Aristote ou le vampire du théâtre occidental. Paris: Aubier.
Düringer, Philipp Jakob/Barthels, Heinrich Ludwig (1841): Theater-Lexikon. Theoretisch-practisches Handbuch für Vorstände, Mitglieder und Freunde des deutschen Theaters. Leipzig: Otto Wigand.
Edwards, Thomas (1970): The Canons of Criticism and Glossary. Being a Supplement to Warburton's Edition of Shakespear. An Account of the Trial of the Letter Y, alias Y. And Sonnets. London: Cass.
Ehrmann, Daniel (2022): Kollektivität. Geteilte Autorschaften und kollaborative Praxisformen 1770–1840. Vienna/Cologne: Böhlau.
Eickmeyer, Angela (2017): "Ich hab' ihn gereizt, seine Vorwürfe verdient." Schröders Hamburger "Kaufmann von Venedig" – eine philosemitische Bearbeitung? In: Bernhard Jahn/Alexander Košenina (eds.): Friedrich Ludwig Schröders Hamburgische Dramaturgie (Publikationen zur Zeitschrift für Germanistik 31), 89–104.
Eigenmann, Susanne (1994): Zwischen ästhetischer Raserei und aufgeklärter Disziplin. Hamburger Theater im späten 18. Jahrhundert. Stuttgart/Weimar: Metzler.
Ermann, Kurt (1983): Goethes Shakespeare-Bild. Tübingen: Niemeyer.
[Eschenburg, Johann Joachim (tr.)] (1779): Wilhelm Shakespears Schauspiele. Neue verbesserte Auflage. Neunter Band. Mannheim: [without publisher].
Eschenburg, Johann Joachim (1787): Ueber W. Shakespear. Zürich: Drell, Geßner, Füßli und Comp.

Etzold, Jörn (2023): Textuelle Infrastrukturen des Theaters. Dramaturgie als Vermittlung. In: Journal of Literary Theory (17/1), 88–110.

Fischer-Lichte, Erika/Schönert, Jörg (eds.) (1999): Theater im Kulturwandel des 18. Jahrhunderts. Inszenierung und Wahrnehmung von Körper – Musik – Sprache. Göttingen: Wallstein.

Foucault, Michel (1995): Discipline and Punish. The Birth of the Prison. New York: Vintage Books.

Friedrich, Michael/Schwarke, Cosima (eds.) (2016): Introduction – Manuscripts as Evolving Entities. In: Michael Friedrich/Cosima Schwarke (eds.): One-Volume Libraries. Composite and Multiple-Text Manuscripts. Berlin/Boston: De Gruyter, 1–26.

Fuchs, Tobias (2021): Die Kunst des Büchermachens. Autorschaft und Materialität der Literatur zwischen 1765 und 1815. Bielefeld: transcript.

Gallop, Jane (2002): Anecdotal Theory. Durham: Duke University Press.

Gazdar, Aban (1979): Deutsche Bearbeitungen der Shakespeare-Tragödien "Othello", "Macbeth", "Hamlet" und "King Lear" im achtzehnten Jahrhundert. München: LMU [Dissertation].

Geffcken, Johannes (1851): Der Streit über die Sittlichkeit des Schauspiels im Jahre 1769 (Goeze, Schlosser, Nölting). In: Zeitschrift des Vereins für Hamburgische Geschichte (3), 56–77.

Gibson, James J. (1986): The Ecological Approach to Visual Perception. Hillsdale, N. J.: Lawrence Erlbaum Associates.

Giesecke, Michael (1998): Der Buchdruck in der frühen Neuzeit. Eine historische Fallstudie über die Durchsetzung neuer Informations- und Kommunikationstechnologien. Frankfurt am Main: Suhrkamp.

Goethe, Johann Wolfgang von (1998a): Wilhelm Meisters Lehrjahre. Goethes Werke. Band VII. München: C. H. Beck.

Goethe, Johann Wolfgang von (1998b): Wilhelm Meisters Wanderjahre. Goethes Werke. Band VIII. München: C. H. Beck.

Graf, Ruedi (1992): Das Theater im Literaturstaat. Literarisches Theater auf dem Weg zur Bildungsmacht. Tübingen: Niemeyer.

Grésillon, Almuth (2008): La mise en œuvre. Itinéraries génétiques. Paris: CNRS Éditions.

Grésillon, Almuth (2010): "Critique génétique". Gedanken zu ihrer Entstehung, Methode und Theorie. In: Kai Bremer/Uwe Wirth (eds.): Texte zur modernen Philologie. Stuttgart: Reclam, 287–307.

Grésillon, Almuth (2016): Éléments de critique génétique. Lire les manuscrits modernes. Paris: CNRS Éditions.

Greub, Thierry (ed.) (2018): Cy Twombly. Image, Text, Paratext. Paderborn: Fink.

Gumbert, Johan Peter (2004): Codicological Units: Towards a Terminology for the Stratigraphy of the Non-Homogeneous Codex. In: segno e testo. International Journal of Manuscripts and Text Transmission (2), 17–42.

Habicht, Werner (1994a): Shakespeare and the German Imagination. International Shakespeare Association Occasional Paper (5).

Habicht, Werner (1994b): Topoi of the Shakespeare Cult in Germany. In: Péter Dávidházi/Judit Karafiáth (eds.): Literature and Its Cults. An Anthropological Approach/La Littérature et ses cultes. Approche anthropologique. Budapest: Argumentum, 47–65.

Haider-Pregler, Hilde (1980): Des sittlichen Bürgers Abendschule. Bildungsanspruch und Bildungsauftrag des Berufstheaters im 18. Jahrhundert. Vienna/Munich: Jugend u. Volk.

Halliwell, Stephen (1986): Aristotle's Poetics. London: Duckworth.

Harwell, Drew (2023): Tech's Hottest New Job: AI Whisperer. No Coding Required. In: The Washington Post, 25 February, 2023 (https://www.washingtonpost.com/technology/2023/02/25/prompt-engineers-techs-next-big-job, last accessed on December 23, 2023).

Häublein, Renata (2005): Die Entdeckung Shakespeares auf der deutschen Bühne des 18. Jahrhunderts. Adaption und Wirkung der Vermittlung auf dem Theater. Tübingen: Niemeyer.

Hebenstreit, Wilhelm (1843): Wissenschaftlich-literarische Encyklopädie der Aesthetik. Ein etymologisch-kritisches Wörterbuch der ästhetischen Kunstsprache. Wien: Carl Gerold.

Heeg, Günther (1999): Der Faden der Ariadne. Ursprung und Bedeutung des Malerischen in der theatralen Darstellung des 18. Jahrhunderts. In: Erika Fischer-Lichte/Jörg Schönert (eds.): Theater im Kulturwandel des 18. Jahrhunderts. Wallstein: Göttingen, 361–383.

Hellmich, Christine (2014): Die Hamburger Bühnenmanuskripte von Schillers Drama "Die Jungfrau von Orleans". Frankfurt am Main: Peter Lang.

Herder, Johann Gottfried (1993): Shakespear. In: Werke in zehn Bänden. Band 2: Schriften zur Ästhetik und Literatur 1767–1781. Frankfurt am Main: Deutscher Klassiker Verlag, 498–521.

Hess, Volker/Mendelsohn, J. Andrew (2013): Paper technology und Wissensgeschichte. In: NTM. Zeitschrift für Geschichte der Wissenschaften. Technik und Medizin (21), 1–10.

Heßelmann, Peter (2002): Gereinigtes Theater? Dramaturgie und Schaubühne im Spiegel deutschsprachiger Theaterperiodika des 18. Jahrhunderts (1750–1800). Frankfurt am Main: Klostermann.

Hoffmann, Christoph (2017): Schreiber, Verfasser, Autoren. In: Dvjs (91/2), 163–87.

Hoffmann, Paul F. (1939): Friedrich Ludwig Schröder als Dramaturg und Regisseur. Berlin: self-published by Gesellschaft für Theatergeschichte.

Hoffmeier, Dieter (1964): Die Einbürgerung Shakespeares auf dem Theater des Sturm und Drang. Berlin: Henschel.

Holland, Peter (2010): The Lost Workers: Process, Performance, and the Archive. In: Shakespeare Bulletin (28/1), 7–18.

Holzapfel, Friedrich (ed.) (1823): Neuer Almanach. Erster Jahrgang. 1823. Den Freunden der Kunst gewiedmet von Friedrich Holzapfel. Schauspieler des königlichen Theaters an dem Isarthore in München. München: Seraph Hübschmann.

Höyng, Peter (2007): Die Geburt der Theaterzensur aus dem Geiste bürgerlicher Moral. Unwillkommene Thesen zur Theaterzensur im 18. Jahrhundert? In: Wilhelm Haefs/York-Gothart Mixa (eds.): Zensur im Jahrhundert der Aufklärung. Geschichte – Theorie – Praxis. Göttingen: Wallstein, 99–119.

Huber, Thomas (1968): Studien zur Theorie der Übersetzung im Zeitalter der deutschen Aufklärung. Meisenheim am Glan: Hain.

Issacharoff, Michael (1987): How Playscripts Refer. Some Preliminary Considerations. In: Anna Whiteside/Michael Issacharoff (eds.): On Referring in Literature. Bloomington: Indiana University Press, 84–94.

Itkonen, Kyösti (1971): Die Shakespeare-Übersetzung Wielands (1762–1766). Ein Beitrag zur Erforschung englisch-deutscher Lehnbeziehungen. Jyväskylä: Jyväskylän Yliopisto.

Jahn, Bernhard (2016): Bühne und Bürgertum. Das Hamburger Stadttheater 1770–1850. Einleitung. In: Bernhard Jahn/Claudia Maurer-Zenck (eds.): Bühne und Bürgertum. Das Hamburger Stadttheater (1770–1850). Frankfurt am Main: Peter Lang, 9–20.

Jonson, Ben (1975): Timber viz. Explorata: or Discoveries. In: The Complete Poems. Penguin English Poets. Harmondsworth: Penguin, 373–458.

Kaethler, Mark/Malone, Toby/Roberts-Smith, Jennifer (2023): Polychronic Actants: Modern Promptbooks as Anticipated Acts, Unanticipated Acts, and Ideal Assemblages. In: Shakespeare, DOI: 10.1080/17450918.2023.2207553.

Kershaw, Baz (2011): Practice as Research. In: Baz Kershaw/Helen Nicholson (eds.): Research Methods in Theatre and Performance. Edinburgh: Edinburgh University Press, 63–85.

Kidnie, Margaret Jane (2009): Shakespeare and the Problem of Adaptation. New York: Routledge.

Klingemann, August (1822): Allgemeiner deutscher Theater-Almanach für das Jahr 1822. Braunschweig: G. C. E. Meyers.

Kob, Sabine (2000): Wielands Shakespeare-Übersetzung. Ihre Entstehung und ihre Rezeption im Sturm und Drang. Frankfurt am Main: Peter Lang.

Kofler, Peter (2008): Übersetzungen. Shakespeare. In: Jutta Heinz (ed.): Wieland-Handbuch. Leben – Werk – Wirkung. Stuttgart: Metzler, 394–403.

Kolesch, Doris (2012): Theater als Sündenschule. Für und Wider das Theater im 17. und 18. Jahrhundert. In: Stefanie Diekmann/Christopher Wild/Gabriele Brandstetter (eds.): Theaterfeindlichkeit. München: Fink, 19–30.

Korte, Hermann/Jakob, Hans-Joachim (eds.) (2012): "Das Theater glich einem Irrenhause". Das Publikum im Theater des 18. und 19. Jahrhunderts. Siegener Symposium zur Theaterpublikumsforschung. Heidelberg: Winter.

Korte, Hermann/Jakob, Hans-Joachim/Dewenter, Bastian (eds.) (2014): "Das böse Tier Theaterpublikum". Zuschauerinnen und Zuschauer in Theater- und Literaturjournalen des 18. und frühen 19. Jahrhunderts. Eine Dokumentation. Heidelberg: Winter.

Košenina, Alexander (2011): Das "eigentliche Theatertalent der Deutschen". August von Kotzebue (1761–1819) zum 250. Geburtstag. In: Zeitschrift für Germanistik (21/3), 586–592.

Kotte, Andreas (2013): Theatergeschichte. Wien et al.: Böhlau.

Kotzebue, August von (1791): Die Sonnen-Jungfrau. Ein Schauspiel in fünf Aufzügen. Leipzig: Paul Gotthelf Kummer.

Kotzebue, August von (1795): Die Spanier in Peru oder Rollas Tod. Ein romantisches Trauerspiel in fünf Akten. Leipzig: Paul Gotthelf Kummer.

Kotzebue, August von (1797): Schauspiele. Zweyter Band. Die Sonnenjungfrau. Das Kind der Liebe. Leipzig: Paul Gotthelf Kummer.

Kotzebue, August von (1810): Theater. Zweyter Band. Die Indianer in England. Die Sonnenjungfrau. Wien: Doll.

Kramer, Ursula (2016): Shakespeare, Kotzebue, Beaumarchais: Blicke in die Hamburger Schauspielmusik-Werkstatt. In: Bernhard Jahn/Claudia Maurer-Zenck (eds.): Bühne und Bürgertum. Das Hamburger Stadttheater (1770–1850). Frankfurt am Main: Peter Lang, 555–580.

Krebs, Roland (1985): L'idée de "théâtre national" dans l'Allemagne des Lumières. Théorie et réalisations. Wiesbaden: Harrassowitz.

Krebs, Roland (2005): Der Theologe vor der Bühne. Pastor Goezes *Theologische Untersuchung der heutigen deutschen Schaubühne* als Streitschrift gegen das Theater und Projekt einer Idealbühne. In: Ariane Martin/Nikolas Rossbach (eds.): Begegnungen: Bühne und Berufe in der Kulturgeschichte des Theaters. Tübingen: Francke, 43–52.

Langer, Arne (1997): Der Regisseur und die Aufzeichnungspraxis der Opernregie im 19. Jahrhundert. Frankfurt am Main: Peter Lang.

Latour, Bruno (1986): Visualisation and Cognition: Drawing Things Together. In: H. Kuklick (ed.): Knowledge and Society Studies in the Sociology of Culture Past and Present. Greenwich: Jai Press, 1–40.

Latour, Bruno (2005): Reassembling the Social. An Introduction to Actor-Network-Theory. Clarendon Lectures in Management Studies. 1. Oxford: Oxford University Press.

Lehmann, Hans Thies (2006): Postdramatic Theatre. Milton Park/New York: Routledge.
Lehmann, Johannes F. (2000): Der Blick durch die Wand. Zur Geschichte des Theaterzuschauers und des Visuellen bei Diderot und Lessing. Freiburg im Breisgau: Rombach.
Leon, Mechele (ed.) (2017): A Cultural History of Theatre. Volume 4: In the Age of Enlightenment. London/New York: Bloomsbury.
Lessing, Gotthold Ephraim (1993): Werke 1778–1780. Frankfurt am Main: Deutscher Klassiker Verlag.
Levine, Caroline (2015): Forms. Whole, Rhythm, Hierarchy, Network. Princeton: Princeton University Press.
Litzmann, Berthold (1890–1894): Friedrich Ludwig Schröder. Ein Beitrag zur deutschen Litteratur- und Theatergeschichte. Hamburg: Voß.
Maksimczuk, José/Möller, Berenice/Staack, Thies/Weinstock, Alexander/Wolf, Jana (2024): Multilayered Written Artefacts: Definition, Typology, Formatting. CSMC Occasional Papers, 9. Hamburg: Centre for the Study of Manuscript Cultures.
Malchow, Jacqueline (2022): Die Illusion des Illusionstheaters. Friedrich Ludwig Schröder, Shakespeare und der natürliche Schauspielstil. Berlin: Peter Lang.
Malone, Toby (2021): Using Theatrical Prompt-Books for Cultural Insight. In: Matthew Brand (ed.): Research Methods for Primary Sources (https://www.am-digital.co.uk/learn/am-research-skills, last accessed on December 23, 2023).
Martus, Steffen/Spoerhase, Carlos (2022): Geistesarbeit. Eine Praxeologie der Geisteswissenschaften. Berlin: Surkamp.
Marx, Peter W. (2011): Enter GHOST and HAMLET. Zur Vielstimmigkeit des Hamburger *Hamlet* von 1776. In: Dvjs (85/1), 508–523.
Marx, Peter W. (ed.) (2017): A Cultural History of Theatre. Volume 5: In the Age of Empire. London/New York: Bloomsbury.
Matzke, Annemarie (2012a): Arbeit am Theater: Eine Diskursgeschichte der Probe. Bielefeld: transcript.
Matzke, Annemarie (2012b): Theorien auf die Bühne schmeißen. René Polleschs Lehrstück-Theater. In: Annemarie Matzke/Christel Weiler/Isa Wortelkamp: Das Buch der angewandten Theaterwissenschaft. Berlin/Köln: Alexander, 119–133.
Maurer-Schmoock, Sybille (1982): Deutsches Theater im 18. Jahrhundert. Tübingen: Niemeyer.
Menke, Bettine (1993): "Magie" des Lesens: der Raum der Schrift. Über Lektüre und Konstellation in Benjamins "Lehre(n) vom Ähnlichen". In: Thomas Regehly/Iris Gniosdorsch (eds.): Namen, Texte, Stimmen. Walter Benjamins Sprachphilosophie. Hohenheimer Protokolle: Akademie der Diözese Rottenburg-Stuttgart, 107–135.

Meyer, Friedrich Ludwig Wilhelm (1819a): Friedrich Ludwig Schröder. Beitrag zur Kunde des Menschen und des Künstlers. In zwei Theilen. Theil 1. Hamburg: Hoffmann und Campe.

Meyer, Friedrich Ludwig Wilhelm (1819b): Friedrich Ludwig Schröder. Beitrag zur Kunde des Menschen und des Künstlers. In zwei Theilen. Theil 2. Hamburg: Hoffmann und Campe.

Meyer, Reinhart (2012): Schriften zur Theater- und Kulturgeschichte des 18. Jahrhunderts. Wien: Hollitzer Wissenschaftsverlag.

Meynen, Gloria (2004): Büro. Berlin: Humboldt Universität [Dissertation].

Montesquieu (2004): The Spirit of the Laws. Cambridge: Cambridge University Press.

Moody, Jane (2002): Romantic Shakespeare. In: Stanley Wells/Sarah Stanton (eds.): The Cambridge Companion to Shakespeare on Stage. Cambridge Companions to Literature. Cambridge: Cambridge University Press, 37–57.

Mühle, Friederike (2023): Zwischen Bühnenlied und Sinfonie. Schauspielmusik und hybride Theaterformen am Hamburger Stadttheater 1770–1850. München: Allitera.

Müller, Marion (2004): Zwischen Intertext und Interpretation. Friedrich Schillers dramaturgische Arbeiten 1796–1805. Karlsruhe: Universitätsverlag Karlsruhe.

Müller-Schöll, Nikolaus (2020): Skript-basiertes Theater. In: Karin Nissen-Rizvani/Martin Jörg Schäfer (eds.): TogetherText. Prozessual erzeugte Texte im Gegenwartstheater. Berlin: Theater der Zeit, 77–98.

Münz, Rudolf (1979): Das andere Theater. Studien über ein deutschsprachiges teatro dell arte der Lessingzeit. Berlin: Henschel.

Nantke, Julia (2017): Ordnungsmuster im Werk von Kurt Schwitters. Zwischen Transgression und Regelhaftigkeit. Berlin/Boston: De Gruyter.

Neubacher, Jürgen (2016): Die Aufführungsmaterialien des Hamburger Stadttheaters. In: Bernhard Jahn/Claudia Maurer-Zenck (eds.): Bühne und Bürgertum. Das Hamburger Stadttheater (1770–1850). Frankfurt am Main: Peter Lang, 23–36.

Nichols, Stephen G. (1997): Why Material Philology? In: Zeitschrift für deutsche Philologie (116), 10–30.

Niefanger, Dirk (2021): Die Weimarer Bühnenbearbeitung von Lessings *Nathan* – und die Stuttgarter Regiebücher. In: Martin Schneider (ed.): Das Regiebuch. Zur Lesbarkeit theatraler Produktionsprozesse in Geschichte und Gegenwart. Göttingen: Wallstein, 123–143.

Oltmann, Philipp (2023): Why Is the Prompter Strolling Around the Stage? Meet the Secret Heroes of German Theatre. In: The Guardian, September 26, 2023. (https://www.theguardian.com/stage/2023/sep/26/meet-the-secret-heroes-of-german-theatre, last accessed on December 23, 2023).

Özelt, Clemens/Schneider, Martin (eds.) (2024): Die Kunst der Theatereröffnung. Ästhetik und Sozialgeschichte von Bühnenprologen. Paderborn: Brill/Fink.

Paulin, Roger (2003): The Critical Reception of Shakespeare in Germany 1682–1914. Native Literature and Foreign Genius. Hildesheim: Olms.

Pavis, Patrice (1998): Dictionary of the Theatre: Terms, Concepts, and Analysis. Toronto: Toronto University Press.

Peters, John Durham (2015): The Marvelous Clouds. Towards a Philosophy of Elemental Media. Chicago: The University of Chicago Press.

Pethes, Nicolas (2019): Paper Mythology. Extending the Material "Milieus" of Literature and Philology. In: Pál Kelemen/Nicolas Pethes (eds.): Philology in the Making. Analog/Digital Cultures of Scholarly Writing and Reading. Bielefeld: transcript, 93–107.

Phelan, Peggy (1993): Unmarked. The Politics of Performance. London: Routledge.

Pieroth, Bodo (2018): Theaterrecht im 18. und 19. Jahrhundert. In: Bastian Dewenter/Hans Joachim Jakob (eds.): Theatergeschichte als Disziplinierungsgeschichte? Zur Theorie und Geschichte der Theatergesetze im 18. und 19. Jahrhundert. Heidelberg: Winter, 15–30.

Piquette, K. E./Whitehouse, R. D. (eds.) (2013): Writing as Material Practice: Substance, Surface and Medium. London: Ubiquity Press.

Plumpe, Gerhard (1979): EIGENTUM – EIGENTÜMLICHKEIT. Über den Zusammenhang ästhetischer und juristischer Begriffe im 18. Jahrhundert. In: Archiv für Begriffsgeschichte (23/2), 175–196.

Pope, Alexander/Wieland, Christoph Martin (1762): Alexander Pope's Vorrede zu seiner Ausgabe des Shakespears. In: Shakespear. Theatralische Werke. Aus dem Englischen von Herrn Wieland. Itr. Band. Zürich: Drell, Geßner und Comp, 2–10.

Quenzer, Jörg B. (2014): Introduction. In: Jörg B. Quenzer/Dmitry Bondarev/Jan-Ulrich Sobisch (eds.): Manuscript Cultures: Mapping the Field. Berlin: De Gruyter, 1–7.

Quenzer, Jörg B./Bondarev, Dmitry/Sobisch, Jan-Ulrich (eds.) (2014): Manuscript Cultures: Mapping the Field. Berlin: De Gruyter.

Reckwitz, Andreas (2003): Grundelemente einer Theorie sozialer Praktiken: Eine sozialtheoretische Perspektive. In: Zeitschrift für Soziologie (32.4), 282–301.

Reckwitz, Andreas (2016): Kreativität und soziale Praxis: Studien zur Sozial- und Gesellschaftstheorie. Bielefeld: transcript.

Rentsch, Ivana (2016): "Abgegriffene Musikklappen". Das Melodrama von Pygmalion bis Cardillac in Hamburg. In: Bernhard Jahn/Claudia Maurer-Zenck (eds.): Bühne und Bürgertum. Das Hamburger Stadttheater (1770–1850). Frankfurt am Main: Peter Lang, 279–300.

Roger, Christine (2007): L'introduction de Shakespeare dans les répertoires des scènes viennoises. In: Revue germanique internationale (5), 37–49.

Roselt, Jens (ed.) (2015): Regie im Theater. Geschichte, Theorie, Praxis. Berlin: Alexander.

Rudloff-Hille, Gertrud (1969): Schiller auf der deutschen Bühne seiner Zeit. Berlin/Weimar: Aufbau.

Sadji, Uta (1992): Der Mohr auf der deutschen Bühne des 18. Jahrhunderts. Anif/Salzburg: Ursula Muller-Speiser.

Schäfer, Martin Jörg (2016): Schröders und Bocks *King Lear*-Bühnenadaptionen der 1770er. Eschenburgs Nachwort als dramaturgischer Baukasten. In: Bernhard Jahn/Claudia Maurer-Zenck (eds.): Bühne und Bürgertum. Das Hamburger Stadttheater (1770–1850). Frankfurt am Main: Peter Lang, 517–539.

Schäfer, Martin Jörg (2017): "Die dritte und eigentlich fremde Natur". Zu Friedrich Ludwig Schröders Konzeption und Praxis des Schauspielens. In: Bernhard Jahn/Alexander Košenina (eds.): Friedrich Ludwig Schröders Hamburgische Dramaturgie (Publikationen zur Zeitschrift für Germanistik 31), 143–159.

Schäfer, Martin Jörg (2018): Verschleierte Obszönitäten im deutschsprachigen Shakespeare von Wieland bis Baudissin. In: Pawel Piszczatowski (ed.): Diálogos. Das Wort im Gespräch. Göttingen: V&R unipress, 53–72.

Schäfer, Martin Jörg (2021): "Vu et approuvé": Censorship Notes in Hamburg Prompt Books from the French Period. In: Jörg B. Quenzer (ed.): Exploring Written Artefacts. Objects, Methods and Concepts. Studies in Manuscript Culture. Volume 25. Berlin: De Gruyter, 1041–1058.

Schäfer, Martin Jörg/Weinstock, Alexander (2023): Prompt Books in Use. The Example of Hamburg's Theater-Bibliothek. In: Manuscript Cultures (20), 45–72.

Schechner, Richard (2003): Performance Theory. New York: Routledge.

Schiller, Friedrich (1949): Werke. Nationalausgabe. Dreizehnter Band. Bühnenbearbeitungen. Erster Teil. Herausgegeben von Hans Heinrich Borcherdt. Weimar: Hermann Böhlaus Nachfolger.

Schiller, Friedrich (1984): Werke. Nationalausgabe. Zweiunddreissigster Band. Briefwechsel. Schillers Briefe 1.1.1803 – 9.5.1805. Herausgegeben von Axel Gellhaus. Weimar: Hermann Böhlaus Nachfolger.

Schiller, Friedrich (1985): Werke. Nationalausgabe. Einunddreissigster Band. Briefwechsel. Schillers Briefe 1.1.1801 – 31.12.1802. Herausgegeben von Stefan Ormanns. Weimar: Hermann Böhlaus Nachfolger.

Schiller, Friedrich (1987): Werke. Nationalausgabe. Vierzigster Band. Teil 1. Briefwechsel. Briefe an Schiller 1.1.1803 – 17.5.1805 (Text). Herausgegeben von Georg Kurscheidt und Norbert Oellers. Weimar: Hermann Böhlaus Nachfolger.

Schiller, Friedrich (1988): Werke. Nationalausgabe. Neununddreissigster Band. Teil 1. Briefwechsel. Briefe an Schiller 1.1.1801 – 31.12.1802 (Text). Herausgegeben von Stefan Ormanns. Weimar: Hermann Böhlaus Nachfolger.

Schink, Johann Friedrich (1778): Ueber Brockmanns Hamlet. Berlin: Arnold Wever.

Schink, Johann Friedrich (1790): Dramaturgische Monate. Vierter Band. Schwerin: Verlag der Bödnerschen Buchhandlung.

Schmid, Christian Heinrich (1768): Ueber das bürgerliche Trauerspiel. In: Unterhaltungen (5/4), 308–316.

[Schmid, Christian Heinrich] (1772): Othello, ein Trauerspiel in fünf Aufzügen, nach Shackespear. In: Englisches Theater. Erster Theil. Danzig/Leipzig: Daniel Ludwig Wedeln, 153–288.

Schmidt, Friedrich Ludwig (1875): Denkwürdigkeiten des Schauspielers, Schauspieldichters und Schauspieldirectors Friedrich Ludwig Schmidt (1772–1841). Nach hinterlassenen Entwürfen zusammengestellt und herausgegeben von Hermann Uhde. Zweiter Teil. Hamburg: W. Mauke Söhne.

Schneider, Martin (ed.) (2017): Der Hamburger Theaterskandal von 1801. Eine Quellendokumentation zur politischen Ästhetik des Theaters um 1800. Frankfurt am Main: Peter Lang.

Schneider, Martin (2018): Schauspieldemokratie? Friedrich Ludwig Schröders Hamburger Theatergesetze im Kontext der Bühnenpolitik des späten 18. Jahrhunderts. In: Bastian Dewenter/Hans-Joachim Jakob (eds.): Theatergeschichte als Disziplinierungsgeschichte? Zur Theorie und Geschichte der Theatergesetze des 18. und 19. Jahrhunderts. Heidelberg: Winter, 103–116.

Schneider, Martin (ed.) (2021): Das Regiebuch. Zur Lesbarkeit theatraler Produktionsprozesse in Geschichte und Gegenwart. Göttingen: Wallstein.

Schneider, Martin (2023): Agonalität und Menschenliebe. Gefühlspoetik im Drama des 18. Jahrhunderts. München: Brill/Fink.

Schneider, Martin (2024): Pathosreduktion. Zu politischen Tendenzen von Theaterbearbeitungen um 1800. In: Zeitschrift für Germanistik (34/2), 416–431.

Schneider, Rebeca (2012): Performance Remains Again. In: Gabriella Giannachi/Nick Kaye/Michael Shanks (eds.): Archaeologies of Presence. New York: Routledge, 64–81.

Schöne, Hermann (approx. 1904): Aus den Lehr- und Flegeljahren eines alten Schauspielers. Leipzig: Reclam.

Schönert, Jörg (2008): Der Kaufmann von Jerusalem. Zum Handel mit Kapitalien und Ideen in Lessings *Nathan der Weise*. In: Scientia Poetica (12), 89–113.

[Schröder, Friedrich Ludwig/Shakespeare, William] (1777): Hamlet, Prinz von Dännemark. Ein Trauerspiel in sechs Aufzügen. Zum Behuf des Hamburgischen Theaters. Hamburg: Herold.

Schröder, Friedrich Ludwig (1778a): [Preface]. In: Hamburgisches Theater. Band 3. Hamburg: J. M. Michaelsen, III-VIII.

[Schröder, Friedrich Ludwig] (1778b): Hamlet, Prinz von Dännemark. Nach Shakespear. Hamburgisches Theater. Band 3. Hamburg: J. M. Michaelsen.

[Schröder, Friedrich Ludwig] (1778c): König Lear. Ein Trauerspiel in fünf Aufzügen. Nach Shakespear. Hamburg: J. M. Michaelsen.

[Schröder, Friedrich Ludwig/Shakespeare, William] (1779): Hamlet, Prinz von Dännemark. Ein Trauerspiel in sechs Aufzügen. Zum Behuf des Hamburgischen Theaters. Nebst Brockmann's Bildniß als Hamlet. Hamburg: Heroldsche Buchhandlung.

[Schröder, Friedrich Ludwig] (1781): König Lear. Ein Trauerspiel in fünf Aufzügen. Nach Shakespear. Hamburgisches Theater. Band 4.1. Hamburg: Herold.

[Schröder, Friedrich Ludwig] (1790): Maaß für Maaß. Ein Schauspiel in fünf Aufzügen. Nach Shakespeare. Von Schröder. Sammlung von Schauspielen für das Hamburgische Theater. Theil 1. Schwerin: Bödner.

[Schröder, Friedrich Ludwig] (1792): Gesetze des Hamburgischen Theaters. In: Annalen des Theaters. Neuntes Heft, 3–22.

[Schröder, Friedrich Ludwig] (1798): Gesetze des Hamburgischen Theaters. Hamburg: self-published.

Schröder, Hans/Klose, C. R. W. (1870): Lexikon der hamburgischen Schriftsteller bis zur Gegenwart. Fünfter Band. Hamburg: W. Maukes Söhne.

Schröter, Axel (2016): Zur Kotzebue-Rezeption am Hamburger Stadttheater zu Lebzeiten des Erfolgsautors – unter besonderer Berücksichtigung bürgerlicher und aristokratischer Wertvorstellungen. In: Bernhard Jahn/Claudia Maurer-Zenck (eds.): Bühne und Bürgertum. Das Hamburger Stadttheater (1770–1850). Frankfurt am Main: Peter Lang, 409–437.

Schulze-Kummerfeld, Karoline (1915): Lebenserinnerungen der Karoline Schulze-Kummerfeld. Herausgegeben und erläutert von Emil Benezé. Band 1. Berlin: self-published by Gesellschaft für Theatergeschichte.

Schütze, Johann Friedrich (1794): Hamburgische Theater-Geschichte. Hamburg: Treder.

Shakespeare, William (2016): The Norten Shakespeare. Third Edition. New York/London: W. W. Norten & Company.

Shattuck, Charles H. (1965): The Shakespeare Promptbooks. A Descriptive Catalogue. Urbana: University of Illinois Press.

Sheridan, Richard Brinsley (1809): Pizarro. A Tragedy in Five Acts. Taken from the German Drama by Kotzebue and Adapted to the English Stage. Boston: John West.

Sherman, William H. (2008): Used Books. Marking Readers in Renaissance England. Philadelphia: University of Pennsylvania Press.

Soden, Friedrich Julius Heinrich Graf von (1814): Theater. Zweiter Theil. Medea. Franzesko Pizarro. Viginia. Aarau: Sauerländer.

Spoerhase, Carlo (2018): Das Format der Literatur. Praktiken materieller Textualität zwischen 1740 und 1830. Göttingen: Wallstein.

Spoerhase, Carlo/Thomalla, Erika (2020): Werke in Netzwerken. Kollaborative Autorschaft im 18. Jahrhundert. In: Zeitschrift für deutsche Philologie (139/2), 145–164.

Stadler, Erst (1910): Wielands Shakespeare. Straßburg: Trübner.
Staël Holstein, Mme la Baronne de (1810): De l'Allemagne. Paris: H. Nicolle.
[Steffens, Johann Heinrich] (1770): Das Schnupftuch oder der Mohr von Venedig, Othello. Ein Schauspiel in fünf Aufzügen nach dem Schakespear. Frankfurt am Main/Leipzig: [without publisher].
Stingelin, Martin/Giuriato, Davide/Zanetti, Sandro (eds.) (2004): "Mir ekelt vor diesem tintenklecksenden Säkulum". Schreibszenen im Zeitalter der Manuskripte. München: Fink.
Stoltz, Dominik (2016): Theaterzensur in der Franzosenzeit (1806–1814) (https://blog.sub.uni-hamburg.de/?p=20422, last accessed on June 8, 2023).
Stone Peters, Julie (2000): Theatre of the Book. 1480–1880. Print, Text and Performance in Europe. Oxford et al.: Oxford University Press.
Tatspaugh, Patricia (2003): Performance History: Shakespeare on the Stage 1660–2001. In: Stanley Wells/Lena Cowen Orlin (eds.): Shakespeare: An Oxford Guide. Oxford: Oxford University Press, 525–549.
Tkaczyk, Viktoria (2012): Theater und Wortgedächtnis. Eine Spurensuche nach der Gegenwart. In: Erika Fischer-Lichte/Adam Czirak/Torsten Jost/Frank Richarz/Nina Tecklenburg (eds.): Die Aufführung. Diskurs – Macht – Analyse. München: Fink, 275–289.
Treharne, Elaine (2021): Perceptions of Medieval Manuscripts. The Phenomenal Book. Oxford: Oxford University Press.
Uhde, Hermann (1879): Das Stadttheater in Hamburg 1827–1877. Stuttgart: Verlag der J. G. Cotta'schen Buchhandlung.
Ulrich, Paul S. (2008): The Role of the Prompter in the Professional German-Language Theater in the 18th Century. In: Júlia Demeter/István Kilián (eds.): Színházvilág világszínház. Budapest: Ráció Kiadó, 217–229.
Ulrich, Paul S. (2022): Deutschsprachige Theater-Journale/German-Language Theater Journals (1772–1918): Herausgeberinnen und Herausgeber/Editors. Wien: Hollitzer.
[Voß, Johann Heinrich (tr.)] (1806): Shakespeare's König Lear, übersetzt von Dr. Johann Heinrich Voß, Professor am Weimarischen Gymnasium. Mit zwei Compositionen von Zelter. Jena: Friedrich Frommann.
Wagner, Meike (2023): Theaterzensur. In: Beate Hochholdinger-Reiterer/Christina Thurner/Julia Wehren (eds.): Theater und Tanz. Handbuch für Wissenschaft und Studium. Baden-Baden: Nomos, 459–466.
[Warburton, William (ed.)] (1769): The Works of Shakespear. In Which the Beauties Observed by Pope, Warburton, and Dodd, Are Pointed Out. Together With the Author's Life; a Glossary; Copious Indexes; and, a List of the Various Readings. In Eight Volumes. Volume 8. Edinburgh: Wal. Ruddiman and Company.
Weidmann, Heiner (1994): Ökonomie der 'Grossmuth'. Geldwirtschaft in Lessings "Minna von Barnhelm" und "Nathan dem Weisen". In: Dvjs (68/3), 447–461.

Weigel, Helene (ed.) (1952): Theaterarbeit. 6 Arbeiten des Berliner Ensembles. Dresden: Dresdner Verlag.
Weilen, Alexander von (ed.) (1914): Der erste deutsche Bühnenhamlet. Shakespeare. Die Bearbeitungen Heufelds und Schröders. Wien: Wiener Bibliophilen-Gesellschaft.
Weiman, Robert (2000): Zwischen Performanz und Repräsentation. Shakespeare und die Macht des Theaters. Aufsätze von 1959–1995. Heidelberg: Winter.
Weinstock, Alexander (2019): Das Maß und die Nützlichkeit. Zum Verhältnis von Theater und Erziehung im 18. Jahrhundert. Bielefeld: transcript.
Weinstock, Alexander (2022): Das umgeschriebene Genie. Zum Verhältnis von literarischem Autorschaftsdiskurs und Schriftpraktiken im Theater. In: Journal of Literary Theory (16/1), 51–76.
Weinstock, Alexander/Schäfer, Martin Jörg (2024): Making and Using Manuscripts in Theatre. The Material Dynamics of Two 19th Century *Nathan der Weise* Prompt Books. In: Antonella Brita/Janina Karolewski/Matthieu Husson/Laure Miolo/Hanna Wimmer (eds.): Manuscripts and Performances in Religions, Arts, and Sciences. Studies in Manuscript Cultures. Volume 36. Berlin: De Gruyter, 17–38.
Weinstock, Alexander (2024): "Er sticht sie" – Korrekturprozesse im Soufflierbuch um 1800. In: Iuditha Balint/Janneke Eggert/Thomas Ernst (eds.): Korrigieren. Eine Kulturtechnik. Berlin: De Gruyter (forthcoming).
Weiße, Christian (1776): Trauerspiele. Vierter Theil. Rosemunde. Romeo und Julie. Leipzig: Dykische Buchhandlung.
Weiße, Christian (1836): Richard der Dritte. Trauerspiel in 5 Aufzügen. Stuttgart/Augsburg: Cotta.
Werstine, Paul (2012): Early Modern Playhouse Manuscripts and the Editing of Shakespeare. Cambridge: Cambridge University Press.
Wessels, Hans-Friedrich (1979): Lessings "Nathan der Weise". Seine Wirkungsgeschichte bis zum Ende der Goethezeit. Königstein im Taunus: Athenäum.
[Wieland, Christoph Martin (tr.)] (2003): William Shakespeare. Theatralische Werke in einem Band. Übersetzt von Christoph Martin Wieland. Frankfurt am Main: Zweitausendeins.
Wild, Christopher J. (2003): Theater der Keuschheit – Keuschheit des Theaters. Zu einer Geschichte der (Anti-) Theatralität von Gryphius bis Kleist. Freiburg im Breisgau: Rombach.
Wimsatt, W. K. (ed.) (1960): Samuel Johnson on Shakespeare. London: Hill and Wang.
Wirth, Uwe (2011): Logik der Streichung. In: Lucas Marco Gisi/Hubert Thüring/Irmgard M. Wirtz (eds.): Schreiben und Streichen. Zu einem Moment produktiver Negativität. Göttingen et al.: Chronos, 23–45.

Wollrabe, Ludwig (1847): Chronologie sämmtlicher Hamburger Bühnen. Nebst Angabe der meisten Schauspieler, Sänger, Tänzer und Musiker, welche seit 1230 bis 1846 an denselben engagiert gewesen und gastirt haben. Hamburg: Berendsohn.

Worrall, David (2017): Social Functions: Audiences and Authority. In: Mechele Leon (ed.): A Cultural History of Theatre. Volume 4: The Age of Enlightenment. London/New York: Bloomsbury, 33–54.

Worthen, William B. (2010): Drama. Between Poetry and Performance. Chichester et. al.: Wiley-Blackwell.

Young, Edward (1966): Conjectures on Original Composition. 1759. Leeds: Scolar Press.

Zanetti, Sandro (ed.) (2012): Schreiben als Kulturtechnik. Berlin: Suhrkamp.

Zantop, Susanne (1999): Kolonialphantasien im vorkolonialen Deutschland (1770–1870). Berlin: Erich Schmidt.

Žigon, Tanja (2012): Souffleure und ihre Theaterjournale im deutschsprachigen Theater in Ljubiljana (Laibach) im 19. Jahrhundert. In: Elisabeth Lang/Veronika Pólay/Petra Szmatári/Dóra Takács (eds.): Schnittstellen: Sprache – Literatur – Fremdsprachendidaktik. Hamburg: Verlag Dr. Kovač, 211–220.

Zumthor, Paul (1988): Körper und Performanz. In: Hans Ulrich Gumbrecht/K. Ludwig Pfeiffer (eds.): Materialität der Kommunikation. Frankfurt am Main: Suhrkamp, 703–13.

Printed in the USA
CPSIA information can be obtained
at www.ICGtesting.com
JSHW010740170824
68284JS00004B/25

9 783837 669657